Pensions Simplifi

A complete guide to the current pensions systeı. .... a ıuıı description of current entitlements under the various types of pension scheme available, both from the State and privately, and gives detailed advice on how to set up a tax-efficient scheme to protect your own future. Areas covered include: • how to choose a pension, set it up and care for it • taking account of the tax implications • retirement planning • what choices are offered at retirement • transfers and opt-outs • dealing with divorce and mortgages • death before and after retirement.

Inheritance Tax Simplified

This book is a detailed practical guide to inheritance tax and estate planning. Packed with tips, advice and examples, the book shows how to plan to minimise inheritance taxes, whilst successfully planning for your estate, wills and trusts. Areas covered include • everything you need to know about inheritance tax • estate planning • choices and money-saving options • how not to lose your house whilst staying in it • preserving and protecting your estate assets • how wills work and why you should have one • how to make substantial savings at very low cost • and a host of other relevant information.

Succession Planning Simplified

Succession planning – planning for the future ownership and management of a business after the death or departure of a key executive – is often left until the last minute – or not done at all. However, the benefits of advance planning can be enormous, not only in protecting the value of the business for the owner's heirs and successors, but also in ensuring a viable future for staff and employees. Succession Planning Simplified is a practical guide to the whole area, including a review of legal and taxation implications of the various alternative types of succession plan, and a thorough explanation of the planning methodology involved.

Taxation Simplified

A concise guide to all the basic forms of taxation in the UK. Now in its 105th edition, this is the longest established tax guide of its kind – including practical down-to-earth descriptions of all the principal areas and methods of taxation, and packed with tips and advice for reducing or avoiding tax. Areas covered include: • income tax • corporation tax • capital allowances • capital gains tax • inheritance tax • value added tax • council tax • self-assessment.

For further information on any of these books visit www.mb2000.com or telephone Management Books 2000 on 01285 771441

The full list of titles in the "Simplified" series is:

Business Protection Simplified
Inheritance Tax Simplified
Pensions Simplified
School and University Fees Simplified
Succession Planning Simplified
Taxation Simplified
Tax-Efficient Investments Simplified
Tax-Efficient Wills Simplified

For further information on any of these titles,
or for a complete list of Management Books 2000 titles
visit our web-site, **www.mb2000.com**

TAX-EFFICIENT WILLS SIMPLIFIED

2011/2012

Carl Islam

2000

First published in 2011 by Management Books 2000 Ltd
Forge House, Limes Road
Kemble, Cirencester
Gloucestershire, GL7 6AD, UK
Tel: 0044 (0) 1285 771441
Fax: 0044 (0) 1285 771055
E-mail: info@mb2000.com
Web: www.mb2000.com

The 1st edition of the STEP Standard Provisions appears in this book with the permission of the Society of Trust and Estate Practitioners and James Kessler QC.

Crown copyright material is reproduced with the permission of the Controller of HMSO and the Queen's Printer for Scotland. Any European material in this work which has been reproduced from EUR-lex, the official European Communities legislation website, is European Communities copyright.

British Library Cataloguing in Publication Data is available

ISBN 9781852526887

This book is dedicated with love to my late Father Dr Amin-ul Islam and to my Mother Betty Islam, without whose unconditional love encouragement and great personal sacrifice the author would not have received his education and start in life, and to Sally who has made my life complete.

Acknowledgements

I would also like to thank my secretary Baljit Kaur Matharu for her patience and endurance with the typing of the manuscript, her daughter Harkeerat Kaur Matharu for designing the artwork that appears throughout the book, and Nick and Pippa at Management Books 2000.

Disclaimer

While every care has been taken to ensure the accuracy of this work, no responsibility for loss or damage occasioned to any person acting or refraining from action as a result of any statement in it can be accepted by the author, editors, or publishers. Without limitation to the generality of the above, note that all statutory extracts that appear in this book have been copied from the UK statute law database (www.statutelaw.gov.uk), which may not show all of the amendments introduced by recent Finance Acts. Therefore the reader should always refer to a current consolidated version of a statute before placing any reliance upon its provisions and their meaning.

Contents

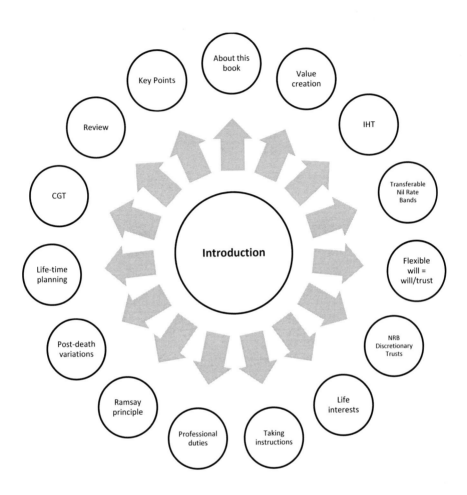

Introduction

- About this book
- Value creation
- IHT
- Transferable Nil Rate Bands
- Flexible will = will/trust
- NRB Discretionary Trusts
- Life interests
- Taking instructions
- Professional duties
- Ramsay principle
- Post-death variations
- Life-time planning
- CGT
- Review
- Key Points

Introduction

- About this book
- Value creation
- IHT
- Transferable Nil Rate Bands
- Flexible will = will/trust
- NRB Discretionary Trusts
- Life interests
- Taking instructions
- Professional duties
- Ramsay principle
- Post-death variations
- Life-time planning
- CGT
- Review
- Key points

About this book

This book discusses how to save Inheritance Tax *('IHT')* by making a tax-efficient will. This is known as testamentary planning. The strategic planning process that results in the drafting of a tax-efficient will is illustrated in **Diagram No.1** – *'Testamentary planning process'*. Planning outcomes cannot be guaranteed. However, by adopting a sensible and flexible approach to testamentary planning, a testator, (the person who makes the will), abbreviated in this book to '**T**':

1. maximises the options available to his executors and trustees to implement a tax-efficient distribution of his estate in accordance with his wishes and intentions; and
2. reduces the practical likelihood of a revenue challenge after his death.

In keeping with these aims, the broad scheme of this book is as follows:

1. this chapter contains an overview of the strategic testamentary planning process and concludes with a summary of key points;
2. Chapter 1 outlines the anatomy of a will/trust (simply referred to throughout this book as a *'will'*);
3. Chapter 2 explains key planning concepts (which for ease of reference are presented in alphabetical order);
4. Chapter 3 discusses the basic planning tools available to the will/trust draftsman;

5. Chapter 4 illustrates the use of basic planning tools to construct a tax-efficient will/trust structure for a testator who is:
   (a) married;
   (b) in a relationship with an unmarried partner; or
   (c) a singleton;
6. Chapter 5 contains an alphabetical menu of additional powers for trustees (which can be used as a check-list);
7. Chapter 6 highlights traps for the unwary (which for ease of reference are presented in alphabetical order); and
8. Chapter 7 alerts the reader to recent developments (including the announcements made in the UK Budget 2011).

Note that planning for non-UK domiciliaries *('non-doms')* is outside the scope of this book. The working assumption made in the book is that **T** and his spouse / civil partner are domiciled in the UK, and that **T's** assets are all located in the UK. Unless otherwise stated:

1. Testator is abbreviated to '**T**' (and a complete list of the abbreviations used in this book is set out in **Appendix 8**);
2. **T's** surviving spouse can be read alternatively as referring to a surviving '*civil partner,*' and are both abbreviated to '**S**';
3. all references to **T's** '*NRB*' (Nil Rate Band) are references to the full amount of his unused Nil Rate Band available on his death either (i) for transfer to **S**; or (ii) to leave to **S** and other beneficiaries under the terms of his will (either absolutely or subject to a trust);
4. in the book the maximum amount of cash that **T** can give without incurring any liability to IHT on his death is called the nil rate amount '*NRA*');
5. a '*minor*' means a person under the age of 18;
6. the term '*settlement*' describes the situation in which property is held in trust for a succession of interests, or the disposition creating that situation, and except in particular contexts (e.g. IHT legislation), the term '*trust*' is used throughout this book to describe trusts created by **T** (i) during his lifetime; and/or (ii) on his death;
7. '*trustees*' include '*executors*';
8. all statutory references (e.g. **s.1**) are to the **Inheritance Tax Act 1984** ('**IHTA 1984**'). The primary legislation is contained in the **IHTA 1984** as amended by subsequent **Finance Acts**; and
9. references e.g. to 'p.1 of the BDO Tax Guide', are references to where supplementary technical commentary appears in a practitioner's text book (and note that an abbreviation appears next to the citation of each book listed in the Bibliography). For example the abbreviation 'the BDO Tax Guide' refers to 'BDO's Yellow Tax Guide 2010-11'.

In this edition technical references appear in the text, statutory extracts are set out in **Appendix 5**, and diagrams are contained in **Appendix 1**. From May 2012 technical updates (including summaries of recent cases) will be free to download at www.wealthplanning.tv.

This book attempts to state the law as at May 30, 2011.

Value creation

When you pay for the drafting of a tax-efficient will, what you get in return is the preservation and effective management of your personal wealth for the benefit of your surviving spouse, descendants, and future generations. This can save substantial amounts of IHT (see **Diagram No.2** – *'IHT Calculations'*) and result in asset protection.

As the *Wealth Triangle* (**Diagram No.3**) illustrates, when effective wealth planning is not undertaken, there can only be one outcome. IHT is not philosophical. By analogy to the laws of physics it is more like the force of gravity, and the amount of **T's** accumulated wealth will fall.

IHT

IHT is a cumulative wealth tax charged on the *'the value transferred by a chargeable transfer'* made by **T**: (i) during his lifetime; and (ii) on death. A chargeable transfer is defined in **s.2(1)** as a *'transfer of value which is made by an individual but is not…an exempt transfer.'* A *'transfer of value'* is defined in **s.3(1)** as, *'a disposition made by a person (the transferor) as a result of which the value of his estate immediately after the disposition is less than it would be but for the disposition; and the amount by which it is less is the value transferred by the transferor.'* Note that **s.3(2)** provides by way of carve out that, *'no account shall be taken of the value of excluded property which ceases to form part of a person's estate as a result of a disposition.'* Note that IHT is calculated on the value transferred, which is usually the reduction in the total value of **T's** estate resulting from the transfer, other than of: (i) excluded property (which is outside the scope of the charge, see **s.5(1)(b)** (Meaning of estate), and s.6 (Excluded property); (ii) property which is exempt; or (iii) property that is potentially exempt. Note that this value is distinct from the value of the asset actually transferred, which may or may not produce the same result.

Therefore three categories of transfer can give rise to IHT: (i) a transfer on death; (ii) a potentially exempt transfer *('PET')*; and (iii) a chargeable transfer made before death. See generally Chapter 2 – *'chargeable transfers'*, and **s.1** *('Charge on transfers')*, **s.2** *('Chargeable transfers and exempt transfers')*, and **s.3** *('Transfers of value')*. IHT does not apply to transactions effected at fair market value (i.e. where no gratuitous intent or element of bounty is involved).

In the tax year that started on the 6th April 2011 *('2011/2012')*, the first £325K of *'chargeable transfers'* made by **T** in any seven-year period is taxable at nil%. This is known as the Nil Rate Band *('NRB')*, and note that the amount of **T's** NRB can become fully replenished every seven years. IHT is payable at the rate of 20% on life-time chargeable transfers above the NRB, and on death at 40% above **T's** remaining (i.e. unused) NRB. Note that the NRB rate of £325K is frozen until 2014/2015. In calculating IHT due on **T's** chargeable transfers of value, his available NRB must be ascertained, which requires aggregation of a transfer on death or during **T's** lifetime, with all chargeable transfers made by him within the previous seven years.

The amount of IHT chargeable on death:

1. is subject to all available *'exemptions'* and *'reliefs'* (see Chapter 2 – *'Exemptions'* and *'Reliefs'*); and
2. depends upon:
    (a) the aggregate chargeable life-time transfers *('CLT's')* and PET's made by **T** within the previous seven years (which is known as the *'principle of cumulation'*); and
    (b) whether the donee of the gift (i.e. the beneficiary), is an exempt beneficiary (for example **S**), or a non-exempt beneficiary (for example a child or grandchild), and see Chapter 1 – *'Beneficiaries'*.

Note that:

- an *'exempt transfer'* is not liable to IHT (and therefore does not affect the rate of IHT charged on later transfers made by **T**);
- a *'PET'* is a life-time transfer that falls within the cumulative total of **T's** NRB within the previous seven year period;
- if **T** survives the making of a PET by seven years or more, it becomes completely exempt;
- however if **T** dies within the seven year period, the PET becomes chargeable at that time, **s.3A;**
- *'taper relief'* applies where a failed PET was made more than three years before **T's** death (which operates to reduce the IHT payable on the PET but not the value of the transfer);
- a life-time transfer that does not qualify as a PET will give rise to an immediate charge to IHT (see **Diagram No.4** – *'IHT categories of lifetime transfer'*);
- that a transfer which benefits from the application of *'relief'* is within the charge to IHT, however the value of the transfer is removed from the charge to the extent that the applicable relief is available, which can be up to 100%; and
- the IHT treatment of property held on trust (known as *'settled property'*) is discussed below.

IHT on death is charged on **T's** estate as if immediately before his death he had made a transfer of value. The value transferred is deemed to be equal to the value of his estate immediately before his death (the *'loss to estate principle'*), see **s.4(1)** (Transfers on death), and **s.5** (Meaning of estate). **T's** chargeable or *'death'* estate for IHT purposes includes:

- the aggregate of all property to which he was beneficially entitled (not counting any excluded property (see below)), known as his *'free'* estate (see Chapter 2 – *'Assets'*); and
- certain settled property in which **T** was beneficially entitled to a life interest (see Chapter 2 – *'Interests in possession'*). However beneficial entitlement does not include property held in a fiduciary capacity.

See **Diagram No.5** – *'Key categories of T's death estate'*. Note that property subject to the IHT gifts with reservation of benefit regime (the *'GWR'* rules) also forms part of **T's** estate by virtue of **s.71A** (see Chapter 2 – *'GWR & POAT'*).

In valuing **T's** estate a liability may be taken into account provided it is legally enforceable, and (i) imposed by law; or (ii) incurred for consideration (in money or money's worth), **s.5(5)**. A mortgage can be deducted from the property if it is charged on it. Note however that the liability reduces the value of the encumbered property, and not of the estate generally, which is significant where (i) an exemption, such as the spouse exemption is available, and (ii) **T's** estate includes property that is eligible for 100% relief (e.g. BPR). Note that the value of property qualifying for BPR cannot be increased by charging business debts on non-business property.

The IHT treatment of *'settled property'* depends upon whether a *'qualifying interest in possession'* exists in the property or not (see **Diagram No.17** – Interest in possession trusts; **Diagram No.18** – Qualifying interest in possession; and Chapter 2 – *'Interests in possession'*).

The only *'qualifying interests in possession'* that can now be created by **T** under his will are: (i) an immediate post-death interest (*'IPDI'*) within **s.49A**; and (ii) a disabled person's interest (*'DPT'*) as defined in **s.89B**. Taxation of these trusts is discussed under the heading 'Special trusts' in Chapter 3 below. See also **Diagram No.6** – *'IHT privileged will/trusts post 22.03.2006.'*

Where what is known as a *'relevant property trust'* is created (e.g. a discretionary trust), no *'qualifying interest in possession'* subsists (see **sections 58 and 59**). IHT is charged on *'Relevant property trusts'* on (i) creation; (ii) every ten years; and (iii) when property leaves the trust. The settlement of property on a relevant property trust is a CLT, precipitating an IHT charge on the date that the property is settled. In the case of a lifetime trust the charge is levied on the value transferred by a chargeable transfer of value (that exceeds the settlor's available NRB) at the rate of 20%.

All lifetime trusts created after 22nd March 2006 are subject to the IHT rules contained in **Part 111, Chapter 3** applicable to the taxation of relevant property (known as the *'relevant property regime'*). Note that where **T** had not made any CLT's within seven years of the creation of a relevant property trust (and provided the amount settled did not exceed **T's** unused NRB), that no exit charge can arise on any appointment made out of the trust within the first ten years, because the effective rate at which IHT will be charged is 0% due to the application of 100% of the full amount of **T's** NRB. See Finney at paragraphs 16.24, and 16.30, where he further observes that if no appointments are subsequently made out of the trusts prior to the first ten year anniversary, and the amount initially settled in the trust equalled **T's** NRB at the time of creation, that no IHT charge arises on the first tenth anniversary. Provided growth in value of trust assets does not exceed the increase in **T's** NRB over that period. In which case the charge can be avoided if growth is stripped out before the first decennial anniversary.

Note that where a *'qualifying interest'* exists:

- property settled on the trust qualifies as a PET (and is not a CLT), therefore where a settlor survives for at least seven years after settling the property, no IHT charge arises on the gift into trust;
- decennial and exit charges do not apply; and
- under what is known as the *'interest in possession principle'* the life-tenant is treated as owning the underlying trust property, which forms part of their estate for IHT.

See paragraphs 16.8 and 16.49 of Finney, and *'Interests in possession'* in Chapter 2.

Where a qualifying interest is created by **T's** trustees appointing property to **S** more than two years after his death:

- the appointment cannot be read back as a spouse-exempt gift under **s.144**;
- an immediate IHT entry charge will be precipitated; and
- the beneficiary principle will not apply (therefore the underlying trust property will not fall into **S's** estate for IHT when she dies.

Transferable Nil Rate Bands

T and **S** are each entitled to one full NRB. However if **S** survives **T**, then on her death, her estate may be entitled to benefit from the maximum amount of the value of two fully available NRB's.

Basic IHT planning for spouses requires that each should make full use of their individual NRB's on death. Where **T** dies leaving part of his NRB unused, then on **S's** death her personal representatives *('PR's')* can make a claim under **s.8 A** for her NRB to be increased by the proportion of **T's** unused

NRB. **s.8A** sets out various formulae for calculating **T's** unused NRB and the increased NRB available to **S's** PR's on her death.

If **T** leaves everything to **S** or to a life interest trust created by his will for **S**, (called an Immediate Post-Death Interest Trust or *'IPDI'* for short), then on her death, **S's** PR's can take advantage of two NRB's. That is because the amount of **S's** NRB is increased by the percentage of **T's** NRB that remains unused at the time of his death.

S can take portions of an unused NRB inherited from any number of spouses or civil partners. Whilst **S's** estate may benefit from the availability of more than one unused transferable NRB, **S** can only inherit the amount of one full NRB. Note the limitation under **s.8A(6)**, and see p.2994 of the BDO Tax Guide. Therefore **S's** death estate cannot benefit by more than the full value of one additional NRB.

Where under his will, **T** makes a gift of his unused NRB(which is referred to in this book as a gift or legacy of the Nil Rate Amount *('NRA')*, to a trust, that results in the full depletion of his NRB, and the amount of his unused NRB ceases to be available for transfer to **S** (unless restored). Strategies involving the making of NRB legacies to discretionary trusts are discussed in Chapter 3.

Note that the introduction of the transferable NRB means that in certain circumstances it is preferable not to include a survivorship clause in a will, which is discussed in Chapter 3.

Flexible will = will/trust

As a testamentary planning tool, the creation of a trust under a will (i.e. a will/trust, which is referred to in this book as a *'will'*), offers flexibility and the opportunity for **T** to posthumously exercise some influence over the application of his property.

A discretionary trust created by a will is the most flexible tool available to the will/trust draftsman when providing for a surviving spouse and children (particularly where **T** is the father of children from an earlier marriage).To an extent it can also provide asset protection. However, **T** must choose his trustees with great care. Although **S**, and adult children can be appointed, and often are, it is usually prudent to appoint a professional trustee to hold the balance between competing interests.

NRB discretionary trusts

Whilst preserving **T's** unused NRB so that it can be transferred to **S** is simple, and involves less cost and risk than planning using a NRB Discretionary Will Trust *('NRBDT')*, the author's view is that:

1. the introduction of transferable NRB's; and

2. the recent changes in the ongoing income tax burden of discretionary trusts,

have not rendered planning using a NRBDT obsolete.

The transferable NRB does not apply to unmarried co-habitees (including siblings), or to singletons, and where **T** has inherited the NRB of a deceased former spouse, NRB planning can prevent the amount of the additional NRB from being wasted.

It is also a wealth preservation strategy that makes intrinsic planning sense for a number of other reasons that we will come to.

In any event, following **T's** death the trustees can unscramble the trust if it is preferable to appoint the NRA legacy directly to **S**.

Where it is unnecessary to put **T's** share of the equitable interest in the matrimonial home (held by **T** and **S** as joint-tenants) into a NRBDT because for example:

1. the balance of advantage favours an absolute transfer of that interest to **S**; or
2. because other assets are available to satisfy the NRA legacy,

then **T's** and **S's** estates do not need to be equalised, by severing any beneficial joint-tenancy that exists over the matrimonial home, in order to create a tenancy in common. **T's** interest will then pass automatically to **S** on his death by survivorship (i.e. outside his will), and be a spouse-exempt transfer for IHT.

Life interests

A complimentary planning tool is the creation of a life interest (known as an interest in possession, see Chapter 2 – '*Interests in possession*') in favour of one or more beneficiaries (known as '*life tenants*').

When coupled with the granting of wide '*overriding powers of appointment*' (see Chapter 1), the trustees can appoint property comprised in the trust on to new trusts, and in favour of different (and additional) beneficiaries. The inclusion of overriding powers in a will confers maximum flexibility on trustees over: (i) the disposition of trust property; (ii) the payment of income; (iii) the advancement of capital; and (iv) the creation (or '*appointment*') of new trusts, for the benefit of beneficiaries.

Planning using a discretionary trust (see Chapter 3 – '*NRB Discretionary Trusts*') essentially involves the creation of a discretionary trust to hold assets equal to the value of **T's** NRA, coupled with gifts of residue (either absolutely or for life).

Taking instructions

Taking instructions usually commences with the completion by **T** of a fact-finding questionnaire about his circumstances, family, assets, and liabilities.

This forms the basis of subsequent investigations and planning discussions with professional advisors until key issues (including the following), have been identified, and investigated:

1. the domicile of **T** and **S** (and their future plans);
2. the composition, nature, ownership, value, and location of both **T's** and **S's** assets (including any life-insurance policies, death in-service benefits, and sums payable under retirement, annuity, and pension policies);
3. debts and liabilities;
4. the couple's life-style, needs, and income;
5. family members and dependants (including their age and domicile, needs, plans, resources, and the state of their relationships with **T**, **S** and with each other). Note that a project management tool that can be used to create a visual road-map is the *'Wealth and Family Tree'*, see **Diagram No.7**;
6. how **T** wishes his estate to devolve on death, including any personal legacies, particularly of chattels (which should include consideration of the incidence of IHT and potential grossing-up);
7. the making of any absolute gifts;
8. the creation of beneficial interests in property subject to a trust of residue, including the creation of any special trusts, and in particular any life interests;
9. **T's** choice of executors, trustees, guardians (if **T** has children under the age of 18), and protectors (in the context of offshore planning);
10. approximate calculation of **T's** unused NRB – which requires tracing his history of giving within the last seven years (and sometimes further back);
11. any excluded property;
12. approximate calculation of the amount of IHT payable on death if **T** dies intestate (as a bench-mark for comparison);
13. the availability of IHT exemptions and reliefs; and
14. approximate calculation of **T's** net residuary estate available for distribution.

T should also be told:

1. about the extent of testamentary freedom under English law, and the potential for a claim being made by a dependant and certain relatives, within six months of his death, under the **Inheritance (Provision for Family and Dependants) Act 1975 ('Inheritance Act')**;

2. that jointly-held property will pass outside **T's** estate by survivorship;
3. that unless specific provision is made in his will, a gift of a specific item will adeem if during his lifetime it: (i) is sold; or (ii) changes in substance;
4. that unless his will provides otherwise, in the event that the recipient (*'donee'*) predeceases **T**, most gifts made in his will to that person will lapse, and either: (i) fall into residue; or (ii) pass under the **Intestacy Rules**;
5. about provision for the making of a *'gift over'* (or *'substitutional gift'*);
6. the *'incidence'* of taxation; *'grossing-up'*; and that unless his will provides otherwise, a beneficiary who takes property subject to a debt, will take it subject to that debt (and that particular care is required where life assurance is linked to debt);
7. that payments from pension funds and insurance policies written in trust for beneficiaries, will pass outside of his will; and
8. about the scope of **s.142** and **s.144** (variations and automatic reading-back).

Professional duties

To avoid any conflict of interest, **T** and **S** should be interviewed separately, and no other beneficiary should be present. Taking instructions from **T** on his own will also provide a defence to any allegation that he did not know or approve of the contents of his will, **Barry v Butlin** (1838). If a testator signs his will without having any knowledge of its contents, the will is invalid. The time when knowledge and approval is required is usually the time of execution.

A solicitor should make a full record of **T's** instructions, ask **T** to confirm them in writing, and then ensure that **T's** will is drawn up accordingly. After **T's** will has been drafted, the provisions of the will should be fully explained to him before he executes the will, to ensure that **T** understands and approves of the contents of his will. A solicitor's duty does not end when the will is drafted, as he must ensure that it is properly and validly executed. Note that the standard of a Solicitor's duty of care is discussed under that heading in Chapter 6 – *'Traps for the unwary'*.

The Ramsay principle

Where an arrangement appears to HMRC to have been artificially engineered with the sole purpose of avoiding tax, and has no basis in reality, they are likely to challenge it under what is known as the *'**Ramsay principle**'*. As the author of Foster's Inheritance Tax has explained, in the current fiscal and political climate, *'tax avoidance schemes are much harder to implement: clients' interests are likely better served by non-aggressive planning which* *ensures that opportunities to reduce the IHT bill using any reliefs available are fully utilised.'* That is the common sense approach advocated by the author and followed in this book.

Post-death variations

The beneficiaries may vary their entitlements after **T's** death (see Chapter 2 – *'Variations and reading-back'*, and **Diagram No.8** *'Post-death alterations'*). A NRA legacy to a discretionary trust made under a will can be unscrambled by an absolute appointment made to **S** within two years of **T's** death, which is automatically read-back into **T's** will under **s.144**. This in effect restores the full amount of **T's** transferable NRB available on death. However, beware of the **Frankland Trap** which is discussed in Chapter 6.

Life-time planning

Tax-efficient wealth structuring also involves life-time planning, which includes:

- if possible, the setting up of what are known as *'pilot trusts'* (see Chapter 3), to create a cascade of additional NRB's (one per settlement) during **T's** life-time, which will be available on **T's** death in addition to the full amount of his unused NRB. The funding of a pilot trust by a legacy made under **T's** will is discussed in Chapter 3 – *'Pilot trusts'*;
- if appropriate, the making of potentially exempt transfers *('PET's')* within **T's** NRB (which can become fully replenished every seven years);
- the structuring of qualifying business assets using for example:
    1. a corporate structure with an underlying shareholders' agreement; or
    2. a limited or a limited liability partnership structure with an underlying partnership or LLP members' agreement,
    however, this requires careful consideration of both the related property rules and the associated operations rules;
- planning surrounding the matrimonial home, which by **T's** election may give rise to either a charge to income tax under the pre-owned assets tax *('POAT')* regime, or to IHT (where for example the gifts with reservation rules *('GWR')* apply; and
- CGT and IHT planning for non-doms using non-resident property ownership structures.

Capital Gains Tax ('CGT')

On death **T's** assets are deemed to be acquired by his PR's at their market value at that time. **T** is not treated as being competent to dispose of assets over which he had a power of appointment (**s.62(1)) TCGA 1992**) but is regarded as being competent to dispose of his share of the equitable interest in jointly-owned property. Death generally wipes out capital gains (unless there are offshore income gains, in which case there is a disposal and the gains are charged).There is an uplift in the value of the assets but no charge to CGT (**s.62(1) TCGA 1992**). **T's** PR's can set his allowable losses against his chargeable gains in the year of assessment of his death (**s.65(2) TCGA 1992**). To the extent that available losses are not exhausted by chargeable gains in the three years of assessment preceding **T's** death then his PR's can claim a rebate.

Review

Planning assumptions can change over time, for example in relation to:

1. the domicile of **T** or **S** and children;
2. **T's** wealth, the nature and ownership of his assets, and asset values;
3. the stability of a marriage at both the level of (i) **T** and **S**; and (ii) between their children/grandchildren and their spouses;
4. the age, character, abilities, and needs of **T's** intended heirs; and
5. the prevailing fiscal environment, and political climate.

Tax legislation may be introduced with retrospective effect. Therefore the drafting of any tax-efficient will should be reviewed periodically, and in the author's view at least once every two years, unless there is an intervening seismic event. Review is also an opportunity for **T's** professional advisors to discuss, update, and assemble, documentation and records required for probate and for the making of a claim by **S's** PR's after her death under **s.8A**, see Chapter 2 – *'Nil Rate Band'*.

Key points

- IHT is a wealth tax levied on:
  1. chargeable lifetime transfers of value made before **T's** death (at the rate of 20%); and
  2. **T's** chargeable death estate (at the rate of 40%).
- IHT must be paid before **T's** remaining estate can be distributed, and delay in payment gives rise to penalties (see **Diagram No.9** – *'Penalties'*).
- If **T** does not leave a will the intestacy rules apply, which can produce unintended results for **S** (see **Diagram No.10** – *'Intestacy rules'*).
- The development of a tax-efficient wealth planning strategy requires the adoption of a *'holistic approach'* that includes consideration of life-time planning.

- The steps in the development of a tax-efficient planning strategy are shown in **Diagram No.12** – 'Master Plan'.
- The pivotal factor in testamentary planning is **T's** domicile (which may change during his lifetime), and note the factors that connect a person to the UK tax jurisdiction for the purposes of other taxes (shown in **Diagram No.11** – 'Fiscal connecting factors').
- The rules that apply to determine a person's domicile for IHT may also change during their lifetime, as may their settled intentions. Therefore where the effectiveness of a person's wealth planning strategy hinges upon their domicile, that status needs to be monitored and reviewed (and appropriate records assembled and kept).
- The planning process is labour intensive, and the provision of professional advice involves high standards of client care and technical expertise, all of which comes at a cost.
- **Rule 2.1** of the **Code of Professional Conduct of the Society of Trust and Estate Practitioners** (see www.step.org) requires that, 'a member shall at all times perform competent work for his or her client. Competent work requires the knowledge, skill, thoroughness and preparation reasonably necessary to perform the work, as well as performing the work conscientiously and diligently in a timely and cost-effective manner.' **Rule 2.3** further states that 'a member should not undertake work for a client if he or she is not competent to handle the work, or is not able to become competent to perform the work without undue delay, risk or expense to the client. Where a member feels he or she is not competent to handle the work, the member should either decline to act, or obtain instructions from his or her client to retain or consult with a practitioner or other advisor who is competent to perform the work.'
- Mandatory Money Laundering due diligence must also be fully complied with. Failure to comply by a solicitor is professional misconduct, and the imposition of criminal sanctions may follow in addition to disciplinary proceedings. Compliance requires thorough due diligence to be completed before legal advice is provided.
- Given that a wealth planning exercise resulting in the execution of a tax-efficient will is likely to save substantial amounts of IHT (see **Diagram No.2**), the cost of obtaining proper professional advice can be viewed as an investment.
- For the taxpayer who thinks that he is getting a bargain by obtaining the cheapest advice, it is sobering to reflect that the ultimate beneficiary of this saving is likely to be HM Treasury, and not his heirs and beneficiaries.

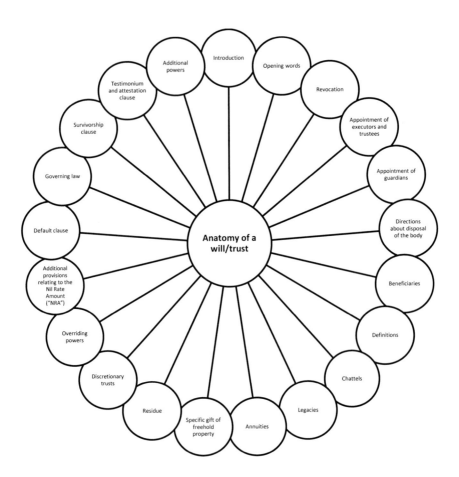

1

Anatomy of a Will/Trust

- Introduction
- Approach
- Opening words
- Revocation
- Appointment of executors and trustees
- Appointment of guardians
- Directions about disposal of the body
- Beneficiaries
- Definitions
- Chattels
- Legacies and devises
- Annuities
- Specific gifts of freehold property
- Residue
- Discretionary trusts
- Overriding powers
- Additional provisions relating to the NRA
- Default clause
- Governing law
- Survivorship clause
- Testimonium and attestation clause
- Additional powers

Introduction

General

It is preferable to set out all the provisions of a will in a single document for execution, and in this chapter we examine the anatomy of a will, standard provisions, and the underlying drafting issues.

Property that T can dispose of by his will

Under his will **T** can dispose of any property vested in him at the date of his death.

s.3 Wills Act 1837 provides that every person may, by his will, devise, bequeath or dispose of:

'all real estate and all personal estate which he shall be entitled to, either at law or in equity, at the time of his death, and which, if not so devised, bequeathed, and disposed of, would devolve upon his executor or administrator; and the power hereby given shall extend to all contingent, executory, or other future interests in any real or personal estate, whether the testator may or may not be ascertained as the person or one of the persons in whom the same respectively may become vested, and whether he may be entitled thereto under the instrument by which the same respectively were created, or under any disposition thereof by deed or will; and also to all rights of entry; and also to such of the same estates, interests, and rights respectively, and other real and personal estate, as the testator may be entitled to at the time of his death notwithstanding that he may become entitled to the same subsequently to the execution of his will.' Note that property held by **T** in a joint tenancy, passes by survivorship and cannot be given by will.

Mental capacity

To execute a valid will **T** must be over 18 and have testamentary capacity. Capacity is determined solely by **T's** state of mind. The criterion of testamentary capacity is that **T** understands, *'the nature of the act and its effects; [and] understands the extent of the property of which he is disposing; [and can] comprehend and appreciate the claims to which he ought to give effect; and, with a view to the latter object, that no disorder of the mind shall poison his affections, pervert his sense of right, or pervert the exercise of his natural faculties – that no insane delusion shall influence his will in disposing of his property and bring about a disposal of it which, if the mind had been sound, would not have been made.'* **Banks v Goodfellow** (1870). **T** must have, *'a memory to recall the several persons who may be fitting objects of [his] bounty, and an understanding to comprehend their relationship to himself and their claims upon him.'* **Broughton v Knight** (1873). Capacity may be lacking because of mental illness or because **T** is under the influence of drugs or alcohol. The relevant time for assessing capacity is the date of execution of the will. **s. 2(1) The Mental Capacity Act 2005** introduces a new statutory test of capacity. The definition does not replace the common law test expounded in **Banks v Goodfellow** (see also **Key v Key** (2010)). However, Judges may use it to develop new common law rules.

Formal requirements

The formal requirements for execution of a will prescribed by **s.9 WA 1837** (as amended by **s.17 AJA 1982**) are as follows:

1. the will must be in writing (note that the **Interpretation Act 1978**

extended the term to include *'typing, printing, photography and other modes of representing words in a visible form'*);
2.   by his signature **T** must intend to give effect to the will (note that the requirement is that **T** knew and approved the contents of his will at the time of signature);
3.   the will must be signed by **T**, or by some other person in his presence and by his direction in the presence of two or more witnesses present at the same time;
4.   each witness must either attest and sign the will in the presence of **T** or acknowledge his signature, in the presence of **T**; and
5.   both witnesses must attest and subscribe or acknowledge after **T's** signature has been made or acknowledged in their joint presence.

T's signature must be written or acknowledged by him in the actual visual presence of both witnesses together before either witness attests and signs the will, or acknowledges **T's** signature. **T** should sign with his usual signature. The signature of another person made on behalf of **T** is only valid if made in his presence, and by his direction. Neither a beneficiary, nor the husband wife or civil partner of a beneficiary should be a witness. The *'golden rule'* is that where there is any doubt about the capacity of an elderly or infirm testator, that a medical practitioner ought to be present to examine the testator, make a note of his findings, and witness the will. For a recent case see *Key v Key* (2010), **Appendix 7**.

Incorporation

A document can be incorporated into a will by reference provided: (i) the document exists when the incorporating testamentary instrument is executed; (ii) the instrument refers to the document as being in existence when that instrument is executed; and (iii) the document is sufficiently described in the will to enable it to be identified. Note that a document incorporated in a duly executed will: (i) is admissible to probate as part of the will; (ii) operates as part of **T's** will (and is subject to all of the rules applicable to wills); and (iii) if the requirements for incorporation are satisfied, an invalid will or codicil executed by **T** may be incorporated into a subsequent testamentary instrument duly executed by him.

Secret trusts

A trust is fully secret if the will does not disclose the existence of the trust, and is half secret if it discloses that there is a trust, but does not disclose the beneficiaries and terms. Secret trusts (which are not considered further in this book) are enforceable even though they do not comply with the **Wills Act 1837**.

Mistake, force, fear, fraud, and undue influence

A will executed by mistake or as a consequence of force, fear, fraud, or undue influence is not admitted to probate. The burden of proof is on the person alleging the irregularity, and there are no legal presumptions to assist. Note that a suspicion of undue influence will arise where **T's** will is drafted by a beneficiary.

Independent advice

Rule 3.04 of the **Solicitor's Code of Conduct** provides,

> 'Where a client proposes to make a lifetime gift or a gift on death to, or for the benefit of:
>> (a) you;
>> (b) any manager, owner or employee of your firm;
>> (c) a family member of any of the above,
> and the gift is of a significant amount, either in itself or having regard to the size of the client's estate and the reasonable expectations of the prospective beneficiaries, you must advise the client to take independent advice about the gift, unless the client is a member of the beneficiary's family. If the client refuses, you must stop acting for the client in relation to the gift.'

Privileged testators

A privileged testator can make a valid will without complying with the prescribed formalities. The will may even be oral. There are three categories of privileged testator: (i) a soldier (including a member of the Air Force) in actual military service (which includes 'not only fighting men but also those who serve in the Forces,' see **Wingham, Re** (1949); (ii) a mariner or seaman being at sea (which appears to be equivalent to being on maritime service); and (iii) a member of the naval or marine forces in actual combat.

Lost wills

Where a will or codicil last known to be in **T's** custody and possession, cannot be found after his death, **T** is presumed to have destroyed it with the intention of revoking it. Note that a will may be deposited with the High Court, for safe keeping, see the **Wills (Deposit for Safe Custody) Regulations 1978 (SI1978/1724)**.

Opening Words

The commencement of a will is intended to identify the testator. Therefore **T's** true and proper name should be stated in full, together with his residential address. Where **T** is known to own property in a different name, or to use a name that is different from his true and proper name, this should be mentioned in the opening words of the will.

Note that the date of the will can be included in the opening words, or at the end, immediately before the attestation clause.

Revocation Clause

A will is always revocable by **T** during his lifetime (even where he declares it to be irrevocable). **T's** intention may be absolute or conditional. An earlier will is revoked by an express clause of revocation in a subsequent will (**s.20 WA 1837**), and by:

1. marriage or registration of a civil partnership;
2. destruction;
3. execution of another valid will or codicil; and
4. any other written declaration of **T's** intention to revoke.

In the event of the dissolution or annulment of a marriage or civil partnership:

1. a provision either appointing the former spouse or civil partner as an executor, or giving them the power to appoint an executor takes effect as if she had died on the date of dissolution or annulment; and
2. any property (or interest in property) bequeathed by **T** to his former spouse passes as if she had died on the date of dissolution or annulment.

A prior will or codicil is impliedly revoked by a later will or codicil, in so far as the latter will or codicil contains provisions that are inconsistent with, or that merely repeat, the terms of the former will or codicil. Under **s.20 Wills Act 1837**, the whole or any part of a will or codicil may be revoked *'by the burning, tearing, or otherwise destroying the same by the testator, or by some person in his presence and by his direction, with the intention of revoking the same.'* This requires both (i) an act of destruction; and (ii) an intention to revoke.

T and **S** may make joint wills that are revocable by either of them (including the survivor) at any time. Where **T** and **S** make mutual wills, joint or separate wills are made as a result of an agreement between them to create irrevocable interests in favour of ascertainable beneficiaries. The agreement is enforced after the death of the first of them to die, by means of a constructive trust (see paragraph 1-012 Theobald).

Appointment of Executors and Trustees

An executor is a person appointed by **T** in his will, to stand in his shoes and administer his estate in accordance with (i) the provisions of his will, and (ii) the law. The person should be named in the will. If the identity of the executor is not clear, the appointment will be void for uncertainty. Any person may be appointed, however a person cannot be compelled to act, and may disclaim the office. It is therefore prudent to choose a person who is both willing and able to take up the office, and probate will not be granted to a minor or to a person of unsound mind. No more than four executors may take out a grant of probate at the same time in respect of the same part of an estate, hence in practice the number of executors is limited to four. Note that a sole trustee cannot give a valid receipt for capital sums derived from land (**s.14 TA 1925** and the **LPA 1925**). A corporation may be named as executor, and probate or administration may be granted to the corporation. However, an offshore trust company will not qualify, because a trust company cannot take out a grant of probate in its own name. A partnership firm may be appointed executor, in which case it is best to appoint the partners of the firm at the date of **T's** death. **T** may also authorise another person to nominate an executor of his will, and effect will be given to such nomination (and the person to nominate may nominate himself).

The executor acquires title and authority from the will. **T's** personal and real property devolves on his executor at death, and the executor derives authority to administer **T's** estate from the grant of probate. Note however that (i) legal title to property held by **T** as a trustee only devolves on the executor if **T** was the sole trustee, otherwise it passes to the surviving trustees; (ii) where property is held on a beneficial joint-tenancy, **T's** interest will pass to the surviving joint-tenant(s) by way of survivorship outside his estate for IHT; (iii) property subject to a nomination (also known as a *'donatio mortis causa'*, see paragraph 1.15 of Volume 1 of Williams) does not devolve on the executor, and can be claimed by the nominee or donee immediately after **T's** death; and (iv) insurance policies written in trust pass outside **T's** estate.

The executor's duties include:

1. collecting **T's** real and personal estate with reasonable diligence;
2. taking reasonable care to preserve the value of **T's** estate;
3. paying **T's** debts; and
4. distributing **T's** net estate to the persons entitled under his will.

However, an executor is not required to distribute **T's** net estate until one year after his death, which is known as the *'executor's year'*.

The minimum number of trustees is one. Even though the duties and functions attaching to executors and trustees are different, and require the conferment of different powers, it is usually convenient to appoint the same persons to act as both executors and trustees. In which case they may appoint another trustee and can delegate trust functions, see **s.11 TA 2000** (discussed in **Appendix 2** – Trustee's duties and powers). Where the executors and trustees are the same, a transfer of personal property *('personalty')* by the executors to the trustees is notional. However in the case of land *('real property')* legal title will not pass unless an assent has been executed.

A trustee's primary duty is to manage the trusts of the will for as long as they continue.

Where the executors and trustees are different people, the executors first liquidate the estate, discharge any debts, and then vest the residue in the trustees by delivery or assent. The appointment of a beneficiary as trustee gives him a direct interest and involvement in his family's financial affairs. However, the appointment of a life-tenant or remainder man as a trustee can give rise to a conflict of interest. It is not appropriate for **S** to wear both hats where **s.103** could be invoked. For IHT it is also preferable if **S** is not a NRA trustee, because if she becomes involved in the exercise of dispositive powers in her favour, HMRC may challenge such transactions on the basis that *the 'self-dealing rule'* applies. A solution is for **S** to be appointed:

1. as an executor and trustee under the will; and
2. to retire as a trustee before any potentially self-dealing transaction is implemented; and
3. then on **S's** retirement as a trustee, a second trustee can be appointed, who for example could be one of **T's** children or an independent professional trustee (see Chapter 6 – the *'Self-dealing rule'*).

TA 1925 codifies the rules that regulate the appointment and retirement of trustees, and it is usual to adopt these rules with specific amendments.

Appointment of Guardians

If **T** has young children, then in his will he can appoint guardians to care for his children after his death. The law of guardianship is set out in **Part 1 of the Children's Act 1989**. Under **sections 5** and **6** a parent who has parental responsibility for his child may by his will appoint a person to be the guardian of the child after his death. Any intended guardian must be aware of his appointment and be willing and able to act. More than one person will usually be appointed to act jointly. The court can also appoint a guardian under **s.5 (1) Children Act 1989** where the children are orphaned on **T's** death. **T's** will may create a trust fund for the maintenance of the children, appointing the guardians as trustees, and conferring upon them the power to apply income and capital for the maintenance, education, advancement, and other benefit of his children.

Directions about disposal of the body

Any directions given in a will about disposal of the body are not binding on **T's** PR's. A person has no property in his body after death, ***Williams v Williams*** (1881). However if **T** wishes any part of his body to be used for medical transplant purposes, he can make a written statement under **s.1(1) Human Tissue Act 1961**, which cannot be rescinded by his relatives. He may also consider making a *'living will'* to provide directions for his care in the event of sudden incapacity. The executors have the right to possession of the body and are under a duty to dispose of **T's** body decently and with reasonable dispatch, ***Dobson v North Tyneside Health Authority*** (1996).

Beneficiaries

If a beneficiary (referred to in this book as a *'legatee'* in relation to a gift of personalty, and as a *'devisee'* in relation to a gift of land), is not clearly described in **T's** will, a gift may be void. Subject to two exceptions (set out under *'Legacies and devises'* below), if the legatee: (i) is not alive when the will is made; or (ii) dies between the date of execution of the will and **T's** death, the gift will lapse, unless **T's** will provided for a *'gift over'* to be made to another person (referred to in this book as a *'substitutional gift'*). See the *'doctrine of lapse'* discussed below. The application of the doctrine cannot be excluded under the terms of a will, however it does not apply where a gift is made to joint-tenants.

There are two types of beneficiary, those who are:

1. exempt from IHT (for example **S** or a charity); and
2. chargeable/non-exempt (for example **T's** son or daughter, or a grandchild).

A gift to either may be left:

1. outright and absolutely ; or
2. in a trust for that person's benefit.

A beneficiary who enjoys a life interest in a trust fund is known as a life tenant or income beneficiary (for example **S**). On the death of a life-tenant, the extent of her interest in the trust fund is aggregated with her chargeable estate for IHT, (**s.5**). A beneficiary under a will has no legal title to or equitable interest in any property comprising an estate under administration.

Legal title refers to the strict legal ownership of an asset. Equitable interest refers to beneficial ownership (the right to enjoy the benefit of an asset). In relation to a house the legal owner is the person registered at HM Land Registry in the proprietorship register with title absolute, and the beneficial owner would be entitled to live in it. Under English law legal title and beneficial ownership (the equitable interest) can be split, so that legal title is held by one person, and the equitable interest is held by another person or persons. The world at large deal with the legal owner, who on the face of it, exercises all of the rights over the asset. However, the legal owner holds the asset on trust for the beneficial owner(s) and exercises his rights over it in accordance with his obligations as trustee.

Where beneficiaries under a discretionary trust include:

1. children (including for example **C.1**); and
2. grand-children,

and trust income is used to pay for **C.1's** school fees, then that income can be attributed to **C.1** resulting in a reclaim of tax paid by the trustees. In 2011/2012 income received by trustees in excess of £1K (the *'standard rate band'*) is subject to income tax in their hands at the rate of 50% (or 42.5% on dividend income of a discretionary trust). A further tax charge may be incurred by trustees when they distribute income to beneficiaries, however, a beneficiary who is taxable on the distribution at his marginal rate is entitled to a credit for the tax paid by the trustees. Therefore a beneficiary whose marginal rate of income tax is lower than the rate applicable to trusts can reclaim all or part of the tax already paid by the trustees.

Class gifts

Where **T** makes a gift to a class of beneficiaries (a *'class gift'*), the members of the class are ascertained after his death. Therefore a person who would have belonged to the class, and who pre-deceases **T** is not included in the class. Class gifts are not the same as gifts made to a distinct group of persons. Note that the doctrine of lapse does not apply to the former, but does apply to the latter.

Class closing rules

If **T** makes a gift to an open class of beneficiaries (to which members may be added) distribution cannot take place until all members of the class have been ascertained. In default of a provision for the closing of the class, default rules apply to different types of gift. For an individual gift to each member the class closes at the date of **T's** death. If there are no living beneficiaries the gift fails. For an immediate gift the class closes at **T's** death. For a postponed gift (i.e. where an absolute gift is preceded by an IPDI), the class includes all living members at the date of **T's** death and those born before the death of the life-tenant. Under a contingent gift the class closes at **T's** death if any member has satisfied the contingency, the rule in ***Andrews v Partington*** (1791). If not, it remains open until a member does, then it closes. For a postponed contingent gift the class closes on the death of the life-tenant provided a member has satisfied the contingency, if not the class remains open until one does, and then it closes. This can produce harsh results therefore consideration should be given to modifying the rules.

Minority and contingent interests

Where a gift is made to **T's** *'children'*, the term includes immediate descendants, but not grandchildren, or remoter issue. Unless a contrary intention is expressed by **T** in his will *'children'* includes adopted children. A child *en ventre sa mere* (in the womb) is included in the description of children born or living at a particular date, where it is to the child's own benefit to be included. *'Descendants'* generally includes any person descended from a particular individual, but does not include collateral relations. Unless restricted by the wording of **T's** will, *'Issue'* means *'descendants in every degree.'* *'Next of kin'* refers to the nearest relative of kin. For IHT and CGT special charging provisions apply to minority and contingent interests under a will (which of course, includes interests created in favour of children and grandchildren).

Definitions

Definitions vary according to the structure of the will. The following definitions are included here to illustrate the basic structure of a NRBDT that can be implemented using either the *'debt'* or *'charge'* scheme, and under which residue is left to **S** absolutely or on a discretionary trust:

- Residuary estate;
- Nil Rate Band *('NRB')*;
- Nil Rate Amount *('NRA')*;
- Trust Fund;
- Trust Property; and
- NRA Trustees.

This is not an exhaustive list, and the drafting of definitions will vary in accordance with the scheme of dispositions made by **T** in his will.

Residuary Estate

Residue, or **T's** *'residuary estate'* is what remains available for distribution after payment of:

1. his debts;
2. testamentary expenses;
3. all taxes and duties; and
4. the distribution of any legacies and devises bequeathed by **T** under his will.

For planning purposes residue is made up of (i) income and (ii) capital (the *'capital fund'*). Note that for: (i) the making of absolute gifts; and (ii) the creation of beneficial interests under a trust fund (i.e. the *'residuary trust fund'* as distinct from the *'NRA Trust Fund'*), residue can be divided into shares.

Nil Rate Band *('NRB')*

The NRB is the upper limit specified in **Schedule 1 IHTA 1984** (which for a testator who dies in 2011/2012 is £325K).

Nil Rate Amount *('NRA')*

Normal practice is to give a legacy of a sum of money fixed by a formula to equal **T's** available NRB. Note that the drafting of the Kessler & Sartin *'nil rate formula'* is discussed in paragraph 18.16 of the current edition of their book. For a discussion of the problems that arise where **T** and **S** have remarried, and either or both have acquired the NRB of a deceased former spouse, see paragraph 18.8 of Kessler & Sartin - *'Untransferable NRB problems'*. Their comments on the decision by the judge at first instance in **RSPCA v Sharp** (2010) (about the construction of a NRB gift) are set out in Chapter 7 below. Note that the decision in **RSPCA v Sharp** was reversed by a unanimous Court of Appeal in December 2010.

Trust Fund

1. If **S** survives **T**, this means the NRA (only).
2. If **S** does not, then it means **T's** residuary estate.
3. In either case it includes all property from time to time representing 1 or 2 above.

The constitution and elements of a trust fund are illustrated by **Diagram No.13** – *'Trust fund.'*

Trust Property

Means any part of the Trust Fund.

NRA Tru#stees

Means the Trustees of the Nil Rate Amount *('NRA')*.

Chattels

The usual bequest is either an absolute gift to an individual, or to executors, to distribute in accordance with a memorandum setting out **T's** wishes. For planning see Chapter 3 – *'Chattels'*.

Legacies and devises

T may make gifts of his property outright or in trust (a *'settled gift'*). A gift made by will of:

1. **T's** personal property *('personalty')* is called a *'legacy,'* and
2. real property is called a *'devise'*.

See **Diagram No.22** – Scheme of dispositions.

A legacy may be:

- *specific* (a gift of a particular item of property owned by **T** at his death), which shows his intention that the property passes to the legatee in specie;
- *general* (a gift of something to be provided out of **T's** general estate, as distinct from a gift of particular property);
- *demonstrative* (a hybrid, which takes the form of a general gift containing a direction for payment out of a designated fund or property);
- *pecuniary* (a gift of money), e.g. an *'annuity'* - which is a pecuniary legacy payable by instalments; and
- *residuary* (a gift that passes all of **T's** property not otherwise disposed of. Note that if no other dispositions have been made it may be a gift of **T's** entire net estate, or it may be a gift of what remains after all specific and general gifts have been paid.

A devise may be:

- *specific* (in which case it will be subject to the rules on ademption – see Chapter 6); or
- *residuary*.

The classification of gifts is pertinent:

1. because of the doctrines of *'ademption'* and *'abatement'*; and
2. in determining what income or interest is carried by the gift, and whether the donee of the gift bears any expenses incurred by **T's** PR's in preserving the assets.

Ademption means the failure of a specific gift when the subject-matter of the gift has ceased to form part of **T's** estate on his death. This may occur for example, as a result of the sale or destruction of an asset or a change in substance (but not merely of form). Note that where **T** during his lifetime enters into a binding contract to sell any real property that the *'equitable doctrine of conversion'* applies, so that from the date of the contract, **T** no longer has an interest in the realty, and instead has an interest in the proceeds of sale.

A demonstrative gift does not adeem if the specified fund or property is insufficient. In that event the legacy will be treated as a general legacy to be paid out of **T's** estate generally. Nor do demonstrative legacies abate with general legacies, but only when such legacies have been exhausted.

When **T** wishes to make a gift of a specific item of property the doctrine of ademption should be explained to him.

Abatement arises where funds available for payment of pecuniary legacies are insufficient, in which case they reduce rateably, subject to any questions of priority between them. Subject to two exceptions for a beneficiary to take a gift under **T's** will, they must survive him. Otherwise the gift lapses (the *'doctrine of lapse'*).

A legacy or specific devise that fails (see **Diagram No.25** – *'Failure of legacies'*) falls into residue unless **T's** will provides for a substitutional gift to be made to another person. Upon the failure of a residuary gift, the property passes to **T's** next of-kin under the *Intestacy Rules* (see **Diagram No.10**). See also *'survivorship clauses'* below and in Chapter 3.

A gift made to joint-tenants or to a class of beneficiaries will lapse after all of the joint-tenants or members of the class have predeceased **T**. However in the case of a gift made to tenants in common, the share of a tenant who pre-deceases **T** will fail.

The two exceptions to the doctrine of lapse are:

1. a gift made by **T** to a beneficiary in discharge of a moral obligation (however the rule may be limited to directions to pay debts, and may not apply to ordinary gifts); and

2. **s.33 Wills Act 1837** (as substituted by **s.9 AEA 1982**), which provides,

    '(1) Where –

    (a) *a will contains a devise or bequest to a child or remoter descendant of the testator; and*

    (b) *the intended beneficiary dies before the testator, leaving issue; and*

    (c) *issue of the intended beneficiary are living at the testator's death,then unless a contrary intention appears by the will, the devise or bequest shall take effect as a devise or bequest to the issue living at the testator's death.*

    (2) Where –

    (a) a *will contains a devise or bequest to a class of person consisting of children or remoter descendants of the testator; and*

    (b) *a member of the class dies before the testator, leaving issue, and*

    (c) *issue of that member are living at the testator's death, then, unless a contrary intention appears by the will, the devise or bequest shall take effect as if the class included the issue of its deceased member living at the testator's death.*

    (3) Issue shall take under this section through all degrees, according

to their stock, in equal shares if more than one, any gift or share which their parent would have taken and so that no issue shall take whose parent is living at the testator's death and so capable of taking.

(4) For the purposes of this section –

(a) the illegitimacy of any person is to be disregarded; and

(b) a person conceived before the testator's death and born living thereafter is to be taken to have been living at the testator's death.'

Where by his will, **T** makes a 'settled gift', the named beneficiary receives income, and capital is preserved until it either vests:

1. on the beneficiary attaining a particular age (for example the age of 25); or in default
2. on the remainder men.

An overriding power can be included in **T's** will to advance capital to a beneficiary before the age of 25).

The planning advantages of a trust include:

1. **T** can provide income for **S** whilst preserving capital for his children;
2. capital is protected from dissipation in the hands of a profligate or irresponsible beneficiary; and
3. by putting the gift into a discretionary trust for his family, **T** creates a vehicle for the implementation of flexible planning after his death.

Common trust structures are:

1. a special trust;
2. a protective trust;
3. a trust under which capital vests upon attainment by the beneficiary of a certain age;
4. a NRB discretionary trust; and
5. a two-year discretionary trust.

Note that the statutory powers of maintenance and advancement under **sections 31** and **32 TA 1925** apply to permit income and capital of a child beneficiary's presumptive share to be advanced to them or applied for their benefit before the contingency is fulfilled.

For planning see Chapter 3 – 'Legacies and devises'.

Annuities

An annuity is a pecuniary legacy payable by instalments.

For planning see Chapter 3 – 'Annuities'.

Specific Gifts of freehold property

Before drafting the will **T's** solicitor needs to check: (i) the nature and extent of **T's** interest in the property (i.e. by reference to office copies in relation to registered land); and (ii) that **T** has the unfettered power to make a disposition of the property.

Where a devise is made to more than one person concurrently, the gift may be of a *'joint-tenancy'*, or of a *'tenancy in common'*. Note that **T** cannot sever an joint-tenancy by his will.

Special provision can be made where for example **T** wishes to:

1. make an absolute or settled gift of property to a particular beneficiary;
2. create special rights of occupation to govern the future use of property; or
3. give a beneficiary or a third party an option to purchase property so that its value can be received by the estate whilst enabling that person to acquire the property.

Otherwise no provision is required where real property devolves with residue. If there is no direction as to payment of tax, then IHT on land is borne by the beneficiary to whom it is given. Where **T** wishes to provide for a gift in trust, the various rights conferred on trustees (and certain beneficiaries) under **TLATA 1996** should be considered (see Chapter 5 – *'Additional powers'*, and **Appendix 2** – *Note on Trustee's duties and powers*).

Unless **T** expresses a contrary intention in his will, IHT on a specific devise of UK property is payable out of residue as a general testamentary expense, **s.221** (which does not apply to UK property which prior to **T's** death was comprised in a settlement), see p.3068 of the BDO Tax Guide.

Residue

A general residuary gift after payment of debts and administration expenses passes everything not specifically disposed of (for planning using residue see Chapter 3 – *'Gifts of residue'*, and **Diagram No.14** – *Gifts of residue*).

Discretionary trusts

To set up a discretionary trust, by his will **T** appoints trustees to hold property (previously in his absolute ownership) for the benefit of a specified beneficiary or class of beneficiaries. The property left by **T** under his will to the trustees becomes the Trust Fund *('Trust property')*. After **T's** death, the trustees acquire all of the common law rights in the trust property *('legal title')*, and to the outside world appear to own it. The beneficiaries acquire equitable proprietary rights against the trust property, and a set of personal claims against the trustees, to ensure compliance by the trustees with the terms of **T's** will (the *'equitable interest'* in the trust property). The proprietary rights include recognition that the beneficiaries hold the property rights in the trust property. Hence the equitable interest is the ultimate ownership interest in the trust property. See **Diagram No.15** - *'Discretionary trust structure'*.

Trustees owe what are called *'fiduciary duties'* (discussed in the note on Trustee's powers and duties in **Appendix 2**), and are liable to the beneficiaries for any loss resulting from a breach of trust. Trustees' duties have to a large extent been codified by the **Trustee Act 2000** (the **'TA 2000'**), which under **s.35** of the Act, apply to *'executors'* as well as *'trustees'*. This section is of broader application than appears at first sight, and for commentary on the full implications see p.332 of Reed. Many administrative powers are also conferred on trustees (which also apply to executors) under: (i) the **Administration of Estates Act 1925** (the **'AEA 1925'**); (ii) the **Trustee Act 1925** (the **'TA 1925'**); and (iii) the **TA 2000**.

Trustees may pay or apply income or capital to any person amongst a defined class of beneficiaries at their discretion by:

1. making a capital distribution or loan;
2. creating new trusts; or
3. permitting a beneficiary to occupy trust property.

A beneficiary has a mere expectation and no fixed entitlement to receive any trust property. For IHT planning using a discretionary trust, see **Chapter 3** – *'Discretionary trusts'*.

Overriding powers

In this book the term *'overriding powers'* is used to describe wide and flexible powers given to trustees, to enable them to achieve **T's** intention to benefit the beneficiaries in the most appropriate way when exercised. The existence of such powers also prevents a profligate beneficiary from selling their interest because the trustees can revoke it on the next day.

A *'power of appointment'* is a power to vary the administrative and beneficial provisions of a trust, or to create new trusts for the beneficiaries. In a standard trust deed, the exercise of a power of appointment would normally require execution of a deed. Note that it is the deed that actually makes the appointment.

A *'power of resettlement'* is a power to transfer trust property to a new and separate trust for the beneficiaries, and may also be used to combine trusts, and to split a trust with sub-funds into separate trusts with separate classes of beneficiary.

A *'power of advancement'* is a power to transfer trust property to a person, or apply it for his advancement or benefit, and may be used:

1. to transfer trust property to a new trust;
2. to create new beneficial interests under an existing trust (which may replace an existing beneficial interest in whole or in part); and
3. to vary the administrative provisions of a trust.

Unlike the transfer of capital to a beneficiary under either a power of (i) appointment or (ii) resettlement, the exercise of a power of advancement does not require the execution of a deed. However, the trustees should record their decision either in a written resolution or in minutes of meeting.

The drafting and exercise of overriding powers is outside the scope of this book and the reader is referred to Chapter 11 of Kessler & Sartin. Great care is required to avoid inadvertent adverse tax consequences resulting from the drafting of a deed of appointment (see paragraph 12.1 of Kessler & Sartin). As a matter of trust law, there may not be much difference between: (i) the alteration of the terms of an existing trust using a power of appointment; and (ii) a transfer of trust property to a new trust by exercising a power of re-settlement. However, there are important differences for tax purposes:

1. a transfer to another trust is a disposal for CGT (whereas the exercise of a power of appointment does not normally involve a disposal); and
2. if only part of the trust fund is transferred to a new trust, the result is two separate trusts.

For a discussion of whether the exercise of a power of advancement or appointment creates a new settlement, and of the CGT consequences, see paragraphs 2.41-2.46 of Whitehouse & King, **SP 7/84** (HMRC's interpretation), and **CGTM 37841**.

Whilst trustees can make an appointment of residue (or of a share of residue) at any time, they cannot make an appointment dealing with particular assets, until those assets have been appropriated or assented to them out of **T's** estate. Therefore **T's** will should provide that his executors may exercise a power of appointment during the course of the administration of his estate. No liability for CGT arises out of the appointment if the power is exercised by executors, because for CGT the appointee takes as legatee.

Additional provisions relating to the NRA LEGACY

These provisions enable the implementation of the *'debt'* or *'charge'* scheme (discussed in **Chapter 3** below) by:

- requiring the NRA Trustees to accept an undertaking from S to pay the NRA (or, if less the value of **T's** residuary estate) to the NRA Trustees on demand;
- authorising **T's** executors to charge all or part of his residuary estate, with payment of all or part of the NRA, to the NRA Trustees on demand;

and
- authorising the NRA Trustees, to refrain from calling in the NRA, or exercising any rights in relation to it, for as long as they think fit.

Default clause

This clause (also known as the *'longstop provision'*) ensures that there is no possibility of the trust failing, so in the (unlikely) event that the trust is not terminated before the end of the perpetuity period there is express provision as to who becomes entitled to capital.

Governing law

The specified law governs the validity, construction, effect, and administration of the will/trust. In principle **T** may choose any governing law which recognises trusts (**Article 6 Hague Convention on the Law Applicable to Trusts and on their Recognition 1985**). A power to change the governing law of a trust is valid under English law, and a choice of a foreign law can create a litigation shield. For the purposes of this book it is naturally assumed that **T** has declared that the proper law and forum for administration is that of England and Wales.

Survivorship clause

A survivorship clause operates to prevent property passing through two estates in close succession. Without such a provision, in the event of simultaneous deaths, and subject to quick succession relief, **T's** assets:

1. are potentially taxable in the estate of both:
   (a) **T**; and
   (b) a beneficiary, i.e. **S**; and
2. will pass according to the will or intestacy of **S**, which may not be what **T** intended.

Where each spouse leaves their respective estate outright to the other (or create an IPDI in their estate for the other), it is more tax-efficient if the survivorship clause does not apply where the order of deaths is uncertain. For planning see **Chapter 3** – *'Survivorship clauses'*.

Testimonium and attestation clause

An attestation clause evidences execution of a will in accordance with **s.9 WA 1837**. If there is no clause **r.12 Non-Contentious Probate Rules** requires an affidavit of due execution before the will can be admitted to proof. **T** must sign or acknowledge his signature before either witness signs the will.

Note that **s.21 WA 1837** provides that, *'no obliteration, interlineations, or other alteration made in any will after the execution thereof shall be valid or have any effect, except so far as the words or effect of the will before such alteration shall not be apparent, unless such alteration shall be executed in like manner as herein-before is required for the execution of the will; but the will, with such alteration as part thereof, shall be deemed to be duly executed if the signature of the testator and the subscription of the witnesses be made in the margin or on some other part of the will opposite or near to such alteration, or at the foot or end of or opposite to a memorandum referring to such alteration, and written at the end of some other part of the will.'* Where an alteration is apparent on the face of the will a rebuttable presumption arises that it was made after execution. To avoid uncertainty, either the alteration should be expressly referred to in the attestation clause as having already been made at the time of execution, or a codicil clarifying the alteration should be executed.

Additional powers

The draftsman needs to consider what if any additional powers need to be conferred on **T's** trustees by his will, for example to implement a super-NRBDT arrangement after **T's** death, see **Chapter 5** – *'Additional Powers'*.

2

Planning Concepts

- Assets
- Chargeable transfers of value
- Domicile
- Exemptions
- Grossing-up
- GWR & POAT
- Inheritance Act claims
- Interests in possession
- Jointly-owned property
- Nil Rate Band ('NRB')
- Reliefs
- Settlement
- Tax mitigation
- Testamentary freedom
- Variations and reading-back

Assets

Free estate

This term is used to describe **T's** own property of which he was free to dispose. However, it does not include: (i) joint-property passing by survivorship; (ii) settled property; (iii) property over which **T** had a general power of appointment; or (iv) nominated property (**IHTM 26003**).

T can dispose of any property vested in him at the time of his death provided his interest does not cease at death. **T's** estate includes the value of all property to which he was beneficially entitled in any part of the world:

1. including certain interests in possession in settled property (see **s.5(1) (a)(ii)**, **(1A), and (1B)**); but
2. excluding any: (i) jointly-owned assets held on a legal and beneficial joint- tenancy; and (ii) excluded property (as defined in **s.5**).

Asset classes

See **Diagram No.16** – '*Assets*'.

Chargeable transfers of value

Subject to the availability of exemptions exclusions and reliefs, IHT is payable:

1. at life-time rates (20%) on the cumulative value of all life-time chargeable transfers that exceed **T's** unused NRB; and
2. at 40% on the value of **T's** chargeable 'free' estate at death, taking into account all chargeable transfers made within the previous seven years.

The cumulative amount of all lifetime transfers of value falls out of charge every seven years, at which point an individual's NRB can become fully replenished. Lifetime chargeable transfers within an individual's NRB are known as potentially exempt transfers ('PET's') and are not reported to HMRC (however, proper records need to be kept).

Three concepts underpin the main charging provisions:

1. 'chargeable transfer' – which may be actual (an estate diminishing disposition) or notional;
2. 'transfer of value'; and
3. 'exempt transfer'.

Taken together **s.2** and **s.3** define a chargeable transfer in terms of a transfer of value that results in loss to an individual's estate (as distinct from the value of the property disposed of), which is known as the 'consequential loss rule.' **s.2 (1)** provides that, 'A chargeable transfer is a transfer of value which is made by an individual but is not (by virtue of Part II of this Act or any other enactment) an exempt transfer.' **s.3 (1)** provides that 'Subject to the following provisions of this Part of this Act, a transfer of value is a disposition made by a person (the transferor) as a result of which the value of his estate immediately after the disposition is less than it would be but for the disposition; and the amount by which it is less is the value transferred by the transfer. **s.3 (2)** provides that 'For the purposes of subsection (1) above no account shall be taken of the value of excluded property which ceases to form part of a person's estate as a result of a disposition.'

Domicile

Introduction

Domicile has been adopted by the UK tax system as a connecting factor limiting the UK tax jurisdiction. Because **T's** liability to IHT depends upon where (i) he is domiciled; or (ii) is 'deemed' to be domiciled (under the IHT rules), consideration of his domicile is a critical priority in developing a tax-efficient wealth planning strategy.

Domicile is also a general legal concept not created solely for tax purposes (see paragraph 2.2 in Volume 1 of Taxation of Foreign Domiciliaries 2010-2011). An individual domiciled in the UK is liable to IHT on their worldwide assets wherever located, whereas a *'non-dom'* is only liable to IHT on chargeable property located within the UK **(s.6(1))**.The place in which an individual is domiciled is not necessarily a nation state in a political sense, but any geographical area governed by a unified system of law. Thus an individual is domiciled in *'England'* or *'Scotland'*, rather than in the *'United Kingdom'*, **Casdagli v Casdagli** (1919). However, throughout this book we refer collectively to individuals domiciled anywhere within the UK as being domiciled in the UK .

Determination of domicile is a question of fact, and because **T's** domicile can change during his lifetime, a final determination can only be made after his death. An individual is generally domiciled in the place where he is considered to have his permanent home, **Whicker v Hume** (1858). However, he may be domiciled in a place even though he does not have his permanent home there, **Bell v Kennedy** (1866). Note that the elements required for the acquisition of a domicile go beyond those required for the acquisition of a permanent home.

Definition of domicile

No individual can be without a domicile. The domicile of a dependant is always dependent on that of an ascertainable independent individual, or is fixed by law. Nor can any person, at the same time, and for the same purpose, have more than one domicile. Where a person has two homes in different countries, in the absence of a contrary intention, he will be domiciled in the country in which he has his principal home, **Forbes v Forbes** (1854), and see **Plummer v CIR** (1987). If an individual has no home nor any intention of residing permanently within the UK, he is domiciled in the country of his domicile of origin. If he has his home in that country, he continues to be domiciled there until he acquires a domicile of choice in another country. Having acquired such a domicile of choice, he retains it until he abandons it. Upon abandonment he may acquire a new domicile of choice, if he does not his domicile of origin revives by operation of law. An existing domicile is presumed to continue until it has been proved that a new domicile has been acquired.

Ascertainment of domicile

a. Domicile of origin

An individual's domicile of origin is in effect his default domicile. Every individual receives a domicile of origin at birth. A legitimate child born during the lifetime of his father has his domicile of origin in the country in which his father was domiciled at the time of his birth. However, a legitimate child born after the death of his father or an illegitimate child, has his domicile of origin in the country in which his mother was domiciled when she gave birth.

A foundling has his domicile of origin in the country in which he was found.

Domicile in an enduring attachment, and a domicile of origin cannot be changed otherwise than as a result of adoption. The burden of proving a change of domicile lies on the individual asserting it, **Winans v A.G.** (1904).

Whilst the standard of proof is the civil standard, the burden of proof is a heavy one to discharge in practice. Practitioners should note that for the purposes of an English rule of the conflict of laws, the question of where a person is domiciled is determined in accordance with English law.

b. Domicile of dependency

The domicile of an individual under 16 changes with that of the relevant parent. The domicile of a legitimate child born during his father's lifetime changes with the domicile of his father. However, the domicile of an illegitimate child, or a child born after the death of his father, changes with that of his mother. The domicile of a legitimate or legitimated child without living parents, or of an illegitimate child without a living mother, probably cannot be changed until he becomes an adult. The domicile of an adopted child is determined as if he were the legitimate child of the adoptive parent or parents. After 16 the domicile of dependency is retained as a domicile of choice. However, it is immediately abandoned if the child does not live in the territory and never intends to live there, and the child's domicile of origin revives. If he is living in a third territory with the intention of remaining there, that territory becomes his domicile of choice.

c. Domicile of choice

Every individual over the age of 16 may acquire a domicile of choice by both: (i) residing in the new country; and (ii) having an intention to make his home in that country, permanently or indefinitely. The conduct of the individual after the alleged change in domicile is equally material in determining his chief residence, as are acts occurring at the time of the change. However, there is nothing inconsistent with the acquisition of a residence in England, and maintenance of a firm intention to return to the place where an individual is domiciled prior to living in England, **Anderson (Anderson's Executor) v CIR** (1998).

An individual cannot be resident in a country where he is present as a traveller or casually resident. A domicile of choice cannot be acquired (where the requisite intention exists) by merely setting out for that country, actual arrival is necessary. When determining whether or not an individual has acquired a domicile of choice, the court must consider any circumstance which is evidence of a person's residence or of his intention to reside permanently or indefinitely in that country.

The absence of any evidence would be conclusive against the acquisition of a new domicile. It is frequently difficult to establish acquisition because neither HMRC nor the courts have laid down a definitive set of criteria by which to resolve the question. Retention of accommodation in the country of origin does not negative the acquisition of a domicile of choice elsewhere if, on the facts, the new country is the main home. But it may be difficult to show that the new country is the individual's chief residence if his accommodation in the old country is his former home, particularly if his social and business activities there continue, and statements made on his behalf indicate that he is looking forward to resuming permanent residence there.

The availability of homes in more than one country may mean that none can be said to be the individual's chief residence. The acquisition of nationality and a passport in the new country can point to the acquisition of a domicile of choice there, but it is not conclusive evidence. An existing domicile is presumed to continue until it is proved that a new domicile has been acquired.

Abandonment of domicile

An adult may abandon his domicile of choice by ceasing to reside in that country or by establishing (to HMRC's satisfaction), a fixed settled intention to live permanently elsewhere, but not otherwise. When a domicile of choice is abandoned, either a new domicile of origin is acquired, or the domicile of origin revives. An individual cannot abandon a domicile of choice simply by becoming dissatisfied with it, without actually leaving the country. Since the enactment of **s.1 (1) Domicile and Matrimonial Proceedings Act 1973**, the domicile of a married woman is ascertained and may change in the same way as that of any other adult. Determination of whether a change of domicile had occurred is fact specific. Note that a list of connecting factors previously considered by the English court is set out in Finney, at paragraph 3.78, which include:

- accompaniment by wife (and children);
- burial;
- business interests;
- health;
- length of time spent in the country;
- lifestyle;
- location of dwellings;
- maintenance of bank accounts;
- membership of clubs; and
- oral statements made to relations and third parties.

IHT deemed domicile rules

For IHT purposes an individual is deemed domiciled in the UK at the date of his death if either:

1. he was domiciled in the UK at any time within the three years preceding

the time at which the question of his domicile was determined (**s.267(1)**) (**a**) – the '*three year rule*'); or

2. he was resident in the UK in not less than 17 out of 20 years of assessment ending with the present one (**s.267(1)(b)** – the '*17 out of 20 rule*').

Income tax rules generally apply to the determination of an individual's residence in the UK in a particular tax year.

Confirmation of domicile

HMRC do not give hypothetical rulings. In the case of a migrant from the UK one solution is to make a gift of foreign assets in excess of his available NRB three complete tax years after migration. A UK domicile is deemed to persist for three years after it is in fact lost, and is retained if the tax payer has been resident in the UK in 17 out of the last 20 years of assessment. In that event IHT will be chargeable unless the individual lost both his actual and his deemed UK domicile following migration. Therefore if HMRC do not charge IHT, it would appear that the individual must have acquired a foreign domicile.

Exemptions

Introduction

The principal exemptions (not all of which are discussed) are:

1. dispositions for family maintenance (**s.11**);
2. dispositions allowable for income tax or conferring retirement benefit (**s.12**);
3. dispositions by close companies for the benefit of employees (**s.13**);
4. transfers between spouses (the '*Spouse exemption*') (**s.18**);
5. annual exemption (**s.19**);
6. small gifts (**s.20**);
7. normal income out of expenditure (**s.21**);
8. wedding gifts (**s.22**);
9. gifts to charities (**s.23**);
10. gifts to qualifying political parties (**s.24**);
11. gifts to registered housing associations (**s.24A**);
12. gifts for national purposes (**s.25**);
13. transfers for maintenance funds for historic buildings (**s.27**);
14. transfers of shares or securities by an individual to an employee trust (**s.28**);
15. transfers of national heritage property (**sections 30-35**); and

16. death on active service exemption (**s.154**).

More than one exemption may apply to a transfer. There are no rules as to the priority given to each exemption. Where possible the best approach is to ensure that a general transfer (which does not fall within an obvious category) falls within **T's** normal expenditure out of income exemption, and failing that, his annual exemption. Where more than one transfer is made in a tax year, it is applied first to the earlier transfers. Where more than one transfer has been made on the same day, the exemptions are pro-rated. See paragraphs 11.58 and 11.59 of Finney.

Annual exemption (s.19)

s.19 provides, '*Transfers of value made by a transferor in any one year are exempt to the extent that the values transferred by them (calculated as values on which no tax is payable) do not exceed £3,000.*' An individual can make transfers of up to £3K per year without incurring IHT. Note that the exemption is only available in relation to transfers made by **T** before his death. Any unused amount can be carried forward by one tax year for use in the next tax year. The exemption applies to transfers into trust as well as to other individuals. It is available in addition to any other lifetime exemptions (so **T** can make gifts of any value to a UK domiciled spouse, and in addition use the exemption to make IHT free gifts to other persons). The exemption is usually applied to a transfer after all other exemptions have been applied. If two transfers are made on the same day the exemption is apportioned between them. If two transfers are made on different days in the same tax year, the exemption is applied first to the earlier transfer. It does not matter whether the transfers are PET's or chargeable when made (**IHTM 14143**). If a transfer is a PET it is left out of account, unless **T** does not survive seven years from the making of the gift. Note that the annual exemption is not set against PET's, even where they are made in the same tax year prior to the making of any chargeable lifetime transfers. The termination of a lifetime '*qualifying interest in possession*' may constitute a PET or a chargeable lifetime transfer. Then **T's** unused annual exemption can be offset against the value of the transfer.

Charities

s.23(1) provides, '*Transfers of value are exempt to the extent that the values transferred by them are attributable to property which is given to charities.*' For a gift to a charity to be exempt under **s.23 (1)** there are two requirements (**IHTM 11111**):

1. the charity must have the requisite charitable status; and
2. the exemption of the gift must not be prevented by any of the exclusions and limitations which are designed to confine the exemption to gifts

which are genuinely charitable, and which can only be used for charitable purposes.

'*Charity*' and '*charitable*' are defined by **s.272** as having the same meaning as in the **Income Tax Acts**. A charity is defined in **s.506 (1) ICTA 1988** as '*any body of persons or trust established for charitable purposes only*'. Note that new definitions were introduced by **FA 2010**.

Income tax case law applies for IHT. This means that the charity must be '*established*' in the UK. The word '*charitable*' in **s.23 (6)** should be construed in its technical legal sense. Therefore a gift to a needy individual, even if made from motives of charity, is not a gift for charitable purposes within the meaning of the subsection. In accordance with a well established series of authorities, a gift for benevolent purposes is not a good charitable gift, because such purposes go beyond the legal definition of charities, ***Att Gen for New Zealand v Brown*** (1917).

In England and Wales the **Charities Act 1993** provided for a register of charities. Registration under the Act raises a conclusive presumption that an institution is or was a charity at any time when it is or was on the register. But not all charities have to be registered under the Act, so a body that is not registered may nevertheless be a charity. The charity exemption is limited by several anti-avoidance provisions, which fall into two groups:

1. **s.23(2)** to **s.23(5)** which apply generally (except to loans to charities), and
2. **s.56** which applies to gifts or transactions involving settled property.

A gift which is caught by these anti-avoidance provisions is not exempt under **s.23** even though the beneficiary is a qualifying charity.

Dispositions by close companies for the benefit of employees (s.13)

s.13 provides,

'*A disposition of property made to trustees by a close company whereby the property is to be held on trusts of the description specified in section 86(1) is not a transfer of value if the persons for whose benefit the trusts permit the property to be applied include all or most of either –*
   (a) the persons employed by or holding office with the company, or
   (b) the persons employed by or holding office with the company or any one or more subsidiaries of the company.'

HMRC Statement of Practice E11. Employee trusts clarifies the application of **s.13(1)**, where employees of a subsidiary company are included in the trust:

'*The Commissioners for Her Majesty's Revenue and Customs regard* **section 13 (1) IHTA 1984** *as requiring that where the trust is to benefit* *employees of a subsidiary of the company making the provision, those eligible to benefit must include all or most of the employees and officers of the subsidiary and the employees and officers of the holding company taken as a single class. So it would be possible to exclude all of the officers and employees of the holding company without losing the exemption if they comprised only a minority of the combined class. But the exemption would not be available for a contribution to a fund for the sole benefit of the employees of a small subsidiary. This is because it would otherwise have been easy to create such a situation artificially in order to benefit a favoured group of a company's officeholders or employees. But even where the participators outnumber the other employees the exemption is not irretrievably lost. The requirement to exclude participators and those connected with them from benefit is modified by **section 13(3) IHTA 1984**. This limits the meaning of 'a participator' for this purpose to those having a substantial stake in the assets being transferred and makes an exception in favour of income benefits. So even where most of the employees are also major participators or their relatives, an exempt transfer could be made if the trust provided only for income benefits and for the eventual disposal of the capital away from the participators and their families.*

*This restriction does not affect the exemptions offered by **section 86 IHTA 1984** from tax charges during the continuance of a trust for employees which meets the conditions of that section.'*

However, **s.13(1)** does not apply if the trusts permit any trust property to be applied at any time for the benefit of (**s.13(2)**):

1. a participator in the company making the disposition;
2. any other person who is a participator in any close company that has made a disposition whereby property became comprised in the same settlement, being a disposition which but for **s.13(1)** would have been a transfer of value;
3. any other person who has been a participator in any company mentioned in (a) or (b) above, either after or within ten years prior to the transfer; or
4. any person connected with a participator within (a) to (c) above.

A participator is defined in **s.102(1)** as meaning, '*in relation to any company, any person who is (or would be if the company was resident in the United Kingdom) a participator in relation to that company for the purposes of [Chapter I of Part XI of the Taxes Act 1988], other than a person who would be such a participator by reason only of being a loan creditor.*' For the purposes of **s.13(2)** a participator does not include a person specified in **s.13(3)**.

Death on active service exemption (s.154)

s.154 provides that **s.4** (the IHT charge on death) will not apply in relation to:

'(1) ...the death of a person in whose case it is certified by the Defence Council or the Secretary of State –

    (a) that he died from a wound inflicted, accident occurring or disease contracted at a time when the conditions specified in subsection (2) below were satisfied, or

    (b) that he died from a disease contracted at some previous time, the death being due to or hastened by the aggravation of the disease during a period when those conditions were satisfied.

(2) The conditions referred to in subsection (1) above are that the deceased was a member of any of the armed forces of the Crown or [a civilian subject to service discipline within the meaning of the Armed Forces Act 2006] and (in any case) was either:

    (a) on active service against an enemy, or

    (b) on other service of a warlike nature or which in the opinion of the Treasury involved the same risks as service of a warlike nature.'

Dispositions for family maintenance (s.11)

Under **s.11** a disposition is not a transfer of value where:

'(1) it is made by one party to a marriage [or civil partnership] in favour of the other party or of a child of either party and is –

    (a) for the maintenance of the other party, or

    (b) for the maintenance, education or training of the child for a period ending not later than the year in which he attains the age of eighteen or, after attaining that age, ceases to undergo full-time education or training;

(2) it is made in favour of a child who is not in the care of a parent of his and is for his maintenance, education or training for a period ending not later than the year in which –

    (a) he attains the age of eighteen, or

    (b) after attaining that age he ceases to undergo full time education or training;

but paragraph (b) above applies only if before attaining that age the child has for substantial periods been in the care of the person making the disposition;

(3) if it is made in favour of a dependant relative of the person making the disposition and is a reasonable provision for his care or maintenance; and

(4) if it is made in favour of an illegitimate child of the person making the disposition and is for the maintenance, education or training of the child for a period not ending later than the year in which he attains

the age of eighteen or, after attaining that age, ceases to undergo full-time education or training.'

A dependant relative is defined by **s.11(6)** as meaning either (i) a relative of the transferor, or of his spouse, who is incapacitated by old age or infirmity from maintaining himself, or (ii) the transferor's mother or father, or the mother or father of his spouse. The exemption only applies to lifetime transfers, and it is uncertain whether it applies where the payer dies.

Normal expenditure out of income (s.21)

A lifetime transfer of value is exempt if made as part of **T's** normal expenditure, and taking one year after another it is made out of his income, provided that on average **T** was left with sufficient income to maintain his usual standard of living (see p.2998 of the BDO Tax Guide). A pattern of giving needs to be established, therefore one-off payments do not qualify. The exemption applies where the gifts are unconditional, and **T** can show that they:

1. formed part of his usual expenditure;
2. were made out of income; and
3. left him with sufficient income to maintain his normal standard of living.

See **IHTM 1431**, and **14243**.

The exemption does not apply to

1. transfers on termination of a life interest in settled property;
2. deemed PET's under **s.102 (4)**, and **s.103 (5) FA 1986**; and
3. apportionments made to persons under **s.94** (transfers by close companies).

Exemption under **s.21** does not prevent the gift which constitutes the transfer from being taxed under the GWR rules. The first condition for exemption is that the transfer should have formed part of **T's** normal expenditure. Normal is considered to mean typical of **T**, not those of the average or reasonable man.

In **Bennett v IRC** (1995) Mr Justice Lightman expressed the view that the term normal *'connotes expenditure which at the time it took place accorded with the settled pattern of expenditure adopted by the transferor.'* He considered that the existence of the settled pattern could be established in two ways, as follows:

1. an examination of **T's** expenditure over a period of time may throw into relief a pattern, for example a payment each year of 10% of all income to charity or members of his family, or
2. **T** may be shown to have assumed a commitment, or adopted a firm resolution, regarding future expenditure and thereafter complied with it.

The commitment may be legal, religious, or moral. The commitment or resolution need have none of these characteristics but may still be effective to establish a pattern, for example to pay the annual premiums on a life assurance policy gifted to a third party or to give a pre-determined part of income to children. Before turning to the facts of the case, the Judge summed up the requirement for expenditure to be normal,

> *'what is necessary and sufficient is that the evidence should manifest the substantial conformity of each payment with an established pattern of expenditure by the individual concerned – a pattern established by proof of the existence of a prior commitment or resolution or by reference only to a sequence of payments.'*

There is no requirement for the expenditure to be reasonable, and there is no quantitative limit on the exemption. In practice it appears that transfers amounting to no more than one third of net income are generally acceptable as falling within the exemption. However it is not clear whether (i) the *'income'* is net after payment of tax; and (ii) whether a claim can be made on the basis that **T's** taxes are paid wholly or partly out of capital. The reference in **s.21(1) (b)** to *'taking one year with another'* means that extraordinary gifts that do not fit within the pattern of giving during normal years will not be made out of income. The same principle applies to the making of interest-free loans. The exemption is applied ahead of marriage gifts and the annual exemption where all three apply to a transfer. Note that use of this exemption enables **T** to gift annual premiums for joint whole life last survivor insurance policies (written on the lives of himself and **S**), in favour of his children, thereby providing for the future payment of IHT.

Potentially exempt transfers *('PET's')* (s.3A)

A PET is an outright gift or transfer at no consideration made by an individual to either:

1. an individual;
2. the trustees of a bare trust (to qualify as a PET the transfer to trustees must be of settled property, see **sections 3A(3)**, **(3A)**, and **(3B)**);
3. the trustees of a disabled person's trust *('DPT')*; or
4. the trustees of a bereaved minor's trust *('BMT')* on the coming to an end of an immediate post-death interest *('IPDI')*.

See **IHTM 04057**.

The basic requirements to be satisfied for a transfer to be a PET are set out in **s.3A**. Certain kinds of transfer are expressly prohibited from being PET's including a disposition within **s.98(1)** by a participator in a close company following an alteration in the company's share capital structure (including voting rights). To qualify as a PET a transfer to trustees must be of settled property, see **sections 3A(3) (3A)** and **(3B)**.

The surrender of a life interest created after 22nd March 2006 is deemed to be a PET provided the interest is either:

1. an IPDI; or
2. a DPT.

See **sections 51** and **52**.

Under **s.3A(5)** it is assumed that a PET will become exempt seven years after the date of the gift. Subject to a gift being unconditional and absolute, the PET becomes an exempt transfer seven years after the gift is made, provided the donor (**T**) is alive, at which point the value of the gift falls out of account for IHT. The contingent liability to tax in respect of a PET can usually be covered by insurance. Before making a PET, liability to CGT should be considered, for example a life-time gift of a shareholding is a disposal for CGT. Note that a gift of an asset, for example the matrimonial home, with continued occupation is subject to IHT under the GWR rules.

Failed PET's

Failure results in:

1. an immediate tax charge on the PET itself; and
2. the retrospective inclusion in **T's** cumulative total of the value transferred by the failed PET.

Consequently:

1. on **T's** death tax may be charged at a higher rate than it would have been if the PET had not failed;
2. if part of **T's** NRB was absorbed by the failed PET, any subsequent lifetime transfers will suffer IHT at a greater rate than they would have done had the PET not failed; and
3. there may be a knock-on effect where a subsequent transfer has been made to a discretionary trust.

Deemed PET's

The following transfers are deemed PET's:

*   the life-time cessation of a reservation of benefit by **T** in a gift of property (**s.102(4) FA 1986** – note the definition of *'Relevant Period'* in **s.102(1)**); and
*   the discharge or reduction of a debt subject to abatement under **s.103 FA 1986**.

Small gifts (s.20)

s.20 provides, '*Transfers of value made by a transferor in any one year by outright gifts to any one person are exempt if the values transferred by them (calculated as values on which no tax is chargeable) do not exceed £250.*' The exemption can be used in addition to the annual exemption so long as it is not used in conjunction with it.

Spouse exemption (s.18)

In general under **s.18(1)** transfers of value between spouses (including civil partners) are wholly exempt to an unlimited extent if both **T** and **S** are domiciled in the UK, or if only the transferee is domiciled in the UK, see **IHTM 11031**.

Where:

1. **T** is domiciled in the UK immediately before the transfer, but
2. **S** is domiciled outside the UK,

then the exemption is limited to £55,000.

That limit is set against the value of **T's** total cumulative transfers to **S** in his lifetime and on death. The exemption is subject to several exclusions designed to prevent it being used for tax avoidance.

As a matter of general law a spouse means anyone to whom a person is legally married, *Holland v. IRC* (2003). **The Tax and Civil Partnership Regulations, SI 2005/3229** amended the tax legislation so that all references to '*spouse*' now read '*spouse or civil partner.*' **s.18** does not apply to co-habiting siblings, note the decision in *Burden & Burden v United Kingdom* (2008), where by a 4-3 majority the European Court of Human Rights held that **s.18** did not breach **Article 14 of the European Convention on Human Rights**.

Note that:

- transfers of value include transfers of settled property in which the transferor had a life interest;
- where a condition must be satisfied before a spouse can take an interest in property, it must be satisfied within 12 months of the transfer; and
- the GWR rules do not apply to spouse exempt transfers.

Exclusions

The main limitations on the spouse exemption are that it does not apply to:

1. postponed gifts, see **s.18(3)(a)** and **IHTM 11092**; and
2. conditional gifts, see **s.18(3)(b)**, and **IHTM 11093**.

Property is treated for these purposes as given to a person if it becomes the property of, or is held on trust for, that person. This provision is expressed to apply for the purposes of **s.18** as a whole, but it is primarily concerned with **subsection (3)**. In addition, the spouse exemption does not apply to certain dealings with settled property (**IHTM 11061**), including reversionary interests (**IHTM 11063**).

CGT

The use of the **s.18** exemption can have an adverse CGT effect.

Transfers of shares or securities by an individual to an employee trust (s.28)

Subject to conditions, a transfer of value by an individual who is beneficially entitled to shares in a company is exempt, to the extent that the value transferred is attributable to shares or securities of the company that become comprised in a settlement.

The conditions are:

1. the settled property must be held on trusts which only permit it to be applied for the benefit of (**s.86(1)**):
   (a) persons of a class defined by reference to employment in a particular trade or profession, or employment by, or office, with a body carrying on a trade, profession, or undertaking; or
   (b) persons of a class defined by reference to marriage, or relationship to, or dependence on, persons of a class defined in (a) above;
   and all or most of the persons employed or holding office with the company can benefit;

2. at the time of transfer (or within one year of it) the trustees:
   (a) must hold more than one half of the ordinary shares in the company; and
   (b) have powers of voting on all questions affecting the company as a whole which if exercised would yield a majority of the votes capable of being exercised on them (**s.28(1)(b)**); and

3. the trust must not permit trust property to be applied at any time for the benefit of either:
   (a) a participator;
   (b) any other person who is a participator in any close company that has made a disposition whereby property became comprised in the same trust, which is relieved from being a transfer of value by **s.13** (see **s.28(4)(b)**);
   (c) any other person who after the transfer or within ten years prior to

the transfer has been a participator in the company or in a close company that has made a disposition of the kind described in (b) above; or

(d) any person connected with any such participator.

Participators and persons connected with them can be given income benefits. Ordinary shares are shares which carry either:

(i) a right to dividends which is not restricted to a fixed rate; or

(ii) a right to conversion into shares carrying such a right.

A close company is defined in **s.102(1)** as, '*a company within the meaning of the Corporation Tax Acts which is (or would be if resident in the United Kingdom) a close company for the purposes of those Acts.*' It is, subject to specified exceptions a UK company in broad terms controlled by either: (i) five or less participators (individuals or bodies corporate); or (ii) participators (however many there are) who are directors. A company can also be regarded as close if more than half of the income which can be apportioned under a shortfall direction can be apportioned to five or fewer participators. However, a company is not to be regarded as close if controlled by a company which is not itself a close company, or by two or more companies none of which is a close company, and it cannot be treated as a close company, except by taking as one of the five or fewer participators requisite for it being so treated, a company which is not a close company (**IHTM 42971**).

Wedding gifts (s.22)

The monetary limit depends upon the identity of the donor. Each parent can give £5,000. £2,500 can be given by each grand-parent, or remoter ancestor, or by either party to the marriage to the other, and £1,000 can be given by any other person. The exemption is applied ahead of the annual exemption where both apply to a transfer.

Grossing-up

IHT is calculated on the loss in value of **T's** estate resulting from a chargeable transfer (**IHTM 14593**). If **T** makes a gift that is expressed to be '*tax-free*' and the value exceeds his unused NRB on death, then the gift must be grossed-up to determine the actual chargeable transfer, because **T** has also made a gift of **IHT** on the gift which results in a further loss to his chargeable estate. Therefore the value of the chargeable gift is calculated on the basis that the beneficiary not only receives the value of the gift itself, but also the value of the IHT paid out of residue that would not otherwise have been incurred. Grossing-up cannot result in IHT being paid on a greater value than the value of the total estate (**s.37(2)**), and if the grossed-up value of the tax-free gift exceeds the value of the total estate it is abated for IHT.

GWR & POAT

GWR

The GWR rules (contained in **sections 102-102C**, and **Schedule 20 FA 1986**) were introduced by **FA 1986** (see **IHTM 24200**).

  s.102(1) provides,

'...this section applies where, on or after 18th March 1986, an individual disposes of any property by way of gift and either –

(a) possession and enjoyment of the property is not bona fide assumed by the donee at or before the beginning of the relevant period; or

(b) at any time in the relevant period the property is not enjoyed to the entire exclusion , or virtually to the entire exclusion, of the donor and of any benefit to him by contract or otherwise;

and in this section the 'relevant period' means a period ending on the date of the donor's death and beginning seven years before that date or, if it is later, on the date of the gift.'

A gift can include a sale at an undervalue (**IHTM 14316**).

  Under **s.102(2)** property is deemed to be subject to a reservation where these requirements are met.

  Then:

1. on **T's** death the property is treated as forming part of his estate for IHT (**s.102(3)**); and
2. if the reservation ends during **T's** lifetime he is treated as having made a PET at that time, and will need to survive seven years to avoid a clawback charge.

Property is not subject to a reservation where **T** pays a full market rent for its continued enjoyment or benefit. If **T** was a non-dom when he died excluded property will not be brought into charge by the clawback. The position in relation to settled property is more difficult. **s.102ZA FA1986** provides that the termination of a life interest will be regarded for the purposes of **s.102** and **Schedule 20**, as a disposal by way of gift by the beneficiary entitled to the interest if the following conditions are met:

1. **T** is beneficially entitled to a life interest in settled property;
2. his interest is treated as part of his death estate because he became beneficially entitled to the life interest either:
   (a) before 22nd march 2006; or

(b) on or after that date, and the life interest is an IPDI or a DPT; and

3. the life interest comes to an end during **T's** lifetime.

Then **T** will be deemed to have made a gift of *'the no longer possessed property'* (see **s.102ZA (2)** and **(3)**). That is the property in which his interest in possession had subsisted immediately before it came to an end, other than any of it to which **T** became absolutely and beneficially entitled in possession upon termination of his life interest. **s.102ZA** treats the termination of an interest in possession by **S** as being a gift by her thereby bringing the GWR rules into play, and specifically targets the abuse of *'peg lives'*, where **S** is younger than **T**, and he can effectively use **S** as a bridge for the making of substantial gifts to his children. For a discussion of the planning implications of **s.102ZA** see paragraphs 5.25 – 5.29 of Whitehouse & King.

The GWR rules do not apply to certain exempt transfers specified in **s.102(5) FA 1986**, including the spouse exemption (except where either **s.102(5)(A)**, or **(B)** apply).

The following exempt gifts can fall within the GWR rules:

1. a PET made more than seven years before **T's** death (and note that if property ceases to be subject to a reservation within the *'relevant period'* **T** is treated as having made a PET on that date);
2. the £3K annual exemption; and
3. the normal gifts out of income exemption.

IHTM 14339 states, that except in relation to insurance policies, the GWR rules do not extend to gifts under which a benefit is reserved to the donor's spouse. However if enjoyment of a gift by **S** is shared by the donor the GWR rules will apply. The associated operations rules may also apply. The **Inheritance Tax (Double Charges Relief) Regulations**, provide relief where a double charge to IHT would otherwise arise under the operation of the GWR rules.

POAT

The Pre-owned assets income charge (the *'POAT regime'*) is an annual charge to income tax on benefits received by a former owner of certain kinds of property, and was introduced with retroactive effect to the 18th March 1986 by the **FA 2004**. The broad structure of the regime is to establish a separate charging system for (i) land; (ii) chattels; and (iii) intangible property comprised in a settlor-interested trust.

There is no IHT *'motive test'* and the rules can catch innocent transactions. The charge arises under three main headings:

1. land;
2. chattels; and
3. intangible property.

Income tax under each head is calculated using different rules.
The POAT regime does not apply:

1. if the relevant property (or property derived from it) is comprised in **T's** estate for IHT **(paragraph 11(1))**;
2. to property indirectly comprised in **T's** estate, to the extent that it is derived from the relevant property, and is not substantially less than the value of the relevant property **(paragraph 11(2))**; and
3. to property subject to and remaining within the IHT GWR charge **(paragraph 11(5), Sch 15 FA 2004**, see also **s.102 FA 1986** as amended by **s.104 FA 1999**, and **s.188 FA 2003)**.

Inheritance Act claims

Broadly speaking the **Inheritance (Provision for Family and Dependants) Act 1975** (the 'Inheritance Act') gives the court the power to order financial provision from **T's** net estate (defined in **s.25(1) Inheritance Act**) for the benefit of any person who falls within one of the following categories of applicant **(s.1(1) Inheritance Act**), where by his will **T** failed to make reasonable financial provision for them:

1. **S**;
2. a former spouse who has not remarried;
3. a person living as **T's** spouse;
4. a child of **T**;
5. a child of the family; and
6. any other person treated as a dependant,
    provided:
    (a) **T** died domiciled in England and Wales;
    (b) the application for the order was made within six months of the grant of representation;
    (c) the claimant falls into one of the six categories; and
    (d) **T** did not make reasonable financial provision for the claimant under his will.

However, a claim by a mature adult child established in life and to whom **T** owes no moral bond greater than the bond between parent and child will usually fail. In **H v Mitson** (2009) Mrs Justice Eleanor King stated that, '*the philosophy of the Act ...is clear; it is designed to provide for those family members and dependants specified in the 1975 Act, in respect of whom the testator has failed to make what is deemed by statute and interpreted by case law, as reasonable provision...The fact remains that unless one or more of the other factors set out in s.3 of the 1975 Act serve to tip the balance in favour of such interference, then for so long as the laws of England and Wales reject* *the concept of forced heirship, its courts will decline to step in and interfere with the validly expressed intention of a testator in relation to his or her adult children albeit in necessitous circumstances.'*

There are two standards of provision, the first applicable to spouses, and the second to all other applicants as follows:

1. Spouses

    'such financial provision as it would be reasonable in all circumstances of the case for a husband or wife to receive, whether or not that provision is required for his or her maintenance' (and note that **s.1(2) (aa) Inheritance Act 1975** applies an identical standard to a civil partner); and

2. Other applicants

    'such financial provision as it would be reasonable in all the circumstances of the case for the applicant to receive for his maintenance.'

The orders that the court can make include:

1. periodical payments;
2. a lump sum payment;
3. the transfer of a particular asset;
4. a settlement of property;
5. the acquisition of property for transfer or settlement; and
6. the variation of any ante-nuptial agreement or post-nuptial settlement.

For tax purposes the alteration of the dispositions made in **T's** will are deemed to take place on death. Any provision should be tax-efficient and under **s.2(4)** the court can order such consequential and supplementary provisions as it thinks necessary or expedient, for the purpose of giving effect to an order, or to secure that the order operates fairly as between one beneficiary and another.

In particular it can:

'(a) order any person who holds any property which forms part of the net estate of the deceased to make such payment or transfer such property as may be specified by the order;

(b) vary the disposition of the deceased's estate effected by the will or the law relating to intestacy, (or by both) in such manner as the court thinks fair and reasonable having regard to the provisions of the order and all the circumstances of the case; and

*(c) confer on the trustees of any property which is the subject of an order under **section [2]** such powers as appear to the court to be necessary or expedient.'*

Interests in possession

General

An interest in possession (referred to in this book as a *'life interest'*) is an interest under a trust which entitles a beneficiary to receive income for life (see **Diagram No.17** – *'Interest in possession trusts'*). The beneficiary is called the *'life tenant'* and the beneficiaries entitled to receive the remainder are called the *'remainder men'*. The true test of the existence of a life interest is whether the interest conferred a present right to present enjoyment being an indefeasible right to net trust income not dependant on a discretionary power exercisable by the trustees, *Pearson v IRC* (1981). Therefore a beneficiary only has a life interest if he is entitled to call for payment of the net trust income as it arises. Where under his will **T** gives his trustees a discretion (without imposing a duty) to allow **S** to occupy the matrimonial home after his death, that does not create an interest in possession, *Judge (Walden's Personal Representative) v HMRC* (2005). Note that the existence of an overriding power of appointment or advancement capable of reducing or eliminating a beneficiary's life interest does not prevent the beneficiary from having a life interest provided the power cannot be exercised to affect the destination of income that has already arisen in the trust. The fact that a life interest is terminable does not prevent it from being a life interest. It remains a life interest unless and until an event occurs that results in the revocation or forfeiture of the interest.

Qualifying interests

A *'qualifying'* life interest (see **Diagram No.18** – *'Qualifying interests in possession'*) benefits from privileged IHT treatment, however, under **s.49** the beneficiary is treated as owning the trust property which is aggregated with her estate on her death for IHT (the *'interest in possession principle'*). The interest created is known as a *'beneficial interest in possession'*. When the principle applies:

1. trust property is exempt from the relevant property regime;
2. transfers of value in favour of trustees of a life interest trust either qualify for the same exemptions as transfers of value in favour of individuals absolutely, or are potentially exempt where the life interest was held by someone other than **S**.

The principle only applies to:

1. an existing interest in possession (i.e. a life interest in settled property to which a person became entitled before 26th March 2006 under a life-time trust or a will/trust that came into operation before that date), **s.49(1), (1A)** ; and

2. a life interest to which a person became entitled on or after 22 March 2006, provided it is:
   (a) an IPDI;
   (b) a disabled person's interest; or
   (c) a transitional serial interest *('TSI')* – which are not discussed further in this book.

Note that a qualifying life interest can only be created by will or within two years of death.

The only qualifying interests that can be created by will are:

1. an immediate post death interest (an *'IPDI'*), **s.49A** - discussed in **Chapter 3** under *'Special Trusts'*); or
2. a disabled person's trust *('DPT')*, **s.89B** - discussed in **Chapter 3** under *'Special Trusts'*).

A life interest trust is subject to income tax at the rate applicable to trusts, and beneficiaries pay tax at the basic rate when the trust receives dividend income.

Non-qualifying interests

If a life interest is not a qualifying interest in possession under **s.59(1) FA 2006** (see **Diagram No.17**), then:

1. where the interest is created more than two years after **T's** death it cannot be read-back as a spouse-exempt git under **s.144**;
2. the trust will be treated as a relevant property trust, and be subject to an immediate entry charge, and to decennial, and exit charges; and
3. **s.49(1)** does not apply.

s.5(1)(ii) and (1A) provide that the estate of a person does not include a non-qualifying interest in possession.

Therefore if an interest in possession trust is created by trustees in favour of **S** more than two years after **T's** death, by the exercise of an overriding power of appointment, she will not be treated as the beneficial owner of the capital in the trust, and the capital will not be aggregated with her estate on death. CGT principal private residence relief (**s.222 TCGA 1992**) is available on the sale of a dwelling house occupied by a beneficiary (as their only or main residence) under the terms of a trust during the trustee's period of ownership **s.225 TCGA 1992**). However, if a beneficiary in occupation holds a share as a tenant in common, HMRC may argue that they occupy by reason of their own interest rather than under the terms of the trust. Non-qualifying status is lost if the interest in possession becomes an IPDI through reading-back under **s.142**.

Rights of residence

If someone has a right to reside in a property under the terms of a trust, he or she will often have a life interest in that property (see **IHTM 16131**).

This has a number of effects for IHT:

1. the death of the beneficiary occupying the property gives rise to a claim to IHT under **s.4**;
2. where the person becomes beneficially entitled to the life interest on or after 22 March 2006, **s.49(1)** will only apply if it is (i) an IPDI, or (ii) a disabled person's interest;
3. if the beneficiary ceases to reside in the property in her lifetime a charge to IHT arises under **s.52 (1)**;
4. where the person becomes beneficially entitled to the life interest on or after 22 March 2006, **s.52(1)** will only apply if it is an IPDI, or a disabled person's interest; and
5. the trusts governing the property after the beneficiary has ceased to live there will be either:
   (a) in favour of an individual, or a disabled person's interest – giving rise to a PET by the beneficiary; or
   (b) in favour of non-interest in possession or non-qualifying interest in possession trusts – giving rise to an immediately chargeable transfer by the beneficiary as deemed transferor.

Statement of Practice 10/79 ('SP 10/79')

HMRC will treat the exercise by trustees of a power under a discretionary trust to provide **S** (for example) with a permanent home, as creating a life interest.
SP 10/79 states,

'Many wills and settlements contain a clause empowering the trustees to permit a beneficiary to occupy a dwelling-house which forms part of the trust property on such terms as they think fit. The Board do not regard the existence of such a power as excluding any interest in possession in the property.

*Where there is no interest in possession in the property in question, the Board do not regard the exercise of power as creating one if the effect is merely to allow non-exclusive occupation or to create a contractual tenancy for full consideration. The Board also takes the view that no interest in possession arises on the creation of a lease for a term or a periodic tenancy for less than full consideration, though this will normally give rise to a charge for tax under **IHTA 1984, s 65(1)(b)**. On the other hand if the power is drawn in terms wide enough to cover the creation of an exclusive or joint residence, albeit revocable, for a definite or indefinite period, and is exercised with the intention of providing a particular beneficiary with a* *permanent home, the Revenue will normally regard the exercise of the power as creating an interest in possession. And if the trustees in exercise of their powers grant a lease for life for less than full consideration, this will be regarded as creating an interest in possession in view of **IHTA 1984 ss 43(3), 50(6)**.'*

Where the implementation of a NRBDT results in **S** being the only discretionary beneficiary living in what was the matrimonial home, HMRC may argue that notwithstanding any right of occupation **S** may have (by virtue of her interest in residue), that **SP 10/79** can be applied so as to treat **S** as having an IPDI in the NRA Trust Fund as well as in the residue. In which case the NRA legacy will be ineffective for IHT, which would be a planning disaster, *IRC v Eversden* (2002). A power authorising trustees to allow **S** to reside in the matrimonial home may be construed as a dispositive provision conferring a life interest on **S**.

In *CIR v Lloyds Private Banking Limited* (1998):

1. Husband ('**H**') and wife ('**W**') owned the matrimonial home as tenants in common;
2. **W** died first;
3. under her will she made a legacy of her equitable share in the property to a trustee, and directed the trustee to permit **H** to live in the matrimonial home until he died (which he did), after which her share passed to her daughter;
4. the Judge held that the purpose and effect of **W's** will had been to create a life interest in her equitable share for **H** (who required the rights attached to **W's** equitable share, because his own rights were not sufficient to entitle him to enjoy exclusive occupation for the rest of his life); and
5. that a determinable life interest (which is what **H** had been granted under **W's** will) was an *'interest in possession'* for the purposes of **s.49(1).**

An IPDI may also arise if the property is sold within the two-year period following death and a replacement purchased for **S** to live in.

Because the legal and equitable interest in **T's** estate vests in his executors until the estate is administered, **T's** unadministered estate is not a trust. Therefore **SP10/79** cannot apply until the property has been appropriated by the executors to the trustees, and prior to the appropriation the trustees do not actually have an interest in it. In other words because prior to the appropriation the property remains part of **T's** estate (as opposed to part of the trust) there cannot be an interest in possession for IHT, because the property is not *'settled'* for the purposes of IHT. An IP cannot exist in the property until there is a trust.

Disposal

s.51 (1) provides,
'...the disposal –
   (a) *is not a transfer of value; but*
   (b) *shall be treated...as the coming to the end of [the life tenant's] interest, and tax shall be charged accordingly under **section 52**...*'

s.52, which applies to the termination of both:
   1. a disabled person's interest; and
   2. an interest under an IPDI,
taxes the capital of the trust fund in which the life tenant's life interest had subsisted.

Note that the section only applies to: (i) an IPDI; (ii) a disabled person's interest; or (iii) a transitional serial interest, within **s.5(1B)**. **s.53** provides for exceptions from the charge under **s.52**. See p.3015 of the BDO Tax Guide.

Jointly-owned property

Property jointly-owned by husband and wife may be held on a joint- tenancy either:

   1. as *'beneficial joint-tenants'* – in which case neither has a distinct share, and on **T's** death his share of the equitable interest in the property passes to **S** by survivorship (at which point she acquires full legal and beneficial ownership of the property); or
   2. as *'tenants in common'* – in which case **T** and **S** will each have a defined share of the equitable interest in the property (based upon their respective contributions to the purchase price which is presumed to be 50:50 unless otherwise stated).

However, a half share of a jointly-owned property is not necessarily a mathematical one half of the vacant possession value of the property. *IRC v Arkwright* (2004) suggests that a discount should be applied. If a debt scheme (see below) is implemented **T's** executors cannot charge a half of the property with a debt for more than the half share is worth. If the share is worth less than **T's** NRA, then additional assets would have to be appropriated to the trustees to make up the difference or be made subject to the charge, unless they decide that any additional amount due is appointed to **S** outright within two years of **T's** death, resulting in automatic reading-back under **s.144**. When **T's** wealth exceeds **S's** their respective estates can be equalised by severing a beneficial joint-tenancy over the matrimonial home in order to re-structure the holding of the asset as a tenancy in common. However, beware of the **SDLT Trap**, see **Chapter 6**. In spite of the introduction of the transferable Nil Rate

Band by the **Finance Act 2006** this remains a useful tool in NRB planning. Note that a beneficial joint-tenancy cannot be severed by will.

Nil rate band ('NRB')

The value of **T's** chargeable estate above £325K is subject to IHT at the flat rate of 40%. Note that the rate has been frozen until 2014/15. Provided **T** has not made any gifts within seven years of death, then the full amount of his NRB is available for use on his death.

T can then either:

1. preserve his unused NRB by making a spouse exempt gift outright to **S**, in which case the unused percentage of **T's** NRB may be claimed under the transfer rules by **S's** PR's on submission of the IHT return, when they administer her estate; or
2. use his NRB to makes gifts to non-exempt beneficiaries outright or subject to a trust.

Where under his will **T** makes a gift of his NRB (referred to in this book as a Nil Rate Amount or 'NRA' legacy) to the trustees of a discretionary trust (the 'NRA Trustees'), then provided the class of beneficiaries includes **S**:

1. during her lifetime **S** can benefit in the discretion of the trustees; and
2. the trust fund will not be aggregated with **S's** estate for IHT on her death.

Planning using NRB Discretionary Trusts is discussed in **Chapter 3** - 'NRA Legacies and NRB Discretionary Trusts'.

NRB Transfer Rules

Under the transfer rules where **T's** NRB has not been fully utilised on his death, the unused portion can be claimed on **S's** death by her PR's. The requirements are set out in **s.2 and Schedule 4 FA 2008** (which inserted sections **8A, 8B, and 8C** into the **IHTA 1984**). See **IHTM 43020, and 43006**. If **T** was married to **S** on his death, even if **S** is separated from **T** before his death, or remarries afterwards, her PR's can still claim the full amount of **T's** unused NRB. A claim can only be made where **S** dies on or after 9 October 2007, however, it does not matter when **T** died. No claim is required on **T's** death, however, detailed records should be kept (for example of payments claimed to be made as normal income paid out of expenditure). The claim must be made within the permitted period, which means:

1. the period of two years from the end of the month in which **S** dies or (if it ends later) the period of three months beginning with the date on

which her PR's first act; or

2. such longer date as an officer of HMRC may in a particular case allow.

The amount of **T's** NRB that can be transferred to **S** is calculated on a percentage basis. The unused percentage of **T's** NRB (the *'multiplier'*) is applied to the NRB rate that is current when she dies (the *'NRB cap'*). **S's** own available NRB up to the NRB Cap (the *'multiplicand'*) is then uplifted by the percentage of the multiplier. Where **S** survives more than one husband, and thereby inherits an additional transferable NRB, the maximum amount that can be transferred to her PR's is the full amount of one additional NRB (or multiplicand). A separate claim must be made for each transfer.

If **T** died domiciled in the UK when **S** was a non-dom, there is a restriction on the spouse exemption, and any life-time gifts made to **S** above that threshold will have eroded the amount of **T's** available NRB. Where a lifetime gift is chargeable on **S's** death (for example a failed PET), then **S's** uplifted NRB is used to calculate any IHT payable on those gifts.

Making the claim

Within the prescribed period after **S's** death, the claim is made by her PR's on **HMRC Form IHT216** (claim to transfer unused IHT nil rate band), which is submitted along with the IHT return for her estate, and specified documents.

Reliefs

The principal reliefs (not all of which are discussed) are:

- taper (**s.7**);
- business property **(sections 103 – 114)**;
- agricultural property **(sections 115 – 124C)**;
- quick succession **(s.141)**;
- related property **(s.176)**;
- sale of shares **(s.178)**;
- sale of land **(s.190)**;
- timber **(sections 125-130)**;
- transfers within seven years before death **(sections 131- 140)**; and
- double charges **(the Inheritance Tax (Double Charges Relief) Regulations 1987 (SI 1987/1130) and the Inheritance Tax (Double Charges Relief) Regulations 2005 (SI2005/3441)**.

Agricultural Property Relief *('APR')*

Provided the conditions summarised below are satisfied, relief from IHT is available on the transfer of agricultural property. APR operates by way of an automatic percentage reduction in the value of the property transferred.

APR is available on the agricultural value (**s.115(3)**) of agricultural property (**s.115(2)**) which has been owned or occupied by T (**s.117**), or by a company of which he has control, for the purposes of agriculture (**s.117** and see **IHTM 24060**), for the required period. In which case the ownership condition for APR must be satisfied in relation to both the property and the shares in the company. For comprehensive guidance see **IHTM 24000**.

APR is due to the extent that the value transferred by a transfer of value is attributable to the agricultural value of agricultural property. Whereas BPR is given on the market value of qualifying assets.

Transfer of value has an extended meaning under **s.3(4)**, so the relief is available on deemed transfers of value.

The relief is specifically made available to the discretionary trust regime by the provisions of **s.115 (1)**, under which a transfer of value includes an occasion on which tax is chargeable on discretionary trusts.

For a transfer to attract APR:

1. it must be attributable, at least in part, to the agricultural value of agricultural property that is situated in (i) the United Kingdom, Channels Islands or Isle of Man, or (ii) an actual EEA state (**s.115(5)**, as amended by **s.122(3) FA 2009**);
2. the agricultural property must not be subject to a binding contract for sale; and
3. the ownership or occupation conditions must be satisfied.

There are also additional conditions for APR when tax is charged under the GWR rules. The purpose of these tests is to prevent exploitation of the relief by a person switching into agricultural property shortly before death or making a transfer. To prevent them from operating unfairly they are relaxed in three types of situation where the:

1. property transferred replaced other relievable property;
2. transferor became entitled to the property on a death; and
3. property transferred had been acquired in an earlier transfer within the relevant period.

Agricultural property

s.115(2) defines agricultural property as meaning, *'agricultural land or pasture and includes woodland and any building used in connection with the intensive rearing of livestock or fish if the woodland or building is occupied with agricultural land or pasture and the occupation is ancillary to that of the* *agricultural land or pasture; and also includes such cottages, farm buildings and farmhouses, together with the land occupied with them, as are of a character appropriate to the property.'*

The required period of occupation or ownership

A requirement for the application of APR is that agricultural property occupied for the purposes of agriculture must have been either:

1. occupied by **T** for the purposes of agriculture throughout the two years preceding the transfer; or
2. owned by **T** throughout the seven years immediately preceding the transfer, and that the property must have been occupied (**IHTM 24071**) throughout the period for the purposes of agriculture (**IHTM 24060**).

In relation to land owned by a farming partnership note the decision in ***Atkinson v HMRC*** (2010). Farmland (including a bungalow built on the land), was let to a farming partnership in which **T** was a partner. Although **T** effectively lived in hospital and a care home during the last four years of his life, he continued to be involved in the decision-making of the farming partnership. Because the occupation was by the partnership the ownership and occupation requirement (**s.117**) was met.

The identity of the occupier does not matter, but the continuity of such occupation is vital.

HMRC consider ownership (**IHTM 24101**) to mean:

1. in the case of property subject to relevant property trusts, legal ownership by the trustees (**IHTM 42165**); and
2. in all other cases, beneficial entitlement (**IHTM 04031**), which includes entitlement to settled property in which **T** had a life interest (**IHTM 16062**).

In view of **s.91**, where an unadministered residuary estate includes agricultural property, a residuary beneficiary is treated as owning the agricultural property, or an appropriate share of it (**IHTM 22022**).

Agricultural purposes

1. Land

Agricultural land or pasture has its natural meaning and is taken to mean bare land used for agriculture (**IHTM 24031**).

2. Farmhouses

Only attract APR if appropriate to the size and nature of the farming business carried on using the land where the land is occupied together with the farmhouse (**IHTM 24036**). The criterion is the purpose of the occupation, which is a functional test, *Arnander and others (executors of McKenna, deceased) v Revenue and Customs Commissioners* (2006), and note *Atkinson v HMRC* (2010).The words *'of a character appropriate to the property'* are ordinary English words. Parliament has not provided any specific criteria to be used in deciding whether the test of being *'of a character appropriate to the property'* has been fulfilled. In *Lloyd's TSB (Personal representative of Antrobus) v IRC* (2002), the test of whether a *'farmhouse'* was *'of a character appropriate'* was framed by the following questions:

1. is the house appropriate by reference to its size, content and layout, to the farm buildings and the particular area of farmland being farmed?;
2. is the house appropriate in size and nature to the requirements of the farming activities conducted on the agricultural land or pasture in question?;
3. is the subject property a family home of some distinction?;
4. would an educated rural layman regard the property as a house with land or as a farm?;
5. how long has the house in question been associated with the agricultural property?; and
6. was there a history of agricultural production?

These issues were examined by the Special Commissioner in *Arnander* (2006), and she made the following general comments on the meaning of *'farmhouse'* in **s.115(2)**:

1. it is a dwelling for the farmer from which the farm is managed;
2. the farmer of the land is the person who farms it on a day to day basis rather than the person who is in overall control of the agricultural business conducted on the land;
3. the status of the occupier is not the test, the purpose of occupation is what matters;
4. if premises are extravagantly large, then even though occupied for the purposes of agriculture they may have become something more grand; and
5. whether a building is a farmhouse is a matter of fact to be decided upon the circumstances of each case, judged by ordinary ideas of what is appropriate in size, content, and layout in the context of the particular farm buildings and the area of land being farmed.

3. Farm Cottages

A farm cottage is eligible for relief if it satisfies two conditions:

1. the occupier has the required status (**IHTM 24034**); and
2. it is of a character appropriate to the agricultural land (**IHTM 24050**).

4. Other buildings

Farm buildings, other than those used for the intensive rearing of livestock or fish (**IHTM 24033**) must be of a character appropriate to the land. The farm buildings must be occupied for the purposes of agriculture (**IHTM 24035**).

Agricultural value

This is defined as the value the agricultural property would have if it were subject to a perpetual covenant prohibiting its use otherwise than as agricultural property (see **s.115(3)**, and **SVM 112050** – IHT Agricultural Property Relief: Agricultural Property, Agricultural Value and Agriculture). Consequently the agricultural value may be less than the open market value of the property because of development value or mineral value (although business property relief may be available instead). The question of what constitutes *'agricultural value'* is a matter for the Valuation Office Agency (the *'VOA'*) (**SVM 112170**).

Rates of relief

APR is applied before any other exemption or relief (including BPR) and operates by reducing the value of the agricultural property transferred with reference to a fixed percentage (see **s.114(1)**).

There are two rates of agricultural relief for IHT:

1. 100%; and
2. 50%.

100% relief applies where:

1. **T's** interest in the property immediately before the transfer carries with it the right to vacant possession or the right to obtain it within the next twelve months (which includes land let on grazing licences which are essentially for less than a year);
2. **Extra Statutory Concession F17** (**IHTM 24144**) applies to extend the period of 12 months specified in **s.116(2)(a)** to 24 months; or
3. property is let on a tenancy beginning on or after 1 September 1995 (**IHTM 24240**).

Note that **ESC F17** provides that, *'On a transfer of tenanted agricultural land, the condition in **section 116(2)(a) IHTA 1984** is regarded as satisfied where the transferor's interest in the property either carries a right to vacant possession within 24 months of the date of the transfer, or is, notwithstanding the terms of the tenancy, valued at an amount broadly equivalent to the vacant possession value of the property.'*

s.39A

A gift of qualifying property should always be dealt with by way of a specific gift made to a chargeable beneficiary. The same point applies to BPR below (for planning see **Chapter 3** – 'Specific gifts of property qualifying for APR/BPR)'.

Shares
APR applies to the transfer of shares in or debentures of a company (to the extent that the value is attributable to the agricultural value of qualifying agricultural property which forms part of the company's assets), provided the conditions set out in **s.122** are satisfied.

Replacement property
Relief is allowed on replacement property under **s.18**, and for a discussion of the requirements see paragraph 5.11 of Golding.

Double dipping
APR and BPR can be re-cycled where:

- **T** leaves the qualifying property (the 'property') to a chargeable beneficiary under his will, for example his son or daughter ('**C**'), which is then inherited tax free;
- after **T's** death **S** purchases the property from **C** for cash; and
- **S** survives **T** by two years (and note the requirement under **s.117**).

Since APR / BPR will then become available on the property in the estate of **S**, because she is not within **s.120**, this enables **S** to make an IHT free gift of the property to **C** under her will.

Business property ('BPR')

Where certain conditions are satisfied, relief from IHT is available on the transfer of 'relevant business property.'

BPR operates by way of a reduction in the 'net value' of 'relevant business property' transferred, **s.104**. Relevant business property is defined in **s.105**, and includes a profession or vocation but does not include a business carried on other than for gain, **s.103(3)**. Note that the following businesses do not qualify for BPR:

1. a business or company that mainly deals with securities, stocks or shares, land or buildings, or in making or holding investments (**s.105(3)**), and note the recent decision in **Brander v HMRC** (2009) – see below;
2. a not-for-profit organisation;
3. a business subject to a contract for sale, unless the sale is to a company that will carry on the business and the transferor will be paid wholly or mainly in shares of the acquiring business; and

4.   a company that is being wound up, unless that is part of a process to enable the business of the company to carry on.

Once a business crosses the line and becomes mainly a business that carries out an excluded activity, all relief is lost. In **Grimwood-Taylor and Mallender v CIR** (2000) shares in two companies did not qualify because the companies had used company funds to buy land for occupation by shareholders, which resulted in the businesses being treated as having been carried on otherwise than for gain.

Note that in **Brander v HMRC** (2009) the upper Tribunal stated that, *'in deciding what the term 'the business of holding investments' means, the test which the decision-maker applies is that of an intelligent businessman who would be concerned with the use to which the asset was being put and the way it was turned to account.'* The question whether a business consists wholly or mainly of making or holding investments is a question of fact. The business must be looked at in the round and, in the light of the *'overall picture'*, to form a view as to the relative importance to the business as a whole of the investment and non-investment activities in that business. This involves looking at the business over a period of time. In so doing, regard can be had to various factors, such as: (i) the overall context of the business; (ii) the turnover and profitability of various activities; (iii) the activities of employees and other persons engaged to assist the business; and (iv) the acreage of the land dedicated to each activity (including the capital value of that acreage). None of these factors is conclusive on their own as the exercise involves looking at the business in the round.

Under **s.112** (Exclusion of value of excepted assets) relief is not available on an *'excepted asset'*. Under **s.112(2)** an asset is excluded where it was;

- neither used wholly or mainly for the purposes of the business during the preceding two years (or period of ownership if less), see **s.112(2) (a)** and **(3)**; nor
- required for future use in relation to those purposes at the time of transfer, see **s.112(2)(b)** and **(3)**.

Note that *'required'* does not mean *'possibly might be required should an opportunity arise to make use of the property'*. It implied, *'some imperative that the money will fall to be used upon a given project or for some palpable business purpose.'* **Barclays Bank Trust Co Ltd v CIR** (1998).

In order to qualify as relevant business property, the property must be owned by the transferor throughout the two years immediately preceding the transfer, **s.106** (Minimum period of ownership). Net value is calculated in accordance with **s.110** (Value of business) which provides:

'(b) the net value of a business is the value of the assets used in the

business (including goodwill) reduced by the aggregate amount of any liabilities incurred for the purposes of the business;

(c)   *in ascertaining the net value of an interest in a business, no regard shall be had to assets or liabilities other than those by reference to which the net value of the entire business would fall to be ascertained.'*

The reduction takes place before any grossing up. Because the relief is granted before IHT is calculated, the tax relief is greater than the nominal percentage if the donor bears the tax on the grossed-up equivalent of the business property transferred (see p.3035 of the BDO Tax Guide).

s.104, provides that,

'Where the whole or part of the value transferred by a transfer of value is attributable to the value of any relevant business property, the whole or that part of the value transferred shall be treated as reduced –

1.   *in the case of property falling within **section 105(1)(a) [(b) or (bb)]** by 100 per cent;*
2.   *in the case of other relevant property, by 50 per cent.'*

All that **s.104** requires is that the value transferred by the transfer of value is attributable to the *'net value'* of the business. Note that in **HMRC v Trustees of the Nelson Dance Family Settlement** (2009) Mr Justice Sales stated (at paragraph 25), that *'…the general principle governing the operation of the IHTA is the loss to donor principle, which directs attention to changes in the value of the transferor's estate rather than in that of the transferee, and that the basic approach in the Act (save in cases where explicit provision is made to the contrary) is that any charge to tax does not turn upon what happens to property transferred when it is in the hands of the transferee.'*

The following *'relevant business property'* (wherever situate) falls within **section 105(1)(a) [(b) or (bb)]** and qualifies for 100% relief:

1.   property of a business or an interest in a business, including: (i) the interest of a sole proprietor; or (ii) of a partner in the business, (see **s.105(1)(a)**, and **IHTM 25051**;
2.   unquoted shares in a company (including shares that are traded on the Alternative Investment Market) which either alone or with other shares owned by the transferor, gave the transferor control of the company immediately before the transfer, **s.105(b)**; and
3.   shareholdings in unlisted companies, **s.105(1)(bb)**.

Note that the test of *'control'* (which is defined in **s.269**) is subjective, and depends upon whether a person can actually exercise control over the company. **s.105(1ZA)** defines unquoted as meaning not listed on a recognised stock exchange (**IHTM 18336** and **18337**).

The following *'relevant business property'* (wherever situate) falls within

s.105(1)(b) and qualifies for 50% relief:

1. listed shares in or securities of a company which gave the transferor control of the company, before the transfer;
2. land or buildings, machinery or plant which, immediately before the transfer, was used wholly or mainly for the purposes of a business carried on by a company of which the transferor then had control or by a partnership of which he was then a partner (**s.105(1)(d)**); and
3. land or buildings, machinery or plant used immediately before the transfer for the purposes of a business carried on by the transferor, which was settled property in which he was then beneficially entitled to an interest in possession, **s.105(1)(e)**.

Under **s.112(3)** an asset is not relevant business property under **s.105(1)(d)** unless either –

1. it was used in the business for two years before the date of the transfer; or
2. 'it replaced another asset so used and it and the other asset and any asset directly or indirectly replaced by that other asset were so used for periods which together comprised at least two years falling within the five years immediately preceding the transfer of value.'

If the transferor owned shares or securities in the company, **s.105(1)(d)**, those shares or securities must themselves have been relevant business property, **s.105(6)**. If the transferor was a partner, his partnership interest must itself have been relevant business property. This means that the transferor must have owned the shares/securities or partnership interest for at least two years prior to the transfer of the land, plant or machinery.

Under **s.108(b)** where **S** acquires business property on **T's** death, her period of ownership is aggregated with that of **T**. Under **s.109** BPR may also be available in respect of a successive transfer of property provided the ownership requirements were satisfied in respect of the first transfer and one of the transfers took place on death.

Note that in relation to a limited liability partnership (an 'LLP') **s.267A** provides that for the purposes of the **IHTA 1984** and any other enactment relating to inheritance tax:

'(a) property to which [an LLP] is entitled, or which it occupies or uses, shall be treated as property to which its members are entitled, or which they occupy or use, as partners;

(b) any business carried on by [an LLP] shall be treated as carried on in partnership by its members; and

(d) any transfer of value made by or to [an LLP] shall be treated as made by or to its members in partnership (and not by or to the [LLP] as such).'

A gift of qualifying business property should always be dealt with by way of a specific gift made to a chargeable beneficiary (see **s.39** under APR above). Where a chargeable or potentially exempt transfer is made by **T** within seven years before his death, **s.113A** (Transfers within seven years before death of transferor) restricts the availability of BPR. The relief is only available where (i) the transferee has retained ownership of the original property gifted by **T**, throughout, from the date of the transfer to the date or **T's** death, and (ii) the property would qualify as relevant business property at the date of **T's** death (despite failure to comply with the minimum ownership requirement prescribed by **s.106**). Note that if the transferee predeceases **T**, the qualification conditions must be met at the date of the transferee's death (see p.3039 of the BDO Tax Guide). **s.113B** specifies the conditions to be met where **s.113A** applies to replacement property, thereby preserving BPR where a transferee disposes of gifted property before **T's** death.

Quick succession relief

Quick succession relief *('QSR')* (**IHTM 22041**), provides relief against two charges to IHT where more than one chargeable transfer has taken place within a five year period (**s.141**), for example where **S's** estate increased in value as a result of a chargeable transfer by **T** made within five years before his death (subject to a survivorship clause in **T's** will).

The relief is given by reducing the tax payable on the death estate by reference to;

1. the amount of tax on the earlier chargeable transfer;
2. the benefit to **S** of that transfer; and
3. the period between the transfer and **S's** death.

The percentage applied depends upon the period between the earlier transfer and **S's** death as follows:

Period between transfer and death	Appropriate percentage
One year or less	100
More than one year but not more than two years	80
More than two years but not more than three years	60
More than three years but not more than four years	40
More than four years but not more than five years	20

If **S's** death takes place more than five years after the earlier transfer, there is no relief.

Related property relief

If property was valued on death as related property under **s.161** and a qualifying sale of the property takes place (**s.176(1)**), within three years of death for less than the related property valuation, then a claim may be made within a six year time limit (**s.241**), to recalculate the tax at death without reference to the related property.

A sale is a qualifying sale (**s.176(3)**) if:

1. the sellers are the persons in whom the property vested immediately after death, or are **T's** PR's;
2. the sale takes place at arm's length for a freely negotiated price, and is separate from any sale of related property;
3. no seller (or person having an interest in the proceeds of sale) is the same as or is connected with the buyer (or any person having an interest in the purchase); and
4. neither the sellers nor any other person having an interest in the proceeds of sale obtain in connection with the sale a right to acquire the property sold or any interest in it or created out of it.

Note the decision of the Fist Tier Tribunal in *Price v HMRC* (2010) about the proper construction of the words *'the appropriate portion of the value of the aggregate of that and any related property'* in **s.161(1)** – extracts from the decision appear in **Appendix 7**. The author understands that an application has been made for leave to appeal, which at the time of writing has not been heard.

Taper relief

On **T's** death IHT is calculated at full death rates on any PET's made within the previous seven years. Taper relief takes the form of a percentage reduction in the tax which would otherwise be payable on a transfer, and under **s.7(4)** applies where:

1. the transfer was made more than three years before **T's** death; and
2. the transfer is chargeable in its own right.

The seven year cumulation rule is not subject to the relief which is given in respect of the rate at which tax is charged. The amount of the taper relief depends upon the length of time by which **T** survived the transfer. The charge to tax on the transfer is reduced by charging the following percentages of the full rate:

Years between transfer and death	Percentage of full tax rate
3 to 4	80
4 to 5	60
5 to 6	40
6 to 7	20

No rebate is payable if this yields a lower figure than the tax originally calculated and paid at life-time rates (**s.7(5)**), see **IHTM14611**, and **14612**.

Settlement

For IHT property is *'settled'* if it is a comprised in a *'settlement'* (i.e. a trust), see **s.43(1)**. For the CGT definition of settled property see **sections 60** and **68** of the **TCGA 1992**. The income tax definition is contained in **s.466** of the **Income Tax Act 2007**. The IHT definition of *'settlement'* is contained in **s.43**, and the definition of *'settlor'* in **s.44**. A settlement exists where:

1. property is held in trust for:
   (a) persons in succession, or
   (b) any person subject to a contingency; or

2. property is held by trustees:
   (a) to accumulate the whole or part of any income of the property, or
   (b) with power to make payments out of that income at: (i) their discretion; or (ii) the discretion of another person,
   either with or without power to accumulate surplus income; or

3. property is charged or burdened with the payment of an annuity or other periodical payment payable for (i) life; or (ii) any other limited or terminable period.

Separate funds held on separate trusts, are treated by HMRC as being separate settlements. Where funds subsequently merge (for example in consequence of the exercise of a power of appointment), this does not prevent HMRC from continuing to treat them as separate settlements. See McCutcheon 11-06, and 11-07.

Tax mitigation

'...The Government have set out a clear strategy on preventing tax avoidance. We will not hesitate to take action to stop those who seek to take unfair advantage of unintended tax loopholes. The measure demonstrates our commitment to act quickly to close these...'
(Extract from a Written Ministerial Statement made in the House of

Commons by David Gauke, the Exchequer Secretary to the Treasury on the 24th May 2011).

'As set out in the Coalition Agreement, the Government is committed to making every effort to tackle tax avoidance. The Government will take a more strategic approach to the risk of avoidance to prevent increasing complexity and reduce the need for frequent legislative change. In this context, the Government is tackling long-standing avoidance risks in a way that makes it clear what result the legislation intends to achieve. The Government will continue to shut down avoidance schemes as they emerge.' **(Budget 2010, Press Notice 3).**

Tax avoidance

'There are cases we know of where transactions are completed solely for the benefit of a tax gain, which of course was not intended by Parliament. The question is, is it avoidance or does the activity go beyond avoidance and cross the boundary between avoidance and evasion? This can sometimes be difficult to decide…It may be that as the legal principles of avoidance become defined in case law , [a person who] implements an avoidance scheme which has been held by the courts to be avoidance could be embarking on a course of conduct which amounts to evasion.' From the text of the 10th Hardman Memorial Lecture delivered on 14 November 2002 by **Richard Broadbent**, former Chairman, Customs & Excise, British Tax Review, Issue No.2, 2003.

[The] *hallmark of tax avoidance is that the taxpayer reduces his liability to tax without incurring the economic consequences that Parliament intended to be suffered by any taxpayer qualifying for such reduction in his tax liability. The haulmark of tax mitigation, on the other hand, is that the taxpayer takes advantage of a fiscally attractive option afforded to him by the tax legislation, and genuinely suffers the economic consequences that Parliament intended to be suffered by those taking advantage of the option.'* Lord Nolan in **Willoughby and another v IRC** (1997) (an Income Tax case).

Artificial tax motivated planning that has no basis in reality, or which hinges upon a perverse interpretation of legislation, amounts to unacceptable tax avoidance and is likely to be challenged by HMRC. However, the ultimate arbiter is the court.

Tax mitigation

Prudent and careful planning involves sensible use of the available exemptions and reliefs that are provided for in the tax legislation (as discussed above).

Anti-avoidance rules

These are rules that are designed to render a planning arrangement ineffective. For IHT the main anti-avoidance provisions are:

1. associated operations (**s.268**);
2. restriction on freedom to dispose (**s.163**);
3. artificial reductions in the value of settled property – depreciatory transactions (**sections 52(3), and 65(1)**));
4. the related property provisions (**s.161**);
5. tax chargeable in respect of certain future payments (**s.262**);
6. free loans (**sections 52(3) , 65(1)(b), and s.103 FA 1986**);
7. back-to-back life policies (**sections 21(2) , (3), and 263**);
8. close companies (**sections 94-102, and s.202**);
9. settlement powers (**s.47A, s.55A, and s.272**);
10. gifts with reservation (**sections 102(5)(a) to (c) FA 1986**); and
11. **s.5(1B)** beneficiary-taxed interests in possession (**s.5(1B)**, added by **s.53 FA 2010**).

Disclosure

Certain IHT planning arrangements must be notified to HMRC under the disclosure rules. The Law for the disclosure regime *('DOTAS')* is contained in a combination of primary and secondary legislation which is usefully set out in Annexe C of the **HMRC Consultation Document Disclosure of Inheritance Tax Avoidance**, published 27th July 2010, available to view on HMRC's website. The following is an extract from the Practice Note - **Disclosure of Tax Avoidance Schemes**, published by the Law Society on the 11th May 2011.

'An inheritance tax (IHT) scheme will be disclosable under the DOTAS regime if the arrangements fall within the prescribed description in the IHT description regulations – see tests 1-3 below, and do not fall out of the scope of the regime as a result of the grandfathering provisions.

Test 1: Do the arrangements result in property becoming relevant property?
The DOTAS regime only applies to IHT arrangements where as a result of those arrangements property becomes 'relevant property'.
Relevant property is defined in section 58(1) IHTA 1984 and does not include, for example, property held on charitable trusts, a qualifying interest in possession or a disabled person's interest.
It does not matter whether or not property becomes relevant property straight away or whether it remains relevant property; a scheme will require disclosure if at any point in the arrangements or proposed arrangements property becomes relevant property.
Where, arrangements do not, at any stage, lead to property becoming

relevant property then the scheme will not require disclosure under the Regulations.

Test 2: Do the arrangements give rise to a 'relevant property entry charge' advantage?

A 'relevant property entry charge' is defined as the charge to inheritance tax which arises on a transfer of value made by an individual during that individual's life as a result of which property becomes relevant property. The DOTAS regime does not apply to deemed or notional transfers of value.

The term 'advantage' is construed very widely and in the context of the relevant property entry charge would mean the avoidance, reduction, relief or deferral of the relevant entry charge.

Where there is no transfer of value and no wider arrangements then no advantage can be obtained in respect of a transaction which results in property becoming relevant property.

Test 3: Is the advantage a main benefit of the arrangements?

This test is objective and you should consider the value of the expected tax advantage compared to the value of any other benefits likely to be enjoyed.

Grandfathering

The purpose of the DOTAS regime is to require disclosure of schemes which are new or innovative.

To reduce the administrative burden on both practitioners and HMRC those schemes which are the same or substantially the same as arrangements made available before 6 April 2011 are exempt from disclosure. This is known as 'grandfathering'.

It is a matter of fact whether an arrangement is grandfathered. To assist you in deciding whether the IHT arrangements are exempt from disclosure under this test, HMRC have produced a list of schemes which they regard as being 'grandfathered' and do not have to be disclosed. See paragraph 9B.6.1 of HMRC guidance.

The fact that any particular scheme is exempted from disclosure should not be taken as an indication that HMRC either finds the scheme acceptable, or that they accept that it has the intended tax effect under current law. It merely signifies that they are already aware of it or that it does not fall within the Regulations.'

In his statement (see above), David Gauke also announced that a consultation will soon take place on proposals to list certain 'high-risk tax avoidance schemes' in regulations. When implemented users of 'listed schemes' will be required to disclose their use to HMRC and be subject to an additional charge on tax underpaid as a result of using the scheme.

The approach of the court

Planning that relies on artificial technical loopholes is questionable. In **WT Ramsay Limited v IRC (1981)** Lord Wilberforce expounded the court's approach to avoidance schemes as follows, *'It is the task of the court to ascertain the legal nature of any transaction to which it is sought to attach a tax, or a tax consequence, and if that emerges from a series, or combination of transactions, intended to operate as such, it is that series or combination which may be regarded.'* The application of the **Ramsay** or *'substance over form'* principle involves a realistic factual analysis of a transaction by the Judge. However, when deciding whether a particular transaction falls within the purpose of any provision of a taxing statute, the court may apply a purposive approach instead of adopting a formulaic or atomistic approach.

In **MacNiven v Westmoreland Investments Ltd** (2001), Lord Hoffmann reviewed the major cases decided since **Ramsay**, and sought to explain the true basis of the case, which for him lay in statutory construction. The **Ramsay** principle involved consideration of what the legislation meant, and whether the particular event in question should properly fall within the statute. This involves deciding whether a transaction is the sort of transaction which the statute has in mind. Commenting on the distinction between *'tax avoidance'* and *'tax mitigation'* Lord Hoffmann said (obiter dictum), *'...when statutory provisions do not contain words like 'avoidance' or 'mitigation', I do not think that it helps to introduce them. The fact that steps taken for the avoidance of tax are acceptable or unacceptable is the conclusion at which one arrives by applying the statutory language to the facts of the case. It is not a test for deciding whether it applies or not.'* Any pre-arranged scheme which involves either tax avoidance, tax deferral or merely the preservation of an existing tax benefit is potentially within the scope of the **Ramsay** principle. However, the application of the principles developed by the **Ramsay** line of authorities depends upon the facts of the case and the wording of the relevant statutory provision in point.

Associated operations

The associated operations provisions are widely drawn and could be applied to almost any series of transactions. *'Associated operations'* is defined by **s.268(1)** as any two or more operations of any kind where the same property is affected, or where one operation affects a further operation (see p.3081 of the BDO Tax Guide).

The operations may:

1.   take place at different times;
2.   involve a number of steps taken at the same time;
3.   be effected by the same or different persons; and

4. be an omission to do something.

s.268 (3) provides,

'Where a transfer of value is made by associated operations carried out at different times it shall be treated as made at the time of the last of them; but where any one or more of the earlier operations also constitute a transfer of value made by the same transferor, the value transferred by the earlier operations shall be treated as reducing the value transferred by all the operations taken together, except to the extent that the transfer constituted by the earlier operations but not that made by all the operations taken together is exempt under s.18.'

A substantial judicial limitation has been placed upon the scope of the associated operations rules by the decision of the Court of Appeal in *Rysaffe* (2003). The court held that the associated operations rule in **s.268** did not apply where five discretionary trusts had been created by the same settlor, on the same terms, and with a nominal amount of £10 each. Mr Justice Park (whose Judgment was unanimously upheld by the Court of Appeal) held that *'...it is up to the settlor who places property in trust to determine whether he wishes to create one trust or several trusts, or for that matter merely to add more property to a settlement which had already been created in the past.* [The associated operations provisions did not apply, because **s.268** was] *not an operative provision which of itself imposes inheritance tax liability. It is a definition of an expression (associated operations) which is used elsewhere. The definition only comes into effect insofar as the expression 'associated operations' is used elsewhere, and then only if the expression in another provision is relevant to the way in which that other provision applies to the facts of the particular case...'* The Judge also stated (obiter dictum), that the mere fact that certain operations all formed part of a single plan or scheme did not of itself necessarily mean that they had been *'effected with reference to each other.'*

Testamentary freedom

Under English Law **T** is free to bequeath his estate as he wishes. However:

1. the arrangements provided for in a will/trust can be altered post death by the entering into of a deed of variation under **s.146**; and
2. the court may re-structure the provision **T** has made for certain persons if a successful claim is made under the **Inheritance Act**.

Variations and reading-back

Under **sections 142, 143,** and **144** it is possible to reorganise and redirect dispositions made by **T** in his will, or under the law of intestacy, provided this is done within two years of **T's** death (see p.3047 of the BDO Tax Guide).

Under **s.142(1)** a deed of variation can be executed by a beneficiary (to rearrange the distribution of **T's** estate by varying or redirecting his entitlement), with the effect that the altered gifts are automatically read-back into the will as having been made by **T**. There can be more than one variation in respect of **T's** estate provided the deeds of variation do not attempt to redirect the same property more than once. Where **T** left a NRB legacy to a discretionary trust under his will and following his death it is decided to preserve his NRB for transfer to **S**, then either:

1. **T's** will can be varied under **s.142** resulting in the fund passing instead to **S** and free of IHT under **s.18** (spouse exemption); or
2. his trustees can appoint the fund to **S** between three months and two years of his death, so that it is read-back into the will under **s.144** and benefits from the spouse exemption.

Where a discretionary trust includes minor or unborn beneficiaries the parties are more likely to use **s.144** to take advantage of the transferable NRB, as unlike **s.142**, there is no requirement for the court's sanction under the **Variation of Trusts Act 1958**.

A beneficiary can also use a disclaimer to vary his entitlement under **T's** will. Whilst a disclaimer may be a way around HMRC's view that a deed of variation cannot be made in relation to a life interest once the life-tenant has died, a beneficiary cannot use a disclaimer to redirect his entitlement to another beneficiary.

Variations (s.142)

Under **s.142** it is possible to:

1. insert a NRA legacy to a discretionary trust into **T's** will, for example to avoid wasting the NRB where one party already has a double NRB as a result of his or her first marriage;
2. posthumously sever a beneficial joint-tenancy in any property, so that **T's** equitable share can pass under his will to **S,** rather than by survivorship;
3. provide in **T's** will that a bereaved minor will become absolutely entitled at the age of 18; and
4. vary a partial interest resulting in a gift of part and retention of the remainder.

Note that following severance of a beneficial joint-tenancy, **T's** interest can pass under his will for example to give **S** an IPDI, however, because **s.142(1)** only provides that a qualifying variation is to be treated as if it had been effected by the deceased, and does not expressly provide that the variation is to be treated as having been made by **T** under his will, then until HMRC provide a clear statement of their view on this matter, caution should be exercised in using **s.142** to create a life interest for **S**.

To be effective for IHT the variation must:

1. be made within two years from **T's** death;
2. be made by a written instrument that contains a statement by all the relevant persons, to the effect that they intend **s.142(1)** to apply to the variation;
3. be a disposition, whether effected by will, under the law of intestacy, or otherwise of property which was comprised in **T's** estate immediately before he died;
4. not be made for any consideration in money or money's worth, other than consideration consisting of the making, in respect of another of the dispositions of the deceased, or a variation or disclaimer which qualifies for relief under **s.142(1)**; and
5. not result in the variation of property that has previously been varied under **s.142**, *Russell v IRC* **(1998)**.

Note that there is a look-through provision if the redirection is to a trust which ends within two years of **T's** death. **s.142(4)** provides:

'*(4) Where a variation to which **subsection (1)** above applies results in property being held in trust for a person for a period which ends not more than two years after the death, this Act shall apply as if the disposition of the property that takes effect at the end of the period had had effect from the beginning of the period; but this subsection shall not affect the application of this Act in relation to any distribution or application of property occurring before that disposition takes effect.*'

Therefore where the variation sets up a trust which lasts for not more than two years, then on termination of the trust HMRC will tax **T's** estate as if the gift to the beneficiary had been made from **T's** estate. This effectively prevents a non-exempt beneficiary from giving a limited interest by deed of variation to his own spouse, and thereby obtaining the spouse exemption under **s.142(1)** as a result. The GWR rules do not apply to the redirection of property in which a beneficiary had a beneficial interest which he continues to enjoy, because for IHT:

(i) the settlor is **T**; and
(ii) the person making the variation is not seen as having at any time owned the property even though the initial beneficial interest was given to him.

s.142 election

s.142 (2) provides that:
> *'Subsection (1) above shall not apply to a variation unless the instrument contains a statement, made by all the relevant persons, to the effect that they intend the subsection to apply to the variation.'*

s.142(2A) provides, *'For the purposes of subsection (2) above the relevant persons are –*
> *(a) the person or persons making the instrument, and*
> *(b) where the variation results in additional tax being payable, the personal representatives.*
>
> *Personal representatives may decline to make a statement under* **subsection (2)** *above only if no, or no sufficient, assets are held by them in that capacity for discharging the additional tax.'*

The effect of the election is to confirm that the disposition being made by the deed of variation is to be treated as if it had been made by **T**. In the real world a gift is being made to the new beneficiary (**'B'**) by the person varying his entitlement. **B** cannot enforce the gift unless he gives consideration. As a general rule the gift will not qualify for relief under **s.142 (1)** if it is made for consideration (**s.142(3)**). Therefore the written notice required by **s.142 (2)** should be executed as a deed, which requires attestation in accordance with the provisions of the **Law of Property (Miscellaneous Provisions) Act 1989** (**'LP(MP)A'**). **s.1(3) of LP(MP)A** provides:

> *'(3) An instrument is validly executed as a deed by an individual if, and only if:*
> > *(a) it is signed –*
> > > *(i) by him in the presence of a witness who attests the signature; or*
> > > *(ii) at his direction and in his presence and the presence of two witnesses who each attest the signature; and*
> > *(b) it is delivered as a deed by him or a person authorised to do so on his behalf.*
> *(4) In subsections (2) and (3) above 'sign', in relation to an instrument, includes making one's mark on the instrument and 'signature' is to be construed accordingly.'*

s.62(6) TCGA 1992 provides:

> *'(6) Subject to subsections (7) and (8) below, where within the period of 2 years after a person's death any of the dispositions (whether effected by will, under the law relating to intestacy or otherwise) of the property of which he was competent to dispose are varied, or the benefit conferred by any of those dispositions is disclaimed, by an*

instrument in writing made by the persons or any of the persons who benefit or would benefit under the dispositions-
  (a) the variation or disclaimer shall not constitute a disposal for the purposes of this Act; and
  (b) this section shall apply as if the variation had been effected by the deceased or, as the case may be, the disclaimed benefit had never been conferred.'

Under **s.62(7) TCGA 1992** an election has to be made for a variation to be effective for CGT. **s.62(7)TCGA 1992** provides, *'subsection (6) above does not apply to a variation [unless the instrument contains a statement by the persons making the instrument to the effect that they intend the subsection to apply to the variation.]'* If an election is not made for CGT the variation will be treated as if it had only been made for IHT, and for CGT will be treated as a disposal by the person(s) making the variation. The situations in which it might not be desirable to make an election for CGT include:

1. where a loss on an asset could be used by PR's or the person(s) making the variation;
2. where an asset is going to be disposed of quickly, because taper relief may be more favourable to the PR's or person(s) making the variation;
3. when the gain is within the annual exemption of the PR's or person(s) making the variation; and
4. where the PR's or person(s) making the variation have losses that can be set against the gain.

Reading-back (s.144)

s.144 allows an appointment from a will/trust to be automatically read-back into **T's** will, so that **T** is treated as having disposed of his property in accordance with the appointment. The section applies where property comprised in **T's** estate immediately before his death is settled by his will and (i) within two years of his death and (ii) before any interest in possession in the property subsists, there occurs either:

- an event on which an exit charge would be imposed; or
- an event which would have resulted in such a charge were it not prevented from being imposed by **s.144.**

Then by virtue of **s.144(2)**:

1. no tax is charged on the event; and
2. the IHT legislation is treated as having effect as if the will had provided that on **T's** death the property should be held as it is held after the event in question.

Note that (i) there can be a **s.144** appointment after a variation has been made within **s.142**; and (ii) **s.142** can apply in relation to property in respect of which **s.144** has applied. See **Diagram No.19** – *'Reading-back'*.

Two year discretionary trusts

s.144 is a flexible and useful method of bequeathing an estate (or part of it), when it is not clear at the time **T** makes his will, what the most beneficial way of making a capital distribution would be. **s.144** allows a distribution to be made under **s.142(1)** within two years of death, without any charge to IHT, out of assets settled on discretionary trusts by **T's** will. Therefore, where **T**:

1. gives his estate (or some part of it) to his trustees to hold on discretionary trusts;
2. under his will conferred wide powers of appointment on the trustees exercisable in favour of a specified class of beneficiaries (leaving it to his trustees to distribute his estate or declare further trusts of trust property);
3. trustees exercise the power within two years of his death; and
4. no-one obtained a life interest within that time, tax will be chargeable as if the gifts or trusts were made by **T** on his death, and the appointment will not be subject to the usual IHT regime for discretionary trusts.

The back-dating operation of **s.144** only applies where, on a distribution from the trust, tax would otherwise have been charged. As a result, if the discretion is exercised within three months of **T's** death, **s.144** will not apply because tax would not otherwise have been chargeable, *Frankland v IRC* (1997) (the *'Frankland Trap'*). However, there is no need to wait three months if the effect of the deed of appointment is to create an IPDI. If an appointment is made within the **s.144** time limit the minimum period of ownership requirements for APR and BPR start afresh from the time of **T's** death, and under **s.144(2) S** should inherit **T's** period of ownership. Note that the two-year discretionary trust only applies on the creation of an interest in possession where that interest is: (i) an IPDI; (ii) a disabled person's interest; or (iii) a TSI under **sections 49A**; **89B**; or **49B** (see p.3048 of the BDO Tax Guide). Where an interest is fully relieved it may be more tax-efficient to appoint it directly (or in trust) for the next generation rather than to **S**, in case there is a change in the nature of the interests owned at the date of **S's** death, or a change in the nature of the relief. For comprehensive commentary on planning using two-year discretionary trusts, see p.422 of Barlow, King and King – *'Settlements Without An Interest In possession – Property Vested Within Two Years Of Death'*.

Unscrambling a NRB Discretionary Trust using s.144.

$\mathbf{T} \rightarrow$ NRA legacy $\rightarrow$ DT
$\downarrow$
Unscrambled by an absolute appointment to **S**

Results in restoration of 100% of **T's** unused NRB.

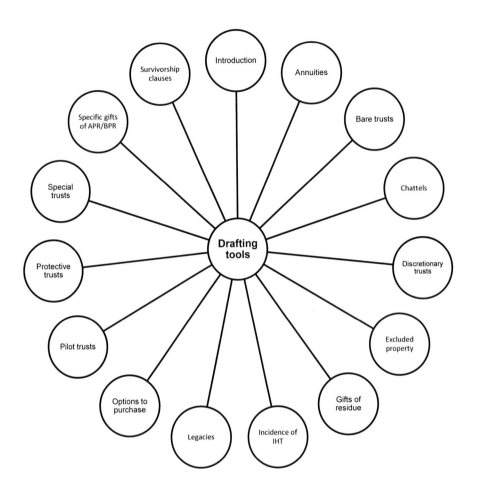

3

Drafting Tools

- Introduction
- Annuities
- Bare trusts
- Discretionary trusts
- Gifts of chattels
- Gifts of excluded property
- Gifts of residue
- Incidence of IHT
- Legacies
- Options to purchase
- Pilot trusts
- Protective trusts
- Special trusts
- Specific gifts of property qualifying for APR / BPR
- Survivorship clauses

Introduction

This chapter describes the principal tools available to the will/trust draftsman. Note that the building blocks of will/trust structures, and a range of basic combinations for planning where **T** is: (i) married; (ii) in a relationship with an unmarried partner; or (iii) a singleton, are illustrated in the next chapter.

IHT planning steps should be fitted around **T's** priorities, and not the other way around. In order to make informed choices **T** must understand the practical consequences of any planning steps and the inherent risks. The assumption made in this book is that **T's** paramount planning objective is to provide for the continued welfare of **S**, taking into account her future financial needs. However in the case of a substantial estate this can result in the bunching of assets on the second death. A gift to **S** may be made outright (an absolute gift) or under a trust (creating a life-interest). If **T** has sufficient liquid wealth or owns qualifying business /agricultural property, he may also wish to preserve value for his children (particularly children of an earlier marriage), and for future generations. In deciding upon a scheme of dispositions to be implemented through his will, and weighing up the corresponding administrative costs, **T** may have to reconcile competing needs, including for example:

1. ensuring that sufficient liquid assets will be available to **S** to enable her

to maintain a reasonable standard of living following his death, and to fund a double NRA legacy (which can be applied by the trustees in their absolute discretion for the benefit of other members of the class of beneficiaries to the entire exclusion of **S**); and

2. ensuring that a balance is kept between the interests of children from **S** and those from an earlier marriage, by for example funding a separate double NRA legacy.

If the most appropriate way of benefiting **T's** family is to transfer his unused NRB to **S**, then in his will **T** simply makes a gift of his entire estate to **S**. As a general principle the use of a trust is not usually appropriate if **T** is young and married with young children, and to provide maximum financial support to **S**, an absolute gift of his entire estate to her is usually the preferred option. An outright gift to **S** would be spouse exempt and 100% of **T's** unused NRB would remain available for the purposes of **S's** PR's making a claim under **s.8A**. Where the gift of the whole of **T's** unused NRB on death is made to trustees under his will, then unless **S** is a beneficiary, and capital is advanced to her:

1. outright; or
2. under a deed of variation that is read-back under **s.142,**

T's NRB will be fully depleted.

However, in the circumstances discussed under Discretionary trusts (below), testamentary planning using a NRB Discretionary Trust remains an attractive alternative to placing reliance on the NRB Transfer Rules.

The following tax-efficient trusts (see **Diagram No.6** – '*IHT privileged will/ trusts post 22.03.2006*'), can also be created under **T's** will:

1. an interest in possession trust that is subject to IHT as a relevant property trust, which is not:
   (a) an IPDI;
   (b) a disabled person's interest; or
   (c) a **s.71A** trust (a trust for a bereaved minor),
   i.e. a life-interest created under a discretionary trust more than two years after **T's** death where certain other conditions are satisfied, see Discretionary trusts below;
2. a disabled person's trust ('*DPT*'), see under Special trusts below;
3. a bereaved minor's trust within **s.71A** (a '*BMT*'), see under Special trusts below;
4. an age 18 to 25 trust within **s.71D,** see under Special trusts below; and
5. an immediate post-death interest trust (an '*IPDI*'), see under Special trusts below.

(Note **Diagram No. 20** – '*Trusts for children and grandchildren*').

The planning tool-box also includes:

1. annuities;
2. bare trusts;
3. gifts of chattels;
4. gifts to chargeable beneficiaries of excluded property;
5. gifts of residue;
6. the making of gifts free of, or subject to, payment of IHT (discussed below under the 'Incidence of IHT');
7. legacies;
8. options to purchase;
9. pilot trusts;
10. protective trusts;
11. specific gifts to chargeable beneficiaries of property qualifying for APR / BPR; and
12. the use of survivorship clauses.

Annuities

An annuity is a right to receive an income stream, and IHT is charged on the underlying capital value generated by the income. Annuities used to be a way of providing maintenance for a person toward whom **T** felt an obligation, and who was not a primary beneficiary under his will. However, in a period of high inflation the real value of an annuity will decline rapidly between:

1. the making of **T's** will and his death; and
2. during the period in which the annuity is payable.

As a general rule a will should not provide for an annuity because:

1. a trust can thereby be created, resulting in an additional liability to tax (see **sections 43(2)(c)**, and **50(2)**);
2. income tax relief on the capital element of a life annuity purchased from an insurance company is not available under **s.717 ITTOIA 2005**; and
3. payments out of capital can become taxable as income.

However in **Stevenson v Wishhart** (1987) the Court of Appeal held that if trustees in the exercise of their power over capital chose to make regular payments out of capital to a capital beneficiary, rather than release a single sum of a large amount, that did not create an income interest.

Alternative methods of providing maintenance are to give a life interest in a:

1. proportionate share of a fund;
2. proportionate share of the income of a fund;

3.   settled legacy; or
4.   legacy of a capital sum with which the legatee may then purchase an annuity.

Bare trusts

Under a bare trust the trustees (as nominees) hold property on trust for a single minor beneficiary absolutely. Capital and income vest at 18. At which time the beneficiary attains a majority and ceases to be a minor. Annuity problems can be avoided by giving a lump sum to an individual or to a third party upon terms that an annuity is to be paid out of the lump sum. The trust property forms part of the beneficiary's estate chargeable to IHT on death. No IHT is payable on death if the beneficiary's estate is below the IHT threshold. The trust property belongs to the minor for CGT, therefore that person's annual CGT exemption is available to offset against any capital gain (and no deemed disposal occurs when he attains the age of 18). If trustees retain income until the beneficiary becomes 18, he has a life interest in the retained income, which forms part of his estate on death if he dies before becoming 18. HMRC have confirmed that a bare trust is not a trust for IHT, and on creation the property transferred to the trust will form part of the minor's estate, however, he is entitled to demand the capital from the trustees when he becomes 18.

Discretionary trusts

Introduction

1.   The transferable nil-rate band *('NRB')* does not apply to:
    1.1 unmarried co-habitees; and
    1.2 singletons (including siblings).

2.   Use of a nil-rate band discretionary trust *('NRBDT')* can result in:
    2.1   freezing the value of an asset likely to grow by a greater percentage than the percentage increase in the NRB between the death of **T** and **S** (note that for the calculation of decennial and exit charges, the value of **T's** share of the equitable interest in the family home is frozen on appropriation by the executors to the trust);
    2.2   prevention of **T's** share of the *'equitable interest'* in the family home (his *'share'*) being collapsed into residue;
    2.3   the ring-fencing of capital value for the benefit of children of an earlier marriage; and
    2.4   NRB maximisation by:
        2.4.1 avoiding **S's** NRB being wasted where **T** has one NRB and **S** already has two; and
        2.4.2 the sheltering of more than two NRB's.

If **T** has one NRB and **S** already has two NRB's (her own and that of her first husband), then if **T** leaves everything to **S** his NRB is wasted. A solution is for **T** to make a gift of his unused NRB to a NRBDT, and to leave residue to **S** either outright or on an IPDI. However there must be sufficient assets in **T's** estate to fund the legacy, which can be achieved by reverse equalisation if necessary (i.e. by **S** making a spouse exempt life-time gift to **T** of cash or other assets to cover the short-fall). Where **S** has more than one, but less than two full NRB's, a solution is for **T** to make a gift to non-exempt beneficiaries and to leave residue to **S** which she can use to top up her own NRB. Where **T** has two NRB's and **S** has one, half of his double NRB will be wasted if he leaves everything to **S**. A solution is for **T** to make a gift equal to one full NRB to a NRBDT, and to leave residue to **S** on an IPDI. This results in consumption of half of **T's** double NRB by the gift made to the NRBDT, and the transfer of the remaining one full NRB to **S**, who then acquires a double NRB. If **T** has more than one but less than two full NRB's, a solution is for **T** to make a gift equal to one full NRB to a NRBDT (which uses up his NRB), and to leave the residue to **S** (so as to increase her maximum NRB shelter). If both **T** and **S** have double NRB's, a solution is for **T** to give a legacy equal to double his NRB to a NRBDT, leaving residue to **S** either absolutely or on an IPDI. However the trust will be subject to a small decennial charge on the tenth anniversary following **T's** death.

3. If not required following **T's** death:
    3.1 provided the necessary powers have been conferred upon the trustees by **T** under his will, they can appoint the legacy directly to **S**, and provided an appointment is made within two years of **T's** death:
        3.1.1 the gift will be automatically read-back into **T's** will under **s.144**, and will benefit from the spouse exemption, resulting in no IHT being payable;
        3.1.2 the NRA legacy will at that point merge with residue; and
        3.1.3 **T's** NRB will not have been used on his death and can be transferred to **S's** personal representatives *('PR's')* on her death; or
    3.2 if all of the beneficiaries are adults, they can enter into a deed of variation after **T's** death to change the dispositions created under his will, resulting in property being advanced e.g. to **S** outright under a deed of appointment.

Note that in this book the maximum amount of cash that **T** can give without incurring any liability to IHT is called the nil rate amount (*'NRA'*), and the *'legacy'* is referred to as the *'NRA Legacy.'*

4. The actual tax treatment of a NRBDT is determined by:

4.1   how the trust is constituted; and

4.2   how the underlying planning arrangement is implemented.

5.   The administration of the following planning arrangements is considered below after a summary of the general principles applicable to the taxation of NRBDT's:

5.1   a simple NRB gift;

5.2   the debt scheme;

5.3   the charge scheme;

5.4   the super-NRBDT; and

5.5   a two-year discretionary trust for a so-called *'distribution legacy'* (i.e. gift of cash for the benefit of a class of beneficiaries with the *trustees* having the power to decide on the size of the benefit to be taken by any particular beneficiary).

Taxation of NRBDT's

1.   The settlement of assets on trust is a chargeable event and under the relevant property regime will trigger IHT as follows:

1.1   on creation of the trust, as part of **T's** estate;

1.2   throughout the duration of the trust, relevant property is taxed on every tenth anniversary;

1.3   an exit charge will arise when assets are appointed out absolutely to beneficiaries; and

1.4   an exit charge will arise at the end of the trust.

Note that during the continuance of a discretionary trust IHT is payable at up to 6% of the value of the trust assets every ten years, and at a proportion of that rate if trust property leaves the trust between ten year anniversaries.

2.   The rate of tax charged on each anniversary depends upon:

2.1   **T's** cumulative total immediately before the trust was created;

2.2   any transfers made from the trust in the previous ten years (except in the first ten years when these are ignored);

2.3   the value of the relevant property in the trust at the anniversary;

2.4   whether **T** created any related settlements (see **s.62(1)**); and

2.5   whether the trust includes any non-relevant property.

3.   Decennial and exit charges will be nil if there was a nil entry charge, and growth is stripped out before the charges arise (i.e. to keep the value of the trust below the original trust value).

4.   The chargeable transfer of value on creation will be charged at 0% if all previous life-time transfers have dropped out of account so that the full

amount of **T's** NRB is available, provided the value of the gifted trust property does not exceed the amount of **T's** unused NRB at the time of his death. Note that for the purposes of the IHT definition of the starting date of the trust (**s.60**), **s.83**, provides that in the case of a trust created by will the starting date is the date of death (see **IHTM 4221**).

5. Distributions are charged at:
   5.1 a proportion of the effective rate charged at the first decennial or,
   5.2 if a distribution is made prior to the first decennial on the rate fixed on the date of creation of the trust.

6. The proportion is $1/40^{th}$ for each complete quarter from the last decennial (or the creation of the trust) and the date of distribution, (**s.69**). The value of the distribution is calculated by reference to the fall in value of the property comprising the trust fund. If IHT is to be paid out of property remaining in the trust, the reduction in value includes the amount of IHT payable.

7. If:
   7.1 no chargeable transfers were made within a seven year period prior to the creation of the trust; and
   7.2 the value of property comprised in the trust immediately after it commenced (together with the value of later additions), did not exceed the maximum amount that can (at the time of distribution) be transferred without incurring a charge to IHT,

   then distributions from a *'special trust'* can be made free of IHT before the anniversary date at the end of the first decennial period.

8. Note that as a general rule all trusts set up on or after 22 March 2006 are subject to the relevant property regime with four exceptions (the *'Special Trusts'*):
   8.1 trusts created on death for a disabled beneficiary;
   8.2 trusts for bereaved minors;
   8.3 trusts for the benefit of a minor who becomes absolutely entitled to capital between the ages of 18 and 25; and
   8.4 trusts created on death with an immediate interest in possession (life interest), known as immediate post-death interest trusts *('IPDI's')*.

9. An IPDI exists where a will/trust provides for a tenant for life, and not for bereaved minors, or for a disabled person, and the life interest exists continuously from **T's** death. A trust created on death where a person becomes immediately entitled to an interest for life will be:
   9.1 treated as that beneficiary's property;
   9.2 aggregated with her estate; and
   9.3 if the interest is created in favour of a spouse, or passes on the

death of a beneficiary to a spouse, will be a spouse exempt gift.

10. Trust property is not treated as being owned by a beneficiary and therefore is not aggregated with their estate on death. The trust is treated as a separate entity.

11. An appointment made between three months and two years of death is automatically read-back into the will under **s.144**, as if **T** had left the property in accordance with the terms of the appointment.

12. Note that dividend income of a discretionary trust is taxed at 42.5%, rather than the normal trust income rate of 50%, subject to a standard rate band which for 2011/2012 is £1,000 (see the summary of Budget announcements made 23rd March 2011 set out in Chapter 7). However as a result of the IHT changes introduced by the **FA 2006** it is possible to combine IHT discretionary trust treatment with income tax interest in possession (life interest) treatment.

13. Where this treatment is desired under a will there needs to be an initial discretionary trust for just over two years to prevent the intended beneficiary from having an IPDI.

How the trust is constituted

1. A NRBDT can be constituted by:
   1.1 appropriating assets to that value to the Trust (including **T's** share of the equitable interest in the matrimonial home (his '*share*'); or
   1.2 with a debt or charge instead (see the '*debt*' or '*charge*' schemes below).

2. If **T's** share is worth less than the NRA, and he owns other assets there are three options:
   2.1 the balance of the NRA legacy can be waived;
   2.2 further assets can be appropriated; or
   2.3 the money owed to the Trust Fund can be left outstanding as a debt from **S** (which is the '*debt*' or '*charge*' scheme).

3. To avoid creating an immediate post-death interest *('IPDI')* in the Trust Fund in favour of **S**, during the first two years following **T's** death, the trustees must not do anything that could be construed as an appointment to **S** of an interest in possession.

4. In HMRC's view (see **SP 10/79**) if a trustee appointed by **T** under his will allows a beneficiary to occupy trust property this creates an IPDI.

5. There is an argument that an IPDI cannot be deemed to arise in the nil

rate band legacy by reason of the surviving spouse's occupation of the property, if the assent of the property to the NRA legacy does not take place until after the end of the two year period following **T's** death.

6. Once two years have expired the trustees can give **S** a right to receive trust income, or to occupy the former matrimonial home, because an IPDI cannot be created thereafter. Note the commentary about **SP 10/79** in Chapter 2 above. Provided the property is not appropriated to the trustees within two years of **T's** death, **S** cannot have an IP in it, because the property remains part of **T's** unadministered estate, which is not a trust. In short, because there is no trust, there cannot be an IP. The appropriation of the property must therefore take place more than two years after **T's** death.

Simple NRB gift

1. Where **T's** share is to be used to fund the NRA legacy, then no earlier than two years after **T's** death (i.e. to avoid creation of an IPDI under **s.144**), the executors and trustees may execute a deed of appropriation and appointment whereby they:
   1.1 appropriate **T's** share to the trust in satisfaction of the NRA legacy; and
   1.2 appoint a life interest in the NRA Trust Fund to **S**.

   Note that the Trustees appropriate either: (i) the whole of **T's** share (if its value is less than his NRA); or (ii) a share of the matrimonial home equal in value to **T's** NRA (if the value of his share exceeds the NRA).

2. The tax consequences of the appointment are as follows:
   2.1 it has no IHT consequences;
   2.2 because the continuing life interest trust would not qualify as an IPDI (as it has not been created by will or been automatically *read-back* into **T's** will), the value of **T's** share is not aggregated with **S's** estate for IHT on her death;
   2.3 it avoids the application of **s.103 FA 1986**;
   2.4 it does not incur Stamp Duty Land Tax; and
   2.5 it results in the preservation of CGT principal private residence relief under **s.222 TCGA 1992** by virtue of **s.225 TCGA 1992**. This also avoids the limitation issues raised by the *debt* and *charge* schemes and the possibility that the *debt* may become irrecoverable.

The debt scheme

1. Under this arrangement, instead of an immediate payment, the NRA legacy is satisfied by a debt owed to the NRA Trustees by either:

1.1   **S** (where residue passes outright to her); or

1.2   the trustees of the residuary trust fund (where residue has been left on trust for **S**).

2. On **T's** death **S** promises to pay the NRA personally to the NRA Trustees by giving them an IOU, and in return receives the whole of **T's** unencumbered residuary estate, but incurs a debt that is deductible against her chargeable estate for IHT on her death.

3. Under the terms of **T's** will the NRA Trustees must be:

    3.1   required to accept the debt (i.e. a written undertaking from **S** to repay it on demand) in satisfaction of the NRA legacy; and

    3.2   permitted to waive interest on the debt, however they must not allow the debt to become statute barred.

    Note that (i) a power to add administrative provisions will not enable the incorporation of a clause requiring the NRB Trustees to accept a debt in satisfaction of the cash gift; and (ii) an existing discretionary trust cannot be varied to add the debt provisions.

4. To avoid the risk of **S** having an interest in possession in it, the debt is repayable on demand.

5. To avoid HMRC arguing that the debt is not repayable on demand because repayment can be prevented by **S,** she should not be a NRA Trustee.

6. Ideally the executors and NRA Trustees under either the debt or the charge scheme should not be the same persons.

7. In particular under the debt scheme, **S** should not be an executor and a NRA Trustee.

8. To be deductible from **S's** estate on her death the debt must: (i) be incurred for full consideration in money or money's worth (**s.5(5)**); and (ii) not infringe the artificial debt rules contained in **s.103 FA 1986**. Which it might, if the loan carried interest or was index-linked, where liability was not incurred for money or money's worth, **sections 5(3)-(5)**. Note that **s.103 FA 1986** disallows the deduction of artificial debts and applies where: (i) on death there is an outstanding liability arising from a debt incurred by **T**; or (ii) the outstanding liability arises from an encumbrance created by a disposition made by **T**.

9. **s.103** is activated if all or part of the consideration for the liability has been derived from property originating with **S** (whether directly or indirectly).

10. **s.103** is therefore likely to be invoked where:

10.1 **T** owned the matrimonial home;

10.2 created a tenancy in common with **S** (conferring upon her an equitable half share in the house);

10.3 they subsequently created reciprocal NRBDT's (without provision for an executor's charge to be created); and

10.4 **S** predeceased **T** (as in the **Phizackerley** case).

11. Therefore the debt scheme should not be used where **S** has made substantial lifetime gifts to **T**.

12. In the opinion of **James Kessler QC** '*s.103 only applies to liabilities made by the debtor: it does not apply to the executor's charge, which is made by the executors, not by the survivor herself.*'

13. If instead of **S** receiving residue outright it is held for her on an IPDI, **s.103(1)** does not apply. That is because **S's** liability for the debt operates to reduce the value of the residuary trust fund that is aggregable with **S's** estate on her death, rather than reducing her estate. Therefore, it is not, '*a liability consisting of a debt incurred by [her] or an encumbrance created by a disposition made by [her]*', within **s.103(1)**. However, because the debt (and also any charge) is incurred by the trustees of the residuary fund and not by **S**, she must not be an executor or trustee of the residuary trust fund.

14. Where **s.103 FA 1986**, applies, **S** should not be a trustee of the residuary estate. Because the risk of **s.103** applying can be avoided if the residuary estate is held on trust for **S** for life, the debt is incurred by the trustees of the residuary estate and not by **S**, see McCutcheon, paragraph 4-26. The property can then be transferred to the trustees of the residuary estate charged with a debt to the NRA Trustees. There is also an argument that the same body of persons cannot grant an interest in land to themselves, which was one of the grounds in **Ingram v. IRC** (1999). Even where **s.103** cannot apply the choice of trustees is important because the arrangement could still be challenged as a sham on the grounds that the parties have rejected the thinking behind the scheme. HMRC may ask to see a letter explaining the scheme to the client. Trustees should ensure that:

14.1 trust minutes are kept setting out acceptance of the debt instead of immediate assets;

14.2 the debt is charged on the house;

14.3 they decide whether or not to charge interest and minute their decision; and

14.4 they notify HMRC of the existence of the trust and complete tax returns.

The trustees should not be subject to the control or choice of **S**. It is preferable for at least one trustee to be independent.

15. The trustees should also behave like trustees and meet at regular intervals to consider whether or not to call in the debt. As far as **S** is concerned, there must always be a frisson of uncertainty that the trustees could call in the debt.

16. Where **s.103 FA 1986** could apply and render a debt scheme ineffective, the charge scheme is the only NRBDT option.

17. If either the debt or charge scheme is used then on **S's** death her estate will either include:
    17.1 her share in the house and an IPDI in **T's** share; or
    17.2 the whole house.

18. The debt or charge (including any interest or additional value if index-linked) due to the NRA Trustees can then be offset against either the share of the matrimonial home held by:
    18.1 the trustees of the residuary trust fund; or
    18.2 by **S**.

The charge scheme

1. Under this arrangement the executors:
   1.1 impose an equitable charge over either:
       (i)   the property; or
       (ii)   **T's** equitable interest in the property (his *'share'*), so **S** does not incur a debt; and
   1.2 transfer the charge to the NRA Trustees in satisfaction of the NRA legacy.

2. **S** does not receive the entire unencumbered residuary estate, but the assets that are transferred to her are reduced in value by the charge on **T's** property. If **T** was the sole owner of the matrimonial home then a legal charge can be imposed on the property, otherwise if the property was held as tenants in common in equity the charge must be an equitable one.

3. Under the terms of **T's** will:
   3.1 the NRA Trustees must be required to accept the benefit of the charge in satisfaction of the NRA legacy; and
   3.2 the executors should be:
       (i)   given an express power to assent assets to the beneficiaries subject to an executor's charge;
       (ii)   permitted to allow the debt to remain outstanding; and
       (iii) relieved from liability for recovering the debt.

4. The charge must be repayable on demand and only be enforceable by the NRA trustees against either:
   4.1 the property; or
   4.2 **T's** share (where **S** takes the residue outright).

5. However whilst **S** remains in occupation of the matrimonial home and the charge is growing in value it is unlikely that the NRA Trustees would succeed in persuading the court to enforce the charge if **S** objected.

6. Under the charge documents, the debt must not be enforceable against either:
   6.1 **S** as the ultimate owner of the property (where residue passes to her outright); or
   6.2 the trustees of the residuary trust fund (where the residuary estate is held on any continuing trusts).

7. Provided the executors have power to charge the NRA legacy on any property passing to **S** they will be protected from claims by the NRA Trustees if they do so.

8. They may then assent the charged property to **S** who is not personally liable for the debt.

9. If this procedure is followed then although there is an encumbrance it was not imposed by a disposition made by **S**, and **S** has never personally incurred a debt, in which case there is no room for the application of **s.103**.

10. **S** must not acquire a life interest in the NRA Trust fund within two years of **T's** death, otherwise the entire advantage of the charge arrangement is lost, because the interest will automatically be read-back under **s.144**, and therefore will be an IPDI.

11. If the charged property is sold, the debt falls to be repaid to the NRA Trustees.

12. Provided that **S** does not need the use of the repaid money, no problems arise, but if she requires any part to be loaned back then the loan will fall foul of **s.103** because **S** then incurs a debt personally. It is at this point that the **FA 2006** changes are helpful since if the NRA Trustees were to purchase a share in the replacement property with **S**, and at the same time appoint a life interest in it to **S**, then –
    12.1 for IHT purposes that appointment is a 'nothing', and
    12.2 **s.103** issues do not arise.

CGT

13. Under either the debt or charge scheme the property ends up being wholly owned by **S**, or by the trustees of the residuary trust fund in which **S** has an IPDI.

14. If the property is occupied by **S** as her principal private residence then:
    14.1 no CGT arises on a sale during **S's** lifetime; or
    14.2 an uplift in the base cost of the property occurs for CGT on her death.

Stamp Duty Land Tax *('SDLT')*

15. Under the debt scheme an SDLT charge arises on the value of the debt.

16. To mitigate the amount of the potential SDLT charge the legacy can be funded with:
    16.1 a debt limited to the maximum amount upon which SDLT is charged at 1% (currently £250K), and
    16.2 by funding the balance with cash.

17. Under the charge scheme the documentation can be drawn up so as to avoid liability to SDLT.

18. As a general rule no chargeable consideration for SDLT arises where:
    18.1 the executors charge **T's** property with the payment of the legacy;
    18.2 it is agreed that the NRA Trustees cannot enforce payment of the legacy personally against the owner of the property;
    18.3 the NRA Trustees accept the charge in satisfaction of the legacy; and
    18.4 the property is transferred to **S** subject to the charge.

The super-NRBDT

1. This is a planning arrangement developed by the author and first outlined in his article *Tax-Efficient Wills* published by Taxation Magazine, 6th March 2008. If this arrangement is adopted an amount of SDLT is payable. The reader should note that the arrangement has not been tested in court and it is not known whether HMRC would accept it. A possible ground on which HMRC might challenge is where the life interest appointed in the IPDI trust fund has no basis in reality, and appears to HMRC to be an artificial step taken purely for the purpose of reducing tax. In the opinion of the author the arrangement is a legitimate form of planning where **T's** objectives are (i) to enable **S** to acquire a 100% equitable interest in the matrimonial home; and (ii) to preserve capital for the benefit of his children from an earlier marriage. Please note that the points made above in relation to **s.103 FA**

1986 (under the commentary dealing with the debt and charge schemes) apply equally to the implementation of a super NRBDT arrangement. The application of **s.102ZA** is discussed below.

2. This arrangement is attractive where **T** wishes to preserve capital for the benefit of children of an earlier marriage, and has sufficient wealth to make reasonable financial provision for **S**. It results in restoration of 100% of **T's** unused and transferable NRB, whilst preserving capital for **T's** children without relying on the continued goodwill of **S**.

3. The maximum IHT shelter that can be achieved using this strategy is £975k in 2011/2012.

4. Please note that in the following commentary it is assumed that **T's** will contains all the necessary powers to implement the following planning steps.

5. On death, **T's** will creates a nil rate band discretionary trust *('NRBDT')* in favour of **S** and each of his children.

6. The principal asset of the NRBDT is the gift by **T** of his NRA plus a nominal amount, for example £10, held by the NRA Trustees on the terms of the NRA Fund (the *'Trust Fund'*).

7. Under the terms of **T's** will, residue (the *'residuary trust fund'*) is gifted to **S** on an immediate post death interest trust *('IPDI')* and then absolutely to each of his children in equal shares.

8. **T's** children are also named as the ultimate default beneficiaries of the residuary trust fund (e.g. in equal shares).

9. After **T's** death, upon the exercise of a power of appropriation by **T's** executors, **T's** equitable share in the matrimonial home (the *'property'*) plus the nominal amount of £10 is transferred to the NRA Trustees, and thereby become assets of the Trust Fund.

10. This results in the full depletion of **T's** unused NRB. Note that **T's** equitable interest in the matrimonial home is appropriated by **T's** executors in satisfaction of his NRA legacy, who then transfer it to the NRA Trustees. The NRA Trustees then enter a Form A restriction on the property at HM Land Registry. This will remain on the title register after **T's** equitable interest in the property has been sold to **S** with the purchase price left outstanding, and whilst the property is subject to a charge. After the transfer of **T's** equitable interest to the NRA Trustees they become co-owners of the property with **S** in equity.

11. The NRA Trustees can then exercise an overriding power of appointment (provided for under **T's** will) to appoint the property plus the nominal amount of £10, on to **S** under an IPDI (which become the sole assets of the IPDI trust), with remainder to the children.

12. The IPDI will automatically be read-back into **T's** will under **s.144**, and the spouse exemption will apply to the whole gift, with the result that **T's** NRB will be treated as having been unused.

13. This restores 100% of **T's** unused NRB.

14. Subject to the issue of self-dealing, the Trustees can then exercise a power under the will to sell the property to **S** (i.e **T's** share of the equitable interest in the matrimonial home (the *'property'*). Note that under the will the trustees have an express power of sale and may sell all or part of the land. They also have a statutory power of sale.

15. This requires execution of a bespoke deed of transfer. Note that if **T's** share in the equitable interest in the property is worth the same amount as his NRA this simply involves execution of a deed of transfer by **T's** executors whereby they transfer his equitable interest to themselves as NRA Trustees in satisfaction of the NRA legacy to the NRBDT. If **T's** equitable interest exceeds the NRA then the NRA is appropriated to the NRA Trustees who sell it to **S,** and the excess (minus £10) can go into the trusts of residue. However beforehand, the NRA Trustees need to calculate the excess so that it can be apportioned between the NRA Trust Fund and the residuary trust fund. They can then record in a single document, the transfer: of (i) whatever is the appropriate percentage of **T's** equitable interest to the NRA Trustees; and (ii) the transfer of the remainder to the trustees of the residuary trust fund.

16. Such a power should expressly permit the trustees to: (i) leave the purchase price outstanding as a debt and; (ii) require interest to be paid, or that the debt be index-linked.

17. The payment of interest would also give rise to an income tax liability. Note that index-linking may also give rise to income tax, and that HMRC's position on this issue is not known.

18. If **T's** equitable share in the matrimonial home exceeds his unused NRB at the time of his death, a share equal to his NRB will need to be appropriated to the Trust Fund.

19. The rest of his share will pass into the trusts of residue but can be appointed out to **S** if the trustees so wish.

20. If **S** then surrenders her life interest in the IPDI trust fund in favour of **T's** children, in effect an amount equal to a third NRB can be sheltered.

21. Subject to any future challenge by HMRC this is theoretically achieved by creating an (interest bearing) debt on deferred payment terms which will reduce **S's** chargeable estate on her death.

22. **s.51(a)** provides that where **S** disposes of her life interest in the IPDI trust fund (whose sole assets are the debt, represented by an IOU, and £10), that there is no transfer of value.

23. Instead, the disposal will be treated for the purposes of **s.52** as the coming to an end of **S's** interest and be charged accordingly under **s.52**.

24. **s.52(1)** provides that when **S's** interest comes to an end, tax shall be charged subject to **s.53**, as if at that time:
    24.1 she had made a transfer of value; and
    24.2 the value transferred had been equal to the value of the property in which her interest in the IPDI had subsisted.

25. If that value is within **S's** NRB, IHT payable at life-time rates on the value of the chargeable transfer will be nil.

26. The surrender will be a potentially exempt transfer *('PET')*, the value of which will fall out of charge after seven years. Please note that under **s.102ZA FA 1986**, termination of **S's** life interest is treated for the GWR rules, as if she had made a gift (i.e. of the £10 and the debt). Therefore if **S** can benefit from those assets (which were the sole assets comprising the IPDI trust fund at the time of the termination of her interest), then the GWR rules apply. However a PET is deemed to have been made should **S** cease to have a reservation of benefit (See McCutcheon, paragraph 5-39). The date the reservation is released is the date of the surrender by **S** of her interest in the IPDI, because at that point the sole assets of the IPDI trust fund (which are £10 and an IOU representing the debt), vest absolutely in the children. On the surrender of her interest, **S** does not reserve to herself any rights in those assets, therefore she cannot continue to enjoy the benefit of any of them (i.e. of the £10 and of the IOU). If it is argued that the IOU does not technically constitute *'no –longer-possessed property'* for the purposes of **s.102ZA**, then the only property to which that section can apply on the surrender of **S's** IPDI is the £10, which falls within **S's** annual exemption.

27. **S** can if necessary procure insurance to cover any potential IHT liability, in the event that the PET fails in whole or in part.

28. The decision to surrender her life interest in any trust property is a matter

for **S**, and she would need to execute a deed of surrender. Note that if the children are named as the remainder men in the appointment, the effect of the surrender by **S** of her life interest is that the property becomes immediately vested in the children absolutely, thereby collapsing the trust, because it will cease to own any assets.

29. However under **T's** will, the trustees can make **S's** life interest in the IPDI trust fund subject to overriding powers, in which case they could terminate it by way of a further appointment if **S** did not co-operate.

30. These steps must take place under **s. 144**, no earlier than three months from death, and within two years of death, and result in **S** owning 100% of the equitable interest in the matrimonial home outright subject to any charge.

31. Prior to implementation the law applicable to the taxation of trusts and in particular SDLT, will need to be reviewed.

32. Whilst in general there is an exemption from SDLT where a transfer is made in satisfaction of a beneficiary's entitlement under a will, the sale of **T's** equitable interest in the property to **S** will be subject to the usual rules.

33. The arrangement cannot be implemented by **T's** will on its own, and further documents need to be drafted.

Two-year discretionary trusts

1. **s.144** allows a distribution to be made under **s.142(1)** within two years of death, without any charge to IHT, out of assets settled on discretionary trusts by **T's** will.

2. Therefore, where **T**:
   2.1 gives his estate (or some part of it) to his trustees to hold on discretionary trusts;
   2.2 under his will, conferred wide powers of appointment on the trustees, exercisable in favour of a specified class of beneficiaries (leaving it to his trustees to distribute his estate or declare further trusts of Trust property);
   2.3 trustees exercise the power within two years of his death; and
   2.4 no-one obtained a life interest within that time,
   then tax will be chargeable as if the gifts or trusts were made by **T** on his death, and the appointment will not be subject to the usual IHT regime for discretionary trusts.

3. The back-dating operation of **s.144** only applies where, on a distribution from the trust, tax would otherwise have been charged.

4. As a result, if the discretion is exercised within three months of **T's** death, **s.144** will not apply because tax would not otherwise have been chargeable, **Frankland v IRC** (1997), see the *'Frankland Trap'* in Chapter 6 below).

5. However there is no need to wait three months if the effect of the deed of appointment is to create an IPDI.

6. If an appointment is made within the **s.144** time limit the minimum period of ownership requirements for APR and BPR start afresh from the time of **T's** death, and under **s.144(2) S** should inherit **T's** period of ownership.

7. Where an interest is fully relieved it may be more tax-efficient to appoint it directly (or in trust) for the next generation rather than to **S**, in case there is a change in the nature of the interests owned at the date of **S's** death, or a change in the nature of the relief.

Conclusion

Whilst the NRBDT remains the most flexible form of tax-efficient will for a married testator who has children from an earlier marriage:

1. implementation and administration involve the incurrence of avoidable costs if **T** simply leaves his entire estate to **S**, whose PR's on her death can then make a **s.8** claim;

2. if **s.103** applies, the benefit of the arrangement in undermined; and

3. a challenge could be made by a disappointed spouse under the **Inheritance Act**.

An alternative method of achieving capital protection is for **T** to leave **S** a terminable life interest in part or all of his estate.

Existing wills that contain a NRA legacy should be reviewed and may be capable of enhancement. For new wills, bespoke planning using a NRBDT can be attractive both for tax, and for non-tax reasons. The NRBDT therefore remains a useful tool in the will/trust draftsman's tool-box.

Gifts of chattels

s. 55 (1)(x) AEA 1925 defines chattels as meaning,
'carriages, horses, stable furniture and effects (not used for business purposes), motor cars and accessories (not used for business purposes), garden effects, domestic animals, plate, plated articles, linen, china, glass, books, pictures, prints, furniture, jewellery, articles of household

or personal use or ornament, musical and scientific instruments and apparatus, wines, liquors and consumable stores, but do not include any chattels used at death of the intestate for business purposes nor money or securities for money.' Note that this does not include shares in chattels which are choses in action, i.e. personal rights of property which can only be claimed by taking legal action, and not by taking physical possession.

s.143 (known as the precatory trust provision) states that,

Where a testator expresses a wish that property bequeathed by his will should be transferred by the legatee to other persons, and the legatee transfers any of the property in accordance with that wish within the period of two years after the death of the testator, this Act shall have effect as if the property transferred had been bequeathed by the will to the transferee.'

Maximum flexibility is achieved where **T's** will provides that the executors may distribute personal chattels amongst a class of beneficiaries in their absolute discretion. Any distribution made by **T's** executors to such a person within that time is then read-back into his will under **s.143**. However, a distribution by executors must be made pursuant to **T's** wishes, otherwise they will be treated as having made a PET themselves.

Unless otherwise provided in **T's** will, IHT on chattels is borne by residue. A gift made to **S** is exempt from IHT. For IHT the value of a chattel bequeathed in a will is usually the market value of the item on the date of death. **s.160** defines market value in the following terms,

'Except as otherwise provided by this Act, the value at any time of any property shall for the purposes of this Act be the price which the property might reasonably be expected to fetch if sold in the open market at that time, but that price shall not be assumed to be reduced on the ground that the whole property is to be placed on the market at one and the same time.'

This value may be higher where an item forms part of a collection, in which case HMRC would expect the collection to be valued together. Any change in the value of an estate that occurred because of death is treated as if it had occurred before death. See **s.171**, which modifies the usual rule that the value of **T's** estate before death is the value transferred by a notional transfer of value of hypothetical property equal to the value of the estate before death.

A chattel that is a wasting asset benefits from CGT exemptions. **s. 132** provides that a chattel is a wasting asset, *'...if, immediately before the chargeable transfer, it had a predictable useful life not exceeding fifty years, having regard to the purpose for which it was held by the transferor ; and plant and machinery shall in every case be regarded as having a predictable useful life of less than fifty years.'* A discount can be applied to the value of **T's** share in any jointly-owned chattels. HMRC may need to be told how the asset was acquired or purchased, and the proportion of any purchase price contributed by **T**. The related property rules under **s.161** will also need to be considered. CGT hold-over relief is available where assets come out of a discretionary trust after two years , and for heritage items where the recipient provides a replacement undertaking under **s.31**. To prevent a gift failing where a beneficiary pre-deceases **T**, his will can provide for a substitutional beneficiary to take the gift, or include provision for the gift to pass to the deceased beneficiary's PR's.

Gifts of excluded property

Introduction

Excluded property is carved out of the charge to IHT by **s.3(2)**, and by virtue of **s.5(1)** is not included in **T's** chargeable estate. Note that: (i) the value transferred by a transfer of value does not take account of the value of excluded property ceasing to form part of **T's** estate as a result of a disposition (**s,3(1), (2)**); (ii) **T's** estate immediately before his death (on which IHT is payable) does not include excluded property, **s.5(1)**; and (iii) if the excluded property is settled property, the termination of an IP in it is not taxable (nor is it *'relevant property'* for the purposes of the rules), see paragraph 20.1 of Golding. However, there is uncertainty about whether ceasing to reserve a benefit in excluded property constitutes a PET, or whether the excluded property rules take precedence so that there is no potential charge.

Excluded property status is determined by reference to:

1. **T's** domicile (whereas in contrast the availability of IHT exemptions is largely dependent upon the tax status of the recipient of a transfer of value);
2. the type of property; and
3. its location.

Excluded property can be classified into three groups:

1. property situated in the UK (see **Diagram No.21** – *'UK situs assets designated as excluded property' (**s.6** and **s.157**)*);
2. property situated abroad; and
3. reversionary interests (see paragraph 20.4 of Golding).

Specific examples include:

1. chattels and real property owned by a non-dom and situated abroad (**s.6(1)**);
2. investments in an authorised unit trust *('AUT')* or open-ended investment company *('OIC')* owned by a non-dom (**s.6(1)**);

3. settled property outside the UK, provided the settlor was a non-dom at the time the trust was made (**s.48(3)**);
4. settled property situated anywhere consisting of investments in an AUT or OIC, provided the settlor was a non-dom at the time the trust was made (**s.48(3)(A)**);
5. a future interest under a trust (a *'reversionary interest'*) (**s.48(1)**), however this is subject to three exceptions, including where the interest has been acquired for consideration; and
6. certain Treasury certificates issued subject to a condition authorised by **s.22 Finance (No.2) Act 1931** (or **s.47 Finance (No.2) Act 1915**) in the beneficial ownership of a non-dom.

Settled property that is excluded property is not relevant property. For high net worth individuals who are non-doms, it is critical for IHT that they maintain excluded property status for as much of their estate as possible through the holding of assets outside the UK. The most tax-efficient form of testamentary planning using excluded property, is to make gifts in favour of chargeable beneficiaries, i.e. **T's** children and grand-children.

Offshore holding structures

IHT charges can be avoided by holding UK assets through a non-UK resident *'shield'* company (which converts the holding of a UK asset by an individual into a holding of a non-UK asset). However, in the case of residential property that is occupied through an offshore holding structure a charge to tax may arise under the benefit in kind legislation. The benefit in kind provisions set out in **ITEPA 2003**, **Chapter 5** can be applied to an individual who is deemed to be a director under **s.67 ITEPA 2003** (including a shadow director), *R v. Allen* (2001). Capital gains of a closely controlled non-UK company are attributable to non-UK domiciled individuals triggering an immediate liability to CGT on a disposal of property at a gain.

Excluded property trusts *('EPT')*

An EPT is a life-time settlement of property situated outside the UK settled by a non-dom before he either: (i) acquires a UK domicile or (ii) is deemed domiciled in the UK for IHT. Property added to an EPT after the settlor becomes a UK domiciliary is not excluded property. **Sections 81** and **82** should also be considered where property moves between trusts after the settlor has become UK domiciled. EPT status is lost where the settlor retains a life interest with the remainder being held on a discretionary trust (or where the trust can be converted into a discretionary trust in the future by the exercise of an overriding power), if the settlor subsequently becomes UK domiciled, or is UK domiciled either at the time of his death, or at the time of any prior termination of his life interest. Where a non-dom creates a Discretionary EPT of which he is a beneficiary and then dies domiciled in the UK, **s.48(3)** overrides the GWR provisions, with the result that the settled property does not form part of that individual's estate on death (see **IHTM 16161**). However, in the current political and fiscal climate this may change.

Gifts of residue

T may leave a gift of residue to:
1. **S** (who is an exempt beneficiary) either:
   (a) outright (by making an absolute gift); or
   (b) on a life interest trust (an IPDI); or
2. children and grandchildren of any age (and thereby skip a generation) of:
   (a) chargeable property outright up to the amount of his unused NRB, which will then become depleted;
   (b) assets qualifying for business or agricultural property relief (APR/BPR); and
   (c) excluded property; or
3. to children who are minors on:
   (a) a bereaved minor's trust (a 'BMT');
   (b) an 18-25 trust;
   (c) an immediate post-death interest trust (an 'IPDI'); or
   (d) a discretionary trust.

An 18-25 trust can be put in place with a maximum charge at current rates of 4.2% payable when capital is distributed, thereby deferring the vesting of capital until the beneficiary becomes 25 years old.

Spouse exempt gifts

The spouse exemption is available (provided the conditions in **s.18** on domicile are satisfied) where residue is left to **S**: (i) outright; or (ii) on an IPDI. This is particularly useful where **T** (i) wants to preserve capital e.g. for children from an earlier marriage; and (ii) in enabling trustees to exercise overriding powers of appointment to cause PET's to be made by the spouse. From 22.03.06 the spouse will only be treated as making a PET (rather than an immediately chargeable transfer) where the appointment is to: (i) another beneficiary absolutely; (ii) a disabled person; or (iii) into a bereaved minor's trust.

In the case of a gift to **S** for life using an IPDI, she becomes entitled to a life interest on **T's** death, the trust does not qualify as a BMT or as a DPT, and must not do so throughout the life of the IPDI. Most intended life interests will take effect as IPDI's except for example where unusually a discretionary trust arises before the life interest can take effect. On **S's** death, the whole of the capital fund constituted by the gift will be aggregated with her estate to calculate IHT payable on her estate.

Absolute gift or IPDI

The points to address when considering leaving residue to **S** either absolutely or on an IPDI include the following:

- if residue is given to **S** outright, she can only make gifts if she has mental capacity or an application is made to the Court of Protection;
- if the house is left on trust the trustees can take the decision as to whether **S's** interest should be terminated in whole or in part and PET's made;
- if **S** is left the residuary estate outright, she can establish IPDI's for the children in her will;
- there may be CGT advantages in transferring the property into trust for **S** because future disposals that might trigger gains can be minimised;
- if property is left outright to **S** she cannot make lifetime gifts on trust for **T's** children to take effect as PET's – and therefore such transfers will be chargeable; and
- by contrast if **S** is given an IPDI in the will which is then terminated so that the property becomes held on a bereaved minor's trust during her lifetime this will be a PET.

Where T is not survived by S

Where **T** is not survived by **S** then to benefit his children **T's** default options include:

- an absolute gift (e.g. to adult beneficiaries);
- a bare trust for example for **T's** grandchildren (who can then take absolutely at 18);
- a bereaved minor's trust *('BMT')* **(s.71A)** ; or
- an 18-25 Trust **(s.71D)**, where **T** wishes to leave assets to children who are under the age of 25.

Incidence of IHT

Unless otherwise stated in a will **s.211(1)** provides,

'(1) Where personal representatives are liable for tax on the value transferred by a chargeable transfer made on death, the tax shall be treated as part of the general testamentary and administrative expenses of the estate, but only in so far as it is attributable to the value of property in the United Kingdom which –
(a) vests in the deceased's personal representatives, and
(b) was not immediately before the death comprised in a settlement.'

s.211(3) further provides that,

'Where any amount of tax paid by a personal representative on the value transferred by a chargeable transfer made on death does not fall to be borne as part of the general testamentary and administration expenses of the estate, that amount shall, where the occasion requires, be repaid to them by the person in whom the property to the value of which the tax attributable is vested.'

Where the disposition of an estate is made partly in favour of an exempt beneficiary (e.g. **S**) and partly in favour of a non-exempt beneficiary (e.g. **C**) the allocation of exemptions between different gifts is determined by reference to **sections 36** to **42**. This requires careful consideration where the:

1. amount of any legacy is large; or
2. non-exempt gift is a share of residue, the balance of which is given under an exempt gift.

In particular **s.41** establishes two rules:

1. no tax falls on any specific gift to the extent that the transfer is exempt; and
2. no tax attributable to residue falls on any gift of a share of residue if or to the extent that the transfer is exempt.

Otherwise to relieve the residuary estate of the liability to IHT there must be an express provision in the will. Under **s.211** real property in the UK which is the subject of a specific gift is free of IHT unless otherwise provided in the will. IHT on chattels situated in the UK is a testamentary expense borne by residue, however, in the case of items situated outside the UK an express direction should be included in the will. Normal pecuniary legacies preceding an exempt gift of residue rarely attract IHT. Tax-free legacies of a specified amount can be given up to the amount of the unused balance of **T's** NRB.

If **T's** will provides that a specific gift bears its own tax (so that IHT is paid out of the gift itself), then the beneficiary receives the net gift, and the tax falls upon residue (whether the residuary beneficiaries are exempt or non-exempt), **s.211(2)**. Unless otherwise provided in **T's** will, a specific gift of UK property is made tax free to the beneficiary, however, a specific gift of non-UK property bears its own tax, **s.211(1)**. Other property bearing its own tax includes: (i) joint-property passing by survivorship; (ii) nominated property; and (iii) property subject to the GWR rules.

If a share of residue is subject to IHT it must bear its own tax. A choice has to be made between providing either for the payment of more tax in equal shares, or for the making of a gift in equal shares before tax is deducted from the non-exempt share that results in a lower payment of IHT but an unequal benefit.

If it is not clear from the will whether the division of residue between exempt and non-exempt beneficiaries is a division of gross or of net residue, this can result in a higher payment of IHT. **s.211** (Burden of tax on death), operates subject to '*any contrary intention shown by the deceased in his will,*' see **s.211(2)**, and **IHTM 26124**. The amount of any tax paid by the PR's on the value transferred on death that does not fall to be borne as part of the general testamentary and administrative expenses of the estate can be reclaimed from the beneficiary in whom the property attributable to the tax paid has vested (**s.211(3)**). A gift of residue usually includes an express direction that IHT be paid from residue. Where a chattel passes by survivorship the surviving joint-owner is liable to pay the IHT on the item unless the will provides otherwise. Where a gift is made in contemplation of the donor's imminent death, tax on the gift is borne by the donee unless the will provides otherwise.

Legacies and Devises

When drafting a specific gift the issues to consider include:

- precise identification of the asset (note that if the subject matter of a gift cannot be identified, it will fail for uncertainty);
- inclusion of a statement that IHT is to be paid out of residue (even though a specific gift will be free of IHT unless otherwise provided in **T's** will);
- **s.35 AEA 1925** (Charges on property of deceased to be paid primarily out of the property charged), which applies where land is subject to a mortgage, and where there is a lien for unpaid purchase monies. Unless **T's** will states otherwise, a beneficiary of a specific gift takes the property subject any charge over it;
- ademption;
- income; and
- costs of delivery and insurance of trust assets after **T's** death.

When drafting a pecuniary legacy the issues to consider include:

- the rules of construction applicable to class gifts, and the operation of **s.33(2) Wills Act 1837** (see under '*Legacies*' in Chapter 1), which applies unless the will expresses a contrary intention;
- substitutional gifts and survivorship clauses;
- the property to be used by **T's** PR's to pay the legacy;
- how the income arising after **T's** death is to be ascertained; and
- payment of interest (note that unless **T's** will provides otherwise, legatees are entitled to interest to compensate them for late payment).

A beneficiary usually takes a gift subject to any outstanding liabilities e.g. a mortgage. Except where during his lifetime **T** entered into: (i) a leasehold covenant as landlord, the beneficiary bears the burden of the covenant; and (ii) a contract to have building work done to the property, then the estate bears the expense of the work. If a contingent or deferred specific gift of property is subject to **s.175 LPA 1925**, then the property carries the right to receive intermediate income unless expressly left elsewhere. This does not apply to a gift of residue. Unless **T's** will directs otherwise the rules applicable to interest are as follows:

1. immediate specific gifts carry the right to income accruing between **T's** death and vesting;
2. contingent and deferred specific gifts carry the right to income (which is added to the capital and transfers with it);
3. contingent pecuniary legacies do not carry interest except in the following cases (where interest is payable from the date of **T's** death):
   - satisfaction of a debt;
   - a vested legacy charged on realty;
   - a legacy to **T's** minor child; and
   - where **T** gives a legacy to any child to provide for their maintenance;
4. immediate residuary gifts carry the right to income accruing after **T's** death; and
5. contingent and deferred residuary gifts also carry the right to income.

Income produced by property that is the subject of a gift must be apportioned between: (i) a primary legatee (who is entitled to income produced after **T's** death); and (ii) a residuary legatee (who is entitled to income arising before that date). However apportionment can be avoided if **T's** will provides that all income received after his death is to be treated as income arising after his death. Where an unlimited gift is made of rents and profits of land the devise takes effect as a gift of the land itself. Likewise, if **T** makes a gift of all the income and benefits of his personal property, the beneficiary is entitled to the capital (except in the case of a gift made to a charity). A devise to a minor is held in trust until the child becomes 18, because during his minority he cannot hold a legal estate in land. Upon attaining his majority at 18 years of age, if the gift remains contingent, the trustees must pay the income of the trust fund to him until the contingency is met or the gift fails. Where in the case of a contingent legacy, **T** has directed the intermediate income or part of it to be paid to or applied for the benefit of the legatee, it is inferred that **T** intended a fund to be set apart and invested to answer the legacy, and in such a case an executor may set apart and invest a sum to carry out **T's** intentions. For a classification of legacies and devises, see Chapter 1.

Options to purchase

By granting a beneficiary an option to purchase trust property at an undervalue

T can ensure that a particular asset is available for acquisition by a beneficiary, without reducing the provision made for the other beneficiaries. IHT is payable if the option price is less than full value, and there is a gift of the excess. However, this is payable out of residue unless otherwise provided in **T's** will.

Pilot trusts

A pilot trust is one established by **T** during his lifetime, by handing a nominal sum of money to trustees, with the intention of adding substantial assets later, i.e. by **T** leaving specific legacies to the existing trusts under his will. A pilot trust will usually be fully discretionary (see Precedent 7.1 on page 251 of Whitehouse & King), but does not have to be. Pilot trusts can reduce (and usually eliminate) IHT charged under the relevant property regime on anniversaries and exits. However they do not reduce IHT payable on the initial creation of a lifetime trust. Where the full amount of **T's** unused NRB is available, and he creates lifetime trusts on consecutive days, for example in favour of his children and grandchildren, transferring a nominal amount to each, (for example £10), then:

1. the trusts are not related; and
2. his cumulative total remains at zero for each transfer (provided the nominal amount settled on all of the pilot trusts created remains within **T's** annual exemption (**s.19**)).

Under **s.62(1)** (the *'Related settlements'* provisions), a related trust is one which commenced on the same day as the main trust and has the same settlor. A settlor can therefore avoid making a related trust where he makes trusts during his life-time by making them on different days. The use of pilot trusts depends upon **T** having an unused NRB when the trusts are established. Note that **T** must not make transfers of value between the creation of the trusts and his death, see **s.67**. Each pilot trust enjoys the benefit of its own full NRB. This enables **T** to increase his IHT shelter by creating a cascade of NRB's in addition to his own, to be funded after his death, by the leaving of a legacy under his will of up to one full NRB to each pilot trust, in effect resulting in no IHT being payable on the cumulative amount of these legacies.

If **T** creates multiple pilot trusts, each trust will have capacity for assets to increase in value without exceeding its NRB. Where life interests are created in a pilot trust the legacy passing to the trust under **T's** will is made to an IPDI. Where after creation multiple trusts are amalgamated for administrative convenience, under **s.81** each will continue to be treated as a separate trust. There is no restriction on the number of pilot trusts that **T** can create. Therefore it is prudent for him to leave room in the trusts for growth in value. Provided additional funds are added to the pilot trusts on the same day by legacies bequeathed under **T's** will, the gifts do not adversely affect the availability of the NRB of each trust (**s.67(3)(b)(i)**). However, the settlor must be the same person who adds to the trusts under his will. Whilst in theory pilot trusts can be jointly created by **T** and **S** (in which case **T** and **S** could subsequently each add assets to the trusts, see **s.44(2)**, and **IHTM 42253**), problems can arise in identifying the destination of funds added by **T** and **S**, i.e. whether, and in what proportions they have been added by **T**(and **S**) to **T's** separate settlement and/or to **S's** fund. Therefore reliance on **s.44(2)** should be avoided and it is better for **T** and **S** to create separate pilot trusts.

Use of this strategy requires careful consideration of:

1. the IHT associated operations rules (in particular **s.272** - definition of *'disposition'*; **s.10(1)** - relief for essentially commercial transactions; **s.263** - back-to-back policies; **s.272** - definition of *'settlement'*; **s.65(1)(b)** (secondary exit charge); **Sch 20, para, 6(1)(c) FA 1986** reservation of benefit; and **s.103 FA 1986** (abatement of liabilities);and
2. the Court of Appeal decision in ***Rysaffe Trustee Co (CI) v I.R.C*** (2003).

Note the **s.80** trap. If **T's** will creates an IPDI for **S**, with remainder going to the pilot trusts, the normal consequence of **T** adding to the pilot trusts does not apply. Instead **S** is treated as the settlor, the pilot trusts are related, and future trusts created by **S** in her will, become related to the pilot trusts. Note that the nominal sum (e.g. £10) must be paid, otherwise the trust will not come into existence before **T's** death. Property of any value or description can be used to establish the trust. An unwanted pilot trust can be unscrambled under **s.144** (see *'Variations and reading-back'* in Chapter 2).

Protective trusts

A protective trust can be created using the form of words prescribed by **s.33 TA 1925.** Under the terms of the trust the beneficiary ('**B'**) enjoys a life interest in the income of the fund until he becomes bankrupt or attempts to sell, mortgage, or assign his interest in the fund, at which point his interest is forfeited and the trust becomes a discretionary trust for the benefit of **B** and his family.

A more flexible solution is for **T's** will to provide that **B's** interest can be terminated by his trustees in their discretion. Then if **B** became insolvent his interest could be terminated and the fund applied for his benefit in the most appropriate way. Before a bankruptcy order is made against **B**, the trustees may convert his interest into a protective trust, which will be tax neutral. On the making of the order **B's** interest will cease and the discretionary trusts of **s.33(1)(ii) TA 1925** take effect with the following tax consequences:

1. no IHT is payable;

2. trust income (except dividends) may in effect continue to be taxed as **B's** income; and

3. on **B's** death there will be no CGT uplift although there will be an IHT charge, however, according to Kessler & Sartin the problem can be overcome if a new life interest is given to **B** with the permission of the Trustee in Bankruptcy (see Footnote 11 on p.55 of Kessler & Sartin).

Special trusts

As a general rule all trusts set up on or after 22 March 2006 are subject to the *'relevant property regime'* with four exceptions (the *'Special Trusts'*):

1. trusts created on death for a disabled beneficiary *('DPT's')* (**s.89(4)**);
2. trusts for bereaved minors *('BMT's')*;
3. trusts for the benefit of a minor who becomes absolutely entitled to capital between the ages of 18 and 25 *('18-25 Trusts')*; and
4. trusts created on death with an immediate interest in possession (life interest), known as immediate post-death interest trusts *('IPDI's')*.

An IPDI exists where a will/trust provides for a tenant for life, and not for bereaved minors, or for a disabled person, and the life interest exists continuously from **T's** death. A trust created on death where a person becomes immediately entitled to an interest for life will be:

1. treated as that beneficiary's property;
2. aggregated with his estate (note that the beneficiary e.g. spouse is treated for IHT as owning the whole of the capital fund see **Inland Revenue Press Notice 12 February 1976**); and
3. if the interest is created in favour of a spouse, or passes on the death of a beneficiary to a spouse, will be a spouse exempt gift.

Disabled person's trusts *(DPT's)*

The definition of a DPT is set out in **s.89B**.
   Four types of interest qualify:

1. a deemed life interest in a trust for a disabled person under **s.89(2)**;
2. a deemed life interest in a *'self-settlement'* (i.e. trust) created by a potentially disabled person under **s.89A**;
3. an actual life interest in settled property (other than an interest within 1 or 2 above) to which a disabled person has become entitled on or after 22nd March 2006; and
4. an actual life interest in a *'self-settled'* trust (other than an interest within 1 and 2 above) into which settled property was transferred on or after 22nd March 2006, which meets the requirements of potential

disability set out in **s.89A(1)(b)**, and which secures that if the capital is applied for the benefit of any beneficiary it is applied only for the benefit of the settlor. See McCutcheon, paragraph 21-13.

Tax treatment

Trusts which create a *'disabled person's'* interest receive **s.49** treatment. For IHT the disabled beneficiary is treated as being beneficially entitled to the trust property. From 22nd March 2006, the lifetime creation of a DPT is a PET provided the settlor is not the person with the disabled interest (**s.49(1)**).

Bereaved Minor's Trusts *(BMT's)*

Under a BMT no IHT is payable:

1. during the bereaved minor's infancy;
2. upon becoming absolutely entitled to capital on or before the age of 18; or
3. if the bereaved minor dies before attaining the age of 18.

To qualify the trust must satisfy the following conditions set out in **s.71A(3)**:

'(a) that the bereaved minor, if he has not done so before attaining the age of 18, will on attaining that age become absolutely entitled to –
  (i) the settled property,
  (ii) any income arising from it, and
  (iii) any income that has arisen from the property held on the trusts for his benefit and been accumulated before that time,
(b) that, for so long as the bereaved minor is living and under the age of 18, if any of the settled property is applied for the benefit of a beneficiary, it is applied for the benefit of the bereaved minor, and
(c) that for so long as the bereaved minor is living and under the age of 18, either –
  (i) the bereaved minor is entitled to all of the income (if there is any) arising from any of the settled property, or
  (ii) no such income may be applied for the benefit of any other person...'

The requirement that the trust be created by will is satisfied if it is created by the exercise of a special power of appointment under the will. While **s.71A** applies to settled property, it is not *'relevant property'*, and no IHT is payable: during the bereaved minor's infancy; on becoming absolutely entitled to capital on or before 18; or where the minor dies before attaining that age.

Where the trust is established by way of a class gift, the trustees may vary the bereaved minors' shares or cross-apply the income attributable to one bereaved minor's share for the benefit of another bereaved minor. If the trust is created by using a power of appointment under **T's** will, then provided there is no prior interest that qualifies as an IPDI, the trust must come into effect:

1. within two years of **T's** death (otherwise **s.144** cannot apply); or
2. immediately upon the termination of an IPDI.

If an IPDI (conferred upon another beneficiary) is terminated during the bereaved minor's lifetime by the exercise of a power of appointment under **T's** will, the termination will be a PET.

18-25 Trusts

Under an 18-25 trust no IHT is payable:

1. until the beneficiary becomes 18 years old;
2. where a beneficiary becomes absolutely entitled to capital before 18; or
3. a power of advancement is exercised before a beneficiary becomes 18, in order to defer his entitlement to capital beyond the age of 25, however, the trust property will become subject to the relevant property regime from the date of the exercise of the power. If the trust continues between the ages of 18 and 25, there will be an exit charge at the rate of 0.6% for each year (up to a maximum of 4.2%) where:
    *   the beneficiary does not become absolutely entitled to capital until 25; or
    *   between the ages of 18 and 25 capital is advanced to him (or for his benefit), which includes the deferral of his capital entitlement beyond the age of 25.

To qualify the trust must satisfy the following conditions set out in **s.71D**:

1. the property is held on trusts for a beneficiary who has not yet attained the age of 25;
2. at least one of the beneficiary's parents must have died;
3. if he has not done so before then, the beneficiary on attaining the age of 25 will become absolutely entitled to:
    (i) the settled property;
    (ii) any income arising from it; and
    (iii) any income that has arisen from the property held on trusts for his benefit and been accumulated before that time;
4. that, for so long as he is living, and under the age of 25, if any of the settled property is applied for the benefit of a beneficiary, that it is applied for his benefit; and
5. that, whilst he is under 25, the income and capital of his presumptive share can only be applied for his benefit, or for the benefit of other members of the class who are also under 25 years old.

Whilst **s.71D** applies to settled property, it is not relevant property. However, a charge similar to an exit charge will apply where a beneficiary becomes absolutely entitled to capital between the ages of 18 and 25. Where the trust is established by way of a class gift, the trustees may vary the beneficiaries' shares, or cross-apply the income attributable to one beneficiary's share for the benefit of another beneficiary. Whilst an 18-25 trust can be created by exercising a power of appointment under **T's** will, a lifetime termination of an IPDI conferred on another beneficiary will be an immediately chargeable transfer by the life-tenant for IHT. If a power of advancement is exercised before a beneficiary becomes 18, to defer his entitlement to capital beyond the age of 25, then the property will fall into the relevant property regime. When the beneficiary becomes absolutely entitled at 25, or where capital is advanced to him between 18 and 25, there will be an exit charge at 0.6% for each year after 18, resulting in a maximum exit charge of 4.2% if capital vests at 25.

Immediate post-death interest trusts *(IPDI's)*

An IPDI exists and will be taxed under **s.49A** where three conditions are satisfied:

1. the trust was effected by will or under the law relating to intestacy;
2. the life tenant (for example **S**) became beneficially entitled to the life interest on the death of **T** ; and
3. the trust must not be for bereaved minors and the interest is not that of a disabled person, which requirement must have been satisfied at all times since **S** became beneficially entitled to the life interest.

The first requirement is satisfied where: (i) under **T's** will funds are transferred into a pre-existing life interest trust; (ii) **T's** will is varied to create a life interest trust; or (iii) an appointment is made within two years of **T's** death that is automatically read-back into his will under **s.144**. If **T** creates an IPDI in favour of **S** the gift is spouse exempt, and on her death **S** will be treated as owning the whole of the capital fund, which is aggregated with the rest of her chargeable estate for IHT. An IPDI can also be created within two years of **T's** death, by trustees exercising an overriding power of appointment (which extends to both income and capital) under **T's** will to give **S** an immediate interest in possession, resulting in the property out of which the income is appointed benefiting from the spouse exemption. An IPDI may be terminated by:

1. the life-tenant (a *'surrender'*);
2. under the express terms of the trust (for example, in the event of re-marriage); or
3. by the trustees (defeasance).

If, as a result of the termination of a life tenant's life interest, the property in which the spouse interest subsisted becomes comprised in the estate of another absolutely, then the life tenant will be treated as having made a potentially exempt transfer *('PET')*. Provided **S** survives for a period of 7 years after the transfer, it will not become chargeable **(sections 3a, 51, 52)**. If the property passes on to further trusts, it will be treated as a chargeable transfer subject to the GWR rules, hence a tax-efficient termination can no longer be on discretionary trusts for the benefit of the life-tenant and issue.

Under **s.102 ZA FA 1986**, termination of **S's** life interest by;

1. her own act;
2. under the terms of the trust; or
3. by the exercise by trustees of overriding powers;

is treated as a gift by **S** for the purposes of the GWR rules.

The effect of these rules is that:

1. **S** is treated as if the subject-matter of the gift was comprised in her estate at its then market value; or
2. if the cessation of the reservation occurred within seven years before her death, **S** is treated as having made a PET of its value at that time.

However, the GWR rules can only apply where **S** continues to enjoy a benefit in some way from the property in which her interest has been lost.

The POAT charge contains no equivalent rule. IPDI's are used to determine the ultimate destination of trust property, and to preserve wealth for the benefit of e.g. **T's** children from a former marriage. On **S's** death the remainder interests in **T's** estate may be in favour of:

1. absolute interests e.g. for **T's** adult children;
2. a discretionary trust e.g. for **T's** children who are minors or for young grand-children; or
3. exempt gifts e.g. to a UK registered charity.

On **S's** death no further IPDI's can be created over residue left to her on an IPDI. However, a surviving spouse who is left a life interest with no right to capital is likely to have a claim under the **Inheritance Act**, therefore this strategy may not protect capital unless **S** remarries.

For a discussion of the relationship between: (i) bereaved minor's trusts; (ii) 18-25 trusts; and (iii) IPDI's, see paragraphs 6.20 – 6.22 of Whitehouse and King, where they state that the pecking order between these trusts (under the IHT legislation) is: 1st a BMT; 2nd an IPDI; and 3rd an 18-25 (**s.71D** trust). Therefore if **T** by his will gives a minor *'an immediate right to income with capital vesting at 25 this is not a s71D trust but instead gives the child an IPDI'*. Whitehouse and King also state that **s.144** can operate to destroy what appears at first sight to be a **s.71D** trust. Where a **s.71D** trust results from conversion of a discretionary trust within two years of **T's** death, it will be read-back to the date of **T's** death under **s.144**, in which case no exit charge will arise on the ending of the earlier relevant property trust. Whereas, if the conversion occurs more than two years after **T's** death, a **s.71D** trust comes into existence on that date, resulting in an IHT exit charge arising on the ending of the relevant property trust. See also pages 3012 and 3025 of the BDO Tax Guide.

Specific gifts of property qualifying for APR/BPR

Where:

1. part of **T's** estate is exempt; and
2. includes property attracting APR or BPR,

then special rules apply in relation to the valuation of specific and residuary gifts. The value of a specific gift of qualifying property is reduced by APR/BPR (**s.39A(2)**). Where however, a gift of residue includes qualifying property, then any specific gift of non-qualifying property (i.e. cash to a child), is entitled to benefit from a due proportion of the relief (**s.39A**). The value of such a specific gift is the *'appropriate fraction'* of its value, calculated in accordance with **s.39A(4)**. See IHTM 26110, and 26158, which contain examples. Note that IHTM 26071 sets out the order in which the partly exempt transfer rules are to be applied, which involves a five stage process, see **Chapter 2 – 'Grossing-up'**.

This is a trap for the unwary as BPR and APR are effectively wasted if given against exempt legacies, and can result in a higher overall IHT bill. Therefore the gift should always be dealt with by way of a specific gift made to a chargeable beneficiary, because any relief on APR / BPR not specifically given is apportioned throughout the estate under **s.39A**. Note that **s.39A(2)** provides for a full reduction in the case of specific gifts of agricultural property and **s.39A(3)** provides for an apportionment in the case of other specific gifts (defined by **s.42(1)** as meaning, *'any gift other than a gift of residue or of a share in residue'*). Furthermore **s.39A(6)** denies relief on the amount of a cash legacy where for example it is charged on relevant property. Therefore if a cash legacy is left to the NRA Trustees, the appropriation by **T's** executors of relevant property to satisfy that legacy will not result in full relief being due under **s.39A(2)**, because the relevant property was not the subject matter of the specific gift. If an unqualified gift of relevant property is bequeathed by **T** to a NRB Discretionary Trust, this will constitute a specific gift of relevant property under **s.39A(2)**. The spouse exemption will not apply, and because (i) tax is at stake; and (ii) the gift exceeds **T's** NRA, HMRC must rule on the availability of the relief.

Survivorship clauses

s.92(1) provides,

> 'Where under the terms of a will or otherwise property is held for any person on condition that he survives another for a specified period of not more than six months, this Act shall apply as if the dispositions taking effect at the end of the period, or if he does not survive until then, on his death (including any such disposition which has effect by operation of law or is a separate disposition of the income from the property) had had that effect from the beginning of the period.'

Therefore if **S** survives **T** by the period of the survivorship clause (which must not exceed six months from **T's** death), the spouse exemption is available in the estate of **T**. If **S** failed to survive that period then the spouse exemption is not available in either the estate of **T** or **S**. In the case of a gift outside the spouse exemption to a non-exempt beneficiary, the possibility of a double charge to IHT is excluded by the inclusion of a survivorship clause, if the same property were to pass through both **T's** and **S's** estates. However, the same result is obtained under **s.141** (which gives relief in the event of a beneficiary dying within five years of **T's** death).

s.184 LPA 1925 (the rule as to commorientes) provides, 'where...two or more persons have died in circumstances rendering it uncertain which of them survived the other or others, such deaths shall (subject to any order of the court), for all purposes affecting the title of the property, be presumed to have occurred in order of seniority, and accordingly the younger shall be deemed to have survived the elder.'

Where it cannot be known who died first under **s.4(2)**, persons are assumed for IHT to have died at the same moment, and their estates are taxed separately (which prevents a double charge to IHT). **s.4(2)** provides, 'where it cannot be known which of two or more who have died survived the other or others they shall be assumed to have died at the same instant.'

s.4(2) does not displace **s.184 LPA 1925**.

Although the estate of each spouse passes under the terms of their own will, because for IHT the estate of the elder is deemed to have passed to his surviving spouse, the **s.18** (spouse exemption) is available to fully relieve IHT on his estate. However, in the case of spouses, where each has left their estate outright to the other (or created an IPDI for the other) it is more tax-efficient if the survivorship clause does not apply where the order of deaths is uncertain. Where the survivor (for example **S**) does not own sufficient assets, the inclusion of a survivorship clause can prevent full utilisation of the NRB's of both spouses. Unless there are residuary beneficiaries who are minors, this can be cured by the redirection of assets post-death using a deed of variation. Under his will **T** could also give a legacy to **S** of an amount of his unused NRB to cover the shortfall with a declaration that the survivorship clause will not apply in relation to the gift. The tax implications of survivorship clauses are discussed in Williams between paragraphs 219.5 and 219.2. The editors of Williams conclude that,

'Survivorship provisions can have a useful role to play but the substantive dispositions affected by the will are more important. Wills of husbands and wives should have the same ultimate destination for their combined assets, or else should give each other life interests only. Where that is so, survivorship conditions imposed on gifts to each other are superfluous and could have an IHT disadvantage. Substantial gifts to issue or to near relations should provide substitution of the issue of the donee in case the latter predecease the testator. In the case of the latter type of gift a survivorship clause can usefully be added.' See also 'Survivorship clauses' in Chapter 1.

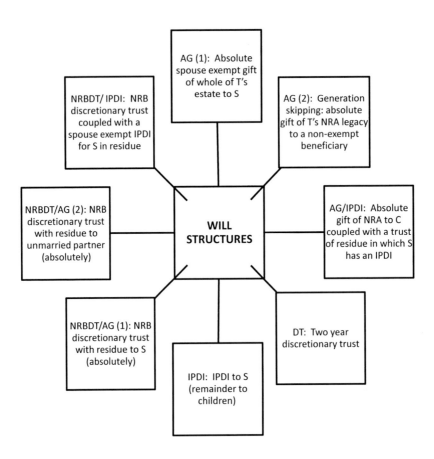

4

Will Structures and Commentary

- Legend
- Index
- Structures & commentary

Legend

C	Child
CB	Class of beneficiaries
DT	A Discretionary trust
GC	Grandchild
IPDI	Immediate post-death interest
NRA	A gift of the maximum amount of **T's** unused NRB on death (his *'Nil Rate Am*ount')
R	Residue
S	Spouse (includes a civil partner)
T	Testator

Index

The following structures illustrate the integration of some of the basic planning tools discussed in **Chapter 3**:

AG (1): Absolute spouse exempt gift of whole of **T's** estate to **S**;

AG (2): Generation skipping: absolute gift of **T's** NRA to a non-exempt beneficiary;

AG / IPDI: Absolute gift of NRA to **C** coupled with a trust of residue in which **S** has an **IPDI**;

DT: Two year discretionary trust;

IPDI: IPDI to **S** (remainder to children);

NRBDT/AG (1): NRB Discretionary Trust with residue to **S** (absolutely);

NRBDT / AG (2): NRB Discretionary Trust with residue to unmarried partner (absolutely); and

NRBDT/ IPDI: NRB Discretionary Trust coupled with a spouse exempt IPDI for **S** in residue.

Note that effective planning is a bespoke process, and that the elements and combinations shown in these structures are not exhaustive of the possible methods for combining and varying the building blocks to construct a tax-efficient will. Note that the planning *'building blocks'* underlying these structures are illustrated in a *scheme of dispositions* set out in **Diagram No.22** in **Appendix 1**.

Structures & Commentary

AG (1): Absolute spouse exempt gift of whole of T's estate to S

Structure

> $T \rightarrow S$ (absolutely)

Commentary

An absolute gift of a specific asset or of residue (an 'AG') is the simplest form of planning.

Where **T** gives his entire estate to **S**:

1. the gift to **S** is spouse exempt; and
2. 100% of the amount of **T's** unused NRB is preserved (and is available for transfer to the PR's of **S** on her death).

S can make PET's during her lifetime that will fall out of account after seven years. Where a couple wish to provide for continuing trusts after **S's** death, a tax-efficient way of arranging this is for **T** to leave assets outright to **S**, which she can then leave, for example to their children or grandchildren. On **S's** death she can leave her estate to children as follows:

1. absolutely, in which case no IHT is payable on:
   (a) gifts equal in value to the amount of **S's** unused NRB multiplied by the percentage of **T's** transferable **NRB**;
   (b) property qualifying for APR / BPR; or
   (c) excluded property;
2. on a bereaved minor's trust ('BMT') under **s.71A** , in which case:
   (a) a child beneficiary will become absolutely entitled to capital (and any accumulated income arising from it) at the age of 18; and
   (b) no IHT is payable on the gift either during the child's minority or upon attaining their majority;
3. on an 18-25 trust, in which case:
   (a) vesting of trust assets can be postponed until the age of 25, then
   (b) between the ages of 18 and 25, IHT will become payable on distributions at the maximum rate of 4.2%;
4. on a discretionary trust:
   (a) which would enable the trustees to postpone the age of vesting beyond 25;

      (b) however, the trust property will then enter the relevant property regime and become subject to decennial and exit charges; or

5. on an IPDI, in which case:

      (a) the trust property will not be subject to the relevant property regime; and

      (b) no IHT is payable when the child becomes entitled to capital at any age. However, if **T** gave **S** an IPDI under his will, then **S** cannot create an IPDI for their children in the same property.

A further advantage of using a discretionary trust, is that the ownership of any relevant property qualifying for APR/BPR remains wholly vested in the trustees at all times (instead of shifting between the life-tenant and the trustees where an IPDI is set up). Whilst **S** cannot set up either a bereaved minor's trust or an 18-25 trust for any grandchildren (because they are not her children) she could create an IPDI for grandchildren or include them in the class of beneficiaries under a discretionary trust.

AG (2): Generation skipping: absolute gift of T's NRA to a non-exempt beneficiary

Structure

    T → GC

Commentary

T's children ('**C**') and grandchildren ('**GC**') are non-exempt beneficiaries.
    No IHT is payable if the gifts are:

1. within **T's** available NRB (although this will erode the amount of **T's** unused NRB if survived by **S**);
2. of excluded property; or
3. or of property that qualifies for APR or BPR.

(See **Diagram No. 20** – '*Trusts for children and grandchildren*').

Wealth is preserved for the next generation. Alternatively, if **T** creates an IPDI for **C** (or makes an absolute gift to **C**), then **C** can make PET's to **GC**, or redirect the gifts to **GC** by executing a deed of variation within two years of **T's** death that will be automatically read-back into **T's** will under **s.142**. In the case of property with an aggregate value greater than the sum of its parts (e.g. a majority shareholding in a family owned company) the value of the property can be spread between **C** and **GC** by making separate gifts to each of them (i.e. of a minority shareholding). This avoids the risk of a substantial liability to IHT arising on the making of PET's by **C** to **GC** (where **C** does not survive the transfer by seven years).

This also avoids the application of the GWR rules to a life-time transfer by **C** to **GC**. If **GC** is a minor, then for income tax purposes, this avoids **C** becoming the settlor of property given to **GC**. If **C** needs the property, a solution is to create an IPDI for **C** coupled with a discretionary trust under which the class of beneficiaries includes: **C** and **GC**. Whilst any distribution of capital is chargeable, IHT may be low or nil, and in the case of **GC** this may be more tax-efficient than a transfer by **C** to **GC** of either (i) absolute property or (ii) settled property in which **C** had a life interest. CGT hold-over relief is available on a distribution out of a discretionary trust but not on a PET. Whilst **GC** receives income, for IHT **C** cannot benefit in future without the **GWR** rules applying to any transfer to him.

AG / IPDI: Absolute gift of NRA to C coupled with a trust of residue in which S has an IPDI

Structure

T → NRA legacy (absolutely) → **C**

↓

R

↓

S (IPDI) → R → **C/GC**

Commentary

This may be appropriate where **S** does not need the amount of **T's** NRB (i.e. because family assets are sufficiently large), and profligacy is not a concern, because the non-exempt beneficiaries are adults and settled in life.

DT: Two year discretionary trust

Structure

T → DT: **CB** (can include **S**)

Commentary

If **T** is a singleton and wishes to build the greatest possible flexibility into his will from the outset, then he can:

1. set up a discretionary trust of residue;
2. leave all of his net assets to the trustees; and
3. require them to make an appointment in writing within two years of his death.

This enables his trustees to distribute his estate as he would have wished amongst a class of beneficiaries chosen by him, within two years of his death, resulting in automatic reading-back under **s.144**. Under a discretionary trust the dispositions are controlled by the trustees, who have an unfettered discretion to choose amongst the beneficiaries, without regard to the capacity and wishes of any member of the beneficial class. Within two years of **T's** death the trust can also be converted into any other form of will/trust. Whilst this structure can be used where **T** is married, the mere inclusion of **S** in the class of beneficiaries under a discretionary trust does not constitute the making of reasonable financial provision for her, and if reasonable financial provision has not otherwise been made, may result in a claim being brought under the **Inheritance Act**.

Where all of **T's** net assets are held on a discretionary trust, a practical disadvantage is that IHT on the full value of the estate has to be paid before probate can be obtained, **(s.25 AEA 1925, and sections 211 and 266)**. Therefore the trustees may have to borrow in order to finance the IHT payment, which will then be repaid with interest, upon the exercise by them (after probate) of their discretionary powers to create an IHT exempt IPDI.

IPDI: IPDI to S (remainder to children)

Structure

     T → **S** (for life) then → **C**

Commentary
The creation by will of a life-interest in residue (an 'IPDI') preserves capital by creating an income interest for life, and determines the ultimate destination of the trust property.

For asset protection, capital is ring-fenced against: (i) future bankruptcy of **S**; (ii) future care home fees levied on **S**; and (iii) the claim of any future spouse of **S** if she remarries after **T's** death.

S cannot makes PET's of that property and the direction of the remainder is fixed by the will thereby preserving wealth e.g. for **T's** children from an earlier marriage who are named as remainder men. The creation of an IPDI for **S** will still attract the spouse exemption, and will not use up **T's** unused and transferable NRB. No IHT is payable on **T's** death where an IPDI is created for **S** (although the property subject to the IPDI is beneficiary taxed on the death of **S**). Because no periodic charges arise whilst an IPDI continues, it can also be used to create a long life-interest for a young beneficiary. It is possible for **T** to create concurrent IPDI's for different beneficiaries in different parts of his residuary estate. If capital is required by **S**, the trustees can exercise overriding powers conferred upon them by **T** under his will, to pay or apply capital for her benefit.

However, **T's** will should not include an overriding power under which the interest in remainder can be altered without the IPDI being terminated, because if trusts continue upon the termination of the IPDI (even in the form of another life interest for the same beneficiary), an immediate IHT charge will arise (i.e. on termination of the IPDI). Where a spouse exempt IPDI is terminated during **S's** lifetime, the deemed transfer of value is a PET if the IPDI is followed by a **s.71A** trust provided for in the will, **s.3A (1A)(C) (iii) 3B**. This is subject to the requirement that the settled property continues to be held on the trusts of the trust when **s.71A** applies **sections 3A** and **(3B) (e) (i)** and **(ii)**). This requirement is satisfied when the **s.71A** trust is created upon the exercise of a special power of appointment provided for under the will, and not by the words of the will itself. Therefore, where **T** leaves behind minor children and stepchildren he can either:

1. create a **s 71 A** bereaved minor's trust (BMT) for children who are minors (to follow the IPDI); or
2. confer overriding powers to enable his trustees to appoint capital to such trusts.

On **S's** death the trustees could also create a **s.71D** trust. If profligacy is a concern, then a discretionary trust can be created instead, which will be subject to entry, decennial, and exit charges under the relevant property regime.

NRBDT/AG (1): NRB Discretionary Trust with residue to S (absolutely)

Structure

T → NRA legacy → DT: **CB** (includes **S**)

↓

R

↓

S (absolutely)

Commentary
Under this arrangement **T** leaves a legacy under his will:

1. that is quantified as the maximum sum that he can give without incurring IHT (described in this book as his nil rate amount or '*NRA*');

2. to the trustees of a Discretionary Trust (the NRBDT);
3. to be held for the benefit of a class of beneficiaries that includes **S**.

This structure can also be used to create an IPDI for future generations. If it is not required, a NRBDT can be unscrambled (and **T's** unused and transferable NRB thereby restored) by:

1. making an absolute appointment between the third and twenty-fourth month after **T's** death, of the whole of the trust fund to **S**, that will automatically be read-back under **s.144** (note however, the *Frankland* Trap discussed in **Chapter 6**); or
2. re-writing **T's** will under **s.142**.

Note that where **T** is a widower who has remarried and has the benefit of two NRB's (one from his earlier marriage), and **S** has only one NRB, then NRB optimisation requires the use of a NRBDT (implemented using either the debt or charge scheme). If used by **S** in her will **T's** additional NRB will remain outside her estate, resulting in **T** and **S's** joint estates being in effect reduced by three NRB's. If used by **T** in his will only one NRB will be transferred to **S**, and the legacy of the other NRB can benefit chargeable beneficiaries under the discretionary trust.

NRBDT /AG (2):   NRB Discretionary Trust with residue to unmarried partner (absolutely)

Structure

T → NRA legacy → DT: **CB** (includes **unmarried partner**)

↓

R

↓

Unmarried partner (absolutely)

Commentary

T's planning options are limited by:

1. his NRA not being transferable; and
2. the non-availability of the spouse / civil partner exemption.

Note that for IHT the concept of a co-habiting couple becoming common law man and wife is a myth. Where one partner has acquired a NRB from an earlier marriage, then if the other partner's estate is below her NRB, consideration should be given to equalising estates by the making of PET's to optimise her available NRB on death. The entitlement of the survivor to remain in occupation of the couple's home must also be addressed, as there is no entitlement on intestacy where the property is held by the partners as tenants in common in equity.

NRBDT/IPDI: NRB Discretionary Trust coupled with a spouse exempt IPDI for S in residue

Structure

T → NRA legacy → DT: **CB** (includes **S**)

↓

R

↓

S (IPDI)

Commentary

This structure can be used when it is not appropriate to give an absolute interest to **S**, (see the debt and charge scheme under NRB Discretionary Trusts in **Chapter 3** above). If the interest is terminable it can be terminated by the trustees before the beneficiary's death by exercising overriding powers. To preserve capital in the event of re-marriage an IPDI can be created over part of the residue. Provided **T's** estate contains sufficient liquid wealth to provide for **S** during her life-time, the amount of his estate that can be passed free of IHT to non-exempt beneficiaries (for example his children and grandchildren) can be increased. This is achieved by giving **S** a short-term interest in possession in part of his estate, which she can then terminate in favour of the children. Termination will be treated as a PET if **S** survives for seven years. This is worth considering where the joint estates exceed £650K. Where **S's** interest is defeated by the exercise of an overriding power of appointment she must be excluded from future benefit in the trust assets (see **s.102ZA FA 1986**).

5

Additional Powers

- Introduction
- Addition
- Agents
- Ancillary powers
- Application of trust income as capital
- Apportionment
- Appropriation
- Borrowing
- Change in governing law
- Charities
- Chattels
- Commitments
- Companies
- Company arrangements & insolvency
- Deferment
- Delegation
- Disclosure
- Distributions
- Duration
- Expenses
- Foreign trustees
- Guarantees
- Incidental acts
- Indemnities
- Insurance
- Investment
- Land
- Lending
- Life insurance
- Litigation
- Maintenance
- Management of companies
- Minors
- Nominees
- Occupation
- Ownership
- Personal interest

- Protection
- Removal
- Release
- Taxes
- Trade
- Trustee charges
- Use of trust property
- Voting

Introduction

The following is an alphabetical menu of additional powers to be included in **T's** will for his executors and trustees (referred to collectively as *'trustees'*). Because an administrative power may incidentally have a dispositive effect, the clause in the main body of the will that applies the administrative powers should specifically provide that no power shall be exercised in a way that conflicts or is inconsistent with the beneficial powers of the will. See **Diagram No.23** – *'Trustee's powers'*, for a classification of powers.

Addition

To allow for necessary administrative powers to be added. The power can also be used to revoke or vary the administrative provisions set out in the will. If there is an administrative step not authorised by the will or by statute, then, if all the beneficiaries who would be affected are of full age and capacity and agree, they may authorise the trustees to act. If there is any doubt about the authorisation of a transaction the trustees can apply to the court under **s.57 TA 1925** for directions to confer any necessary additional powers.

Agents

To extend the statutory powers to appoint agents and proxies conferred by **s.11 (1) and (2) TA 2000**. The statutory duty of care is imposed on trustees when entering into arrangements under which an agent is appointed to act and subsequently when reviewing those arrangements. **s. 23(1) TA 2000 provides**,

'(1) A trustee is not liable for any act or default of the agent, nominee or custodian unless he has failed to comply with the duty of care applicable to him, under paragraph 3 of Schedule 1-

(a) when entering into the arrangements under which the person acts as agent, nominee, or custodian, or

(b) when carrying out his duties under section 22.'

Trustees are under a duty to keep clear and distinct accounts of the property they administer and under **s.11 TA 2000** may employ an accountant to do so on their behalf. Trustees are not obliged to have their accounts audited, but may have the cost of auditing by an independent accountant paid for as a trust expense under **s.22 (4) TA 1925**.

Ancillary powers

To remove doubts raised in connection with a narrow interpretation of any of the trustees' powers.

Application of trust capital as income

This power might be useful if trustees are unsure whether a receipt or an expense is one of income or of capital. It may also be needed for tax planning purposes. If trustees wish to transfer trust capital to a beneficiary they may use:

1. their overriding power to advance the capital to the beneficiary; or
2. this power to treat capital as income, and then pay that *'income'* to the beneficiary.

This enables the trustees to exercise a choice between achieving receipt by the beneficiary of a sum as either income or capital. See **Diagram No.24 –** *'Beneficiary's entitlement to income & profits generated by a trust asset from the date of **T's** death'*.

Apportionment

To exclude the rules requiring that income be apportioned between beneficiaries successively entitled, which impose a disproportionate administrative burden and can result in avoidable expense.

Appropriation

In the context of the administration of an estate, the term *'appropriation'* means a conscious decision taken by **T's** executors to take an asset out of the general pool of unadministered assets, and transfer the equity in it to a specified beneficiary (including the trustees of a trust fund). Whilst the act of *'appropriation'* may not affect the legal title to the asset (which remains with **T's** executors until it is transferred), it will give the beneficiary a beneficial interest in the asset, rather than an inchoate right to compel the administration of the estate. It will therefore act as an assent of the equitable interest in the asset. Appropriation allows:

1. **T's** executors to satisfy any general or residuary legacy by allocating specific assets (without obtaining formal consent); and
2. his trustees to swap assets between separate sub-funds.

Under **s.41 AEA 1925** an executor may, with relevant consents, appropriate assets in order to satisfy a general or residuary legacy (in whole or in part). In the case of a settled legacy, the consent of the trustees is required unless those trustees are also the executors, in which case the consent of the person for the time being entitled to the income of the trust is required (provided that person is of full age and has mental capacity). **s.41 TA 2000**, does not apply to trusts, therefore an express power for trustees to appropriate assets is also usually included. Where a beneficiary acquires assets as a result of an appropriation by **T's** executors in or toward the satisfaction of a share or interest in **T's** estate, the assets are acquired as a legatee (within **s.64 TCGA 1992**), then for CGT the appropriation does not result in a chargeable gain, and the beneficiary takes the asset at the executors' acquisition cost (**s.62 TCGA 1992**). Trustees have an implied power to appropriate assets in satisfaction of a beneficiary's share, **Re Ruddock** (1910). The appropriation or appointment of assets to particular beneficiaries by the exercise of an overriding power is irrevocable unless the trustees reserve a power to subsequently transfer assets between sub-funds. When the same person is an executor and a legatee the will must authorise that person to appropriate assets to himself. A fiduciary may not make an unauthorised profit from their office. Note that all trustees are fiduciaries.

In **Tito v Waddell (No.2)** (1977), Megarry VC stated the rule against self-dealing as follows, '*if a trustee purchases trust property for himself, any beneficiary may have the sale set aside.*' Where the rule against self-dealing applies, with the exception of cash (or assets equivalent to cash), the trustees cannot appropriate assets in specie toward a particular beneficiary's share, without: (i) the consent of the other beneficiaries who are affected; or (ii) an order of the court. For the prohibition on the purchase of trust property by a trustee, see **Holder v Holder** (1968).

If an appropriation is made in breach of this rule a beneficiary may apply to the court to have the appropriation set aside, **Kane v Radley Kane** (1999). Where **T** bequeaths rights in property to a person who is a legatee and a trustee, and his will permits the sale of property to that person the transaction is voidable even where an independent valuation is obtained, **Wright v Morgan** (1926).

Borrowing

To confirm the trustees' power to borrow on security of trust property in the widest possible terms. **s.16 TA 1925** gives trustees express power to mortgage all or part of the trust property to raise any capital money required for any purpose to be applied in any manner authorised by the trust investment. However, it does not authorise trustees to mortgage the trust property to acquire further property for the trust or to acquire further land with the aid of a mortgage over the land being acquired. The general powers of trustees of a trust of land given by **s.6(1) TOLATA 1996** , are not so limited, but do not override any restriction limitation or condition imposed by any other enactment and may be restricted or excluded by the will or be made subject to the obtaining of consent.

Change in governing law

To authorise the trustees to change **T's** choice of governing law and place of administration of the will, to that of another jurisdiction.

Charities

To authorise the release of trust property to a proper officer of a charity. Note the changes introduced by **FA 2010**.

Chattels

To extend limited statutory powers to deal with chattels and to insure, protect, maintain, and repair them in any manner to the extent the trustees think fit.

Commitments

To allow the trustees to give indemnities (which may be secured by trust assets). It also allows the provision of warranties and undertakings in connection with the sale of business assets or shares.

Companies

To confer power to carry on a business through a company. Unless clearly authorised to do so by the will, trustees have in general no power to:

1. put trust assets at risk by commencing to carry on a business with them; and
2. commence an unincorporated business.

Company arrangements and insolvency

To confirm the trustees' powers in relation to the re-organization and liquidation of companies.

Deferment

To allow deferment of payment of the purchase price by **S** for **T's** share of the equitable interest in the matrimonial home, following the sale of that interest to her.

Delegation

To generally extend the trustees' statutory power of delegation and to specifically extend the trustees' powers in relation to the operation of bank accounts. **TA 2000** contains a negative definition of the matters capable of delegation. The primary exclusion is designed to ensure that trustees are not able to delegate their dispositive functions. Under **s.9 TLATA 1996** trustees of land may, by power of attorney, delegate any of their functions as trustees which relate to the land, to any beneficiary of full age who is beneficially entitled to a life interest in land subject to the trust. The power of investment is a delegable function within **s.11 TA 2000** (power to employ agents). However, the trustees retain overall fiduciary responsibility for investment policy, and exercise control over the investment adviser by imposing adequate guidelines and limits within the parameters of which the investment adviser can operate.

An agreement authorising a person to exercise any of the trustees' asset management functions as their agent, must be in writing, or evidenced in writing. Note that **s.15(5) TA 2000** provides that asset management functions relate to: (i) investment of assets subject to trust; (ii) acquisition of property subject to trust; (iii) managing property subject to trust; and (iv) creating or disposing of an interest therein.

s.16 TA 2000 enables the trustees to appoint a person to act as their nominee in relation to *'such of the assets of the trust as they determine (other than settled land)'* and to *'take such steps as are necessary to secure that those assets are vested in a person so appointed.'*

The usual process is for a trust and its documentation to be reviewed, objectives to be set by the trustees, and the **Policy Statement and Guidelines (PSG)** to be produced, so that the Nominated Advisor (usually an IFA or financial planner) can be given explicit instructions on what is required and by when. The Nominated Advisor gives a signed receipt for the PSG, and confirms his or her Client Arrangement/Fee Agreement with the trustees. Only then can advice be given and investments made.

Disclosure

To specify documents which beneficiaries have the right to inspect and to confirm the confidentiality of trust documents, see *Schmidt v Rosewood Trusts Ltd* (2003), and *Breakspear v Ackland* (2008).

Distributions

To exonerate the trustees from personal liability where a claim is made by an illegitimate member of a class of beneficiaries when the trustees were not aware of the existence of the claimant.

Duration

To confirm that the trustees' powers are exercisable whilst the trust subsists.

Expenses

To allow the trustees to pay expenses out of capital or income in their discretion.

Foreign trustees

To allow the appointment of a non-resident trustee (see **s.36(1) TA 1925** and **Re Stoneham's Settlement Trusts** (1953)), and expressly negative the application of **s.36(1) TA 1925**, which allows a trustee to be removed if he remains outside the UK for more than 12 months.

Guarantees

To allow the trustees to guarantee a beneficiary's debts (and likewise borrowings by any company the trust fund has invested in), and to apply trust property in relation to any guarantee.

Incidental acts

To allow the trustees to execute any act permitted by the **s.57 TA 1925** which is not already permitted under the terms of the will or common law without having to execute a further deed or apply to the court for directions and an order.

Indemnities

To allow the trustees to take out indemnity insurance to be billed to the trust fund. Warranties and similar undertakings can also be given in relation to a sale of shares or business assets, see **Jones v Firkin Flood** (2008).

Insurance

To extend the limited statutory power to insure property. The trustees may insure any property, which is subject to the trusts, against risk of loss or damage due to any event, and pay the premium out of the trust funds (capital or income), **s.19 TA 1925 (as substituted by s.34 TA 2000)**. Note that the statutory duty of care does not expressly impose a duty to insure on a trustee.

Investment

To confer wide powers of investment with specific authority to purchase any type of property for use by a beneficiary where this is not justified on investment grounds, to invest the trust property in a single asset or type of asset, and to invest in non-income producing assets. In exercising a power of investment the standard investment criteria ('SIC') contained in **s.4 TA 2000**, should also be considered. The SIC apply to the exercise of any power of investment arising under **Part III TA 2000** *'or otherwise'*. It appears that the duty to consider diversification under **s.4 TA 2000** cannot be excluded . There is some doubt as to whether the SIC can be excluded. The general power of investment contained in **s.3 TA 2000** which does not permit the trustees to invest in land (other than in loans secured on land) can be modified or excluded under the will, **s.6(1) TA 2000**. As a general rule, in the absence of a specific provision to the contrary, trustees have a duty not to allow trust funds to be invested otherwise than in the names of all of them.

Land

To confer full powers of management in relation to any real property comprised in the trust fund. Note that **s.11(1)(a) TLATA 1996** which requires consultation with beneficiaries, may be excluded by the will (**s.11(2)(b)**). Trustees of land have all the powers of the absolute owner **s.6(1) TLATA 1996**. This includes the power to maintain and repair the trust property in order to preserve it in good condition. The cost of periodic maintenance should be paid from income. The cost of major works should be borne by capital. Where trust property includes a lease or a tenancy held by the trustees as joint-tenants, then all must join in any dealing in respect of it. If trustees have power to sell specific property all must concur in a sale.

If trustees hold land on an express trust for sale, then although they have a power to postpone sale (under **s.4 TLATA 1996**) they must be unanimous in their agreement to exercise the power to postpone. If they are not unanimous, then the trust for sale takes effect and the land must be sold. As a general rule the purchase of trust property by a trustee is voidable within a reasonable time at the instance of a beneficiary, *Holder v. Holder* (1968) (the self-dealing rule). However, the rule does not apply if:

1. the will authorises it;
2. the beneficiaries (all being of full age and capacity) consent; or

3. the court authorises the sale.

The rule applies to the exercise of the power of appropriation by a person who is both a trustee and a beneficiary. In *Re Thompson's Settlements* (1986) Mr Justice Vinelott held that the self-dealing rule, whereby a trustee's sale of trust property to himself was voidable, was an application of a wider principle that a man must not put himself into a situation where his duty and interest were in conflict. However, a beneficiary may fail to have a sale set aside if he or she has acquiesced in the transaction, *Holder v Holder* (1968). It is the duty of trustees to obtain the best possible price for trust property, *Buttle v Saunders* (1950).

Lending

To allow lending to a beneficiary on non-commercial terms. A trustee should not lend trust money to himself or to a co-trustee as to do so would be a breach of the self-dealing rule even if the loan were fully secured and on commercial terms. A trustee should exercise caution before lending to a beneficiary and, unless the will provides otherwise, any such loan should be fully secured and on commercial terms. Trustees should not make unsecured loans unless the will specifically authorises them to do so.

Life insurance

To confer wide powers to take out and pay life insurance policy premiums.

Litigation

s.15 TA 1925 confers power on trustees to compromise claims and compound liabilities. Trustees have the title and authority to bring or defend legal proceedings on behalf of the trusts.

Maintenance

It is common to make the following variations to the statutory power of maintenance conferred by **s.31 TA 1925**:

1. to give the trustees a complete discretion as to whether the income should be applied for the maintenance, education, or benefit of a beneficiary; and
2. to postpone the entitlement to income to an age greater than 18.

Management of companies

In *Bartlett v Barclays Bank Trust Co. (No.1)* (1985) trustees were held to be in breach of trust for not involving themselves in the management of a company in which the trust had a majority shareholding. The exclusion or restriction of this duty should be agreed in writing with **T**, following an explanation of the practical implications of including an anti-Bartlett clause to exonerate the trustees or limit their strict obligation to monitor the running of any such company.

Minors

To provide that any receipt given by a minor or by a parent or guardian is valid and operates as a full discharge to the trustees for the transfer of trust capital or income to the minor (to which the minor was beneficially entitled).

Nominees

To allow the trustees to hold any investment in the name of a nominee, e.g. where a trustee delegates investment management functions to an investment advisor.

Occupation

To make allowance for occupation or use of trust property by a beneficiary on any terms. Trustees have a default power to acquire land under **s.8 TA 2000** (which specifically allows land to be acquired for occupation by a beneficiary, which would not otherwise constitute an investment). The trustees must exercise this power and decide the terms in the context of the beneficial trusts created by the will. **s.12 TLATA 1996** entitles a beneficiary who is entitled to a life interest in land (that is subject to a trust of land) to occupy that land (provided it is available and suitable for occupation). This right can be excluded or restricted in the circumstances specified in **s.13**. However, the trustees may not exclude all beneficiaries from occupation and may impose conditions on any beneficiary's occupation. Note that granting a right of occupation creates an IPDI for IHT which may not be tax-efficient.

Ownership

To confirm that the trustees enjoy the same rights as an absolute individual owner of the trust fund.

Personal interest

To ensure that a trustee (who is also a beneficiary) can exercise any power in his own favour, see *Breakspear v Ackland* (2008), and *Thompson v Thompson* (1985).

Protection

To provide that lay trustees are not liable for personal acts unless fraud was involved, see *Armitage v Nurse* (1998). It is the view of the **Law Society** and of other professional bodies, including the **Society of Trust and Estate Practitioners**, that where trust property is not of a specially onerous nature (which is usually the case), that professional trustees should not enjoy any additional relief from liability. It is thought that the statutory duty imposed by **s.1 TA 2000** (which is a higher duty if a trustee is a professional trustee or has special knowledge or experience), still applies unless specifically excluded. The practical implications of this provision should be explained to **T** and express approval to the inclusion of the clause obtained in writing to be kept as a record on the Solicitor's file.

Removal

Under **s.19 TLATA 1996**, (which can be excluded) where all of the beneficiaries are absolutely entitled, and all of full age and capacity, they can direct a trustee to retire provided that at least two individual trustees or a trust corporation remain as trustees. The court also has a general power under **s.41 TA 1995,** to appoint new trustees.

Release

To empower the trustees to modify or release any power if no longer appropriate, as they may not release a fiduciary power unless expressly authorised to do so by the will.

Taxes

To authorise payment of taxes.

Trade

To confer power to trade.

Trustee charges

To empower trustees to charge reasonable fees for the discharge of their functions as trustees. The general rule (modified by **TA 2000**) is that a trustee is not allowed to make a profit from his position of trust, nor place himself in a position where his interest and duty conflict. Where a will contains an express authority to charge, the extent to which the trustees are permitted to charge is determined by the terms of the charging clause. Specific provision needs to be made to allow the trustees to receive payment for services provided as a director of any company in which the trust fund has an investment, and to retain commissions resulting from transactions involving trust assets.

Use of trust property

To extend the trustees' statutory power to acquire land for occupation by a beneficiary.

Voting

To provide that the trustees may exercise voting and any other rights attaching to shares. Unless otherwise provided all decisions made by trustees must be unanimous.

6

Traps for the Unwary

- Abatement
- Acceleration
- Ademption
- Alterations
- Annuities
- Artificial debt rules
- Beneficiaries
- Charities
- Civil partner
- Class gifts
- Conditions
- Delay
- Domicile of surviving spouse
- Duty of care
- Frankland trap
- Governing law
- Joint-bequests
- Joint-property
- Mistake
- No contest clauses
- Occupation
- Partial or total intestacy
- Phizackerley
- Revocation
- SDLT Trap
- Self-dealing rule
- Sham attack
- **s.39A trap**
- **s.199 trap**
- Unincorporated associations
- Valuation reports

The purpose of this chapter is to increase awareness of some of the elephant traps that lie in wait to catch the unwary will/trust draftsman. It is not an exhaustive list, and **Diagram No.25** – *'Failure of legacies'* shows the circumstances in which a legacy can fail.

Abatement

This occurs where the residuary estate remaining after payment of debts and expenses is insufficient to cover payment of the legacies made by **T** under his will in full. In default of any provision in the will specifying the order in which legacies are reduced **s.34 AEA 1925** provides that:

1. general legacies abate first;
2. then demonstrative legacies; and
3. then specific legacies.

Legacies within each class abate rateably.

Acceleration

Where **T's** will purports to give realty or personalty on an IPDI and the gift fails, if there is a vested gift in the remainder, it takes effect immediately in possession. The remainder is not accelerated where after the life-tenant's interest there is only a contingent gift in remainder. However, if the gift in remainder then becomes vested, the remainder is accelerated and takes effect in possession. This may be excluded by a contrary intention.

Ademption

A specific gift in a will of, for example, an investment, will fail if the investment is no longer held by **T** at the date of his death.

Alterations

Alterations often take the form of;

1. interlineations – bequests inserted between the lines;
2. amendments made to figures or words; and
3. the crossing out of words.

These alterations do not take effect unless it can be proved that they were made before execution or that the will was re-executed with these amendments in accordance with the **WA 1837**.

s.21 Wills Act 1837 provides,
'no obliteration, interlineations, or other alteration made in any will after the execution thereof shall be valid or have any effect, except in so far as the words or effect of the will before such alterations shall not be apparent, unless such alteration shall be executed in like manner as hereinbefore is required for execution of the will.'

An alteration made after execution of **T's** will should be (i) executed by him and initialled by two witnesses; or (ii) made by a duly executed codicil. An alteration made before execution of a will is not valid if it was merely deliberative and not final. There is a rebuttable presumption that an unattested alteration was made after execution of a will or subsequent codicil. Republication of a will by its re-execution in accordance with the prescribed formalities validates an alteration made after the will was executed but before it was republished if **T** intends the alteration to form part of his will when republished. If **T's** intention to revoke is conditional, revocation does not take place until the condition is fulfilled.

Annuities

s.50 (2) provides that an annuitant is treated as having a life interest in the same proportion of the capital fund as the proportion that the annuity bears to the income fund, subject to prescribed maximum and minimum rates for the income of the fund. The extent of the life interest therefore varies with the yield from the capital. This can give rise to an IHT charge that is greater than the value of the fund. Alternative methods of providing maintenance include:

1. creation of an IPDI in all or part of the capital sum;
2. creation of an IPDI in all or part of the income from a capital fund; or
3. a legacy of a capital sum with which the legatee may purchase an annuity and claim relief under **s.717 ITTOIA 2005**.

To avoid capital being turned into income as a result of the operation of **s.349 ICTA 1988** PR's should be given the power to apply capital as they see fit, with the result that capital payments are treated as advances of capital rather than as income payments. A provision in a will directing an annuitant to receive a sum free of tax will be construed as an undertaking to pay such sum as, after tax, leaves the annuitant with the stated amount (the rule in *Re Pettit*). This results in the annuitant having to account to the PR's for any tax recovered from HMRC. The effect of this rule can be excluded.

Artificial debt rules

If a substantial inter-spouse gift has been made during **T's** life-time the debt or charge scheme can fail where **s.103 FA 1986** applies. This is discussed in Chapter 3 – *'NRB Discretionary Trusts'* and under *Phizackerley* below.

Beneficiaries

A legatee must be clearly described otherwise the gift may be void. If a beneficiary is dead when the will is made, or dies between execution and **T's** death, the gift is invalid and lapses.

Charities

A charity may receive the benefit of a gift in a will by means of a charitable trust, in which case **T's** intention must be clearly expressed. Whilst precatory words (expressing a hope or wish in relation to a gift) have been held to be sufficient, failure to identify an institution correctly can jeopardise the gift and encourage a disappointed next-of-kin to mount a legal challenge. '*Precatory words are words of entreaty that a* [testator] *uses. They imply an intention to create a trust. They create an express trust if they satisfy three certainties of: (i) words (intent); (ii) subject (the property and beneficial interests); and (iii) object (beneficiaries or benefiting causes)*' (**TSEM Glossary**). A gift to a charity is exempted from IHT by **s.23 (1)** unless any part of it is applied for '*purposes other than charitable purposes,*' **s.23(5)**. However, **s.23 (1)** does not apply to a gift for '*charitable or benevolent purposes*', **Chichester Diocesan Fund and Board of Finance Inc v Simpson** (1944)) or to a body that is not solely charitable and a charity in the UK. Registration under the **Charities Act 1993** is not a requirement, (**IHTM 11134** and **11135**). Note also the new definitions introduced by **FA 2010**.

Civil partner

For drafting purposes this expression is not technically interchangeable with the term '*spouse*'. Whilst this may not affect provisions made by **T** for his civil partner in his will, in the absence of specific words or a special context, the inclusion of '*spouses of beneficiaries*' in a definition of beneficiaries would not include a civil partner of a beneficiary.

Class gifts

If the class of beneficiaries provided for under a will is too large, the whole gift may be void because it cannot practically be administered. Likewise if the terms of any gift appear to be intentionally perverse, the gift can be declared void for capriciousness. In **Re Gestetner Settlement** (1953), see also **Re Gulbenkian's Settlements** (1970), and **McPhail v Doulton** (1971), membership of a class under a discretionary trust was described as a question which must be answerable in relation to any person in the world with the answer '*is*' or '*is not*' a member of the class.

Conditions

If a gift is made subject to fulfilment of a condition precedent, then if the condition is void the whole gifts fails. By contrast a gift subject to a condition subsequent takes effect free from a void condition.

Conditions may be void if they are:

1. contrary to public policy or illegal;
2. repugnant to the interest given to the beneficiary or other gifts or provisions of the will;
3. too uncertain to be enforced;
4. impossible to perform; or
5. made against a beneficiary as a threat to induce him to comply with the condition.

A condition or proviso against alienation or forfeiture on bankruptcy is void, whereas a limitation until bankruptcy or an attempted alienation is valid.

Delay

A will draftsman who delays in drawing up a will owes a duty of care to disappointed beneficiaries. It appears that seven working days is ordinarily an acceptable length of time to prepare a will following completion of fact-finding, and the confirmation of instructions, see *X v Woolcombe Yonge* (2001).

Domicile of surviving spouse

If **T** was domiciled in the UK on his death but **S** was not, the spouse exemption only applies up to a cumulative total of £55,000. Therefore on **T's** death only the first £55K of his chargeable estate plus his unused NRB will be exempt.

Duty of care

Rule 1.05 of the Solicitors Conduct Rules 2007 requires a solicitor to *'provide a good standard of client care and of work, including the exercise of competence, skill and diligence.'* **Rule 2.01(b)** further directs that *'a solicitor cannot act in a matter where he has insufficient resources or lacks the competence to deal with the matter.'* See *Bacon v Howard Kennedy* (2000). The precise scope of the solicitor's duty to advise depends amongst other things upon the extent to which the client appeared to need advice. An inexperienced client is entitled to expect his solicitor to take a much broader view of the scope of his retainer and of his duties than will be the case with an experienced client. The test is what the reasonably competent practitioner would do having regard to the standards normally adopted by his profession, which is directly related to the confines of the retainer, *Midland Bank v Hett, Stubs & Kemp* (1979). In *Cancer Research Campaign and others v Ernest Brown & Co (a firm) and others* (1997) the extent of a solicitor's duty to give tax advice (about the IHT savings that could have been achieved by the making of a post-death variation) was expressed by Mr Justice Harman in the following terms,

'I do not doubt the solicitor, in considering the will, must consider what inheritance tax complications that testator will cause by the bequests for which he is given instructions. But I refuse to hold, extending the duty to advise by, it was said, analogy, that there arises a duty to inform the intended testator, who has come in to instruct a solicitor about his or her will, about tax avoidance schemes in connection with some quite other estate.'

A solicitor who prepares a will is obliged to take any necessary steps to put his client's wishes into effect. He should therefore explain the consequences of implementing **T's** testamentary planning strategy, and cannot abdicate professional responsibility by instructing counsel, *Estill v Cowling Swift and Kitchen* (2000) (see also paragraph 6.30 of Kessler & Sartin). In a client care letter a solicitor can expressly carve out the giving of tax advice from the scope of his retainer. Regarding the existence of a duty to give tax advice see *Carradine Properties Ltd v DJ Freeman & Co* (1999), and *Hurlingham Estates Ltd v Wilde & Partners* (1997) (where a duty to give tax advice was held to exist in a property transaction).

The standard of care that applies to solicitors also applies to non-solicitor will-writers, *Esterhuizen v Allied Dunbar* (1998). Note also **rules 2.1** and **2.3** of the **Code of Professional Conduct of the Society of Trust and Estate Practitioners** (see Key Points at the end of the Introduction). Note that professional indemnity insurance will not apply if a firm of accountants or a trust company draft an English law trust relating to English property. Under **s.22 Solicitors Act 1974** (and subject to minor exceptions contained in **s.22(2)**, and **(2A)** this is a criminal offence. To stamp out negligent will drafting by unregulated will-writers, the Legal Services Board has recommended to the Coalition Government that will-writing becomes a reserved activity. If implemented (which according to commentators is likely), the drafting of any will undertaken by an unregulated will writer for payment will be a criminal offence. In which case any available PI cover cannot apply if a claim in negligence is subsequently brought against the draftsman.

Frankland trap

s.144 only applies where there would otherwise be a charge. No charge arises until three months after death. Therefore an appointment should be deferred until that period has expired. However, an appointment creating: (i) an IPDI; (ii) a trust for bereaved minors; or (iii) an 18-25 trust can be made at any time within the two year period following **T's** death (see paragraph 19.24 of Barlow, King and King).

Governing law

The law governing:

1. capacity and essential validity (for example the transfer of a beneficial share in a jointly-owned asset by survivorship) in relation to moveables, is the law of **T's** domicile; and
2. capacity and essential validity in relation to immoveables, is the law of the state in which the assets are situate.

If the will does not contain a governing law clause it will be construed in accordance with the law of **T's** domicile on the date it was made. The construction of a will is not altered by any change in **T's** domicile after the execution of the will, **s.3 Wills Act 1963**.

Joint- bequests

The creation of interests in a joint gift can take one of two forms: (i) a legal and beneficial joint-tenancy; or (ii) a tenancy in common. Note that a life interest in a half share of income is not the same as a life interest in a half share of capital, *Re Freeston's Charity* (1979).

Joint-property

The terms of a will can be frustrated by the terms upon which property is jointly-owned. A solicitor owes a duty of care to ensure that a beneficial joint-tenancy is severed if **T** intends to make a gift of a defined share of the equitable interest in the matrimonial home. Note *Carr-Glynn v Frearsons* (1968), where the lack of care lay in failing to ensure that the asset fell into the estate by neglecting to advise on the severance of a joint-tenancy. The authors of Risks and Negligence in Wills, Estates, and Trusts, consider that liability could also arise where a substantial part of a residuary gift is frustrated by survivorship (although **T's** intentions are harder to determine where joint-property is not the subject of a specific gift).

Mistake

A will executed by mistake cannot be admitted to probate. Three types of mistake can occur:

1. execution of the wrong document;
2. a mistaken belief held by **T** about the existence of circumstances or facts that influences the scheme of bequests made under his will; and
3. a mistaken belief held by **T** about the effect of the will, or of any of its provisions.

Where **T** includes words in his will, having intended to write other words, they will be omitted from probate. Similarly, if words are included that were not known or approved, they will also be omitted.

Where satisfied that **T's** will fails to carry out his intentions because of (i) a clerical error; or (ii) failure of the draftsman to understand **T's** instructions, the court may order *'rectification'* of **T's** will. Note that the following legal principles were enunciated in **Ashcroft v Barnsdale** (2010):

- the distinction between a mistake as to the *'meaning'* or *'effect'* of a document (which may be amenable to rectification) and one as to its *'consequences'* (which is not) applies to all claims for rectification;
- it is not limited to cases involving voluntary transactions;
- the relevance of the distinction does not depend upon the nature of the document which it is sought to rectify;
- the function of rectification is to enable the court to put the record straight by correcting a mistake in the way in which the parties have chosen to record their transaction;
- it does not empower the court to change the substance of that transaction or to correct an error in the transaction itself;
- so long as a mistake relates to the meaning or effect of a document (rather than the *'consequences'* of, or the *'advantages'* to be gained from entering into it), relief may be available even though the actual words of the document were deliberately adopted by the parties;
- it is firmly established that the fact that the parties intended to use a particular form of words in the mistaken belief that it was achieving their common intention does not prevent the court from giving effect to their true intention;
- where the mistake results from the inadvertent omission of a word or phrase from a document, and it is sought to introduce additional words into the document to cure that mistake, it may in practice prove easier to discharge the evidential burden of establishing the existence of a mistake than in the case where words have been inadvertently included in the document which it is sought to rectify;
- this is because the parties may not always appreciate the legal effect of the omission of particular words;
- it may be more difficult for parties outwardly to express an intention to include a word or phrase when they have failed to appreciate the need for them;
- the court cannot rectify a document merely because it fails to achieve the fiscal objectives of the parties to it;
- a mere misapprehension as to the tax consequences of executing a particular document will not justify an order for its rectification;
- the specific intention of the parties as to how the fiscal objective was to be achieved must be shown if the court is to order rectification;

- the court will only order the rectification of a document if it is satisfied by cogent evidence (sufficient to counteract the effect of the parties' subscription to the relevant document) that:
  1. the document does not give effect to the true agreement or arrangement between the parties; and
  2. there is *'an issue capable of being contested'* between the parties, it being irrelevant that rectification of the document is:
     (a) sought or consented to by all of them; and
     (b) desired because it has beneficial fiscal consequences; and
- conversely, the court will not order rectification if the parties' rights will be unaffected, and if the only effect of the order will be to secure a fiscal benefit for one or more of them.

No contest clauses

These are capable of being valid but cannot oust the making of an **Inheritance Act** claim. See ***Nathan v Leonard*** (2002).

Occupation

If trustees grant a beneficiary a right of occupation in a dwelling owned by the trust this will create an IPDI. To avoid this outcome **T** can devise the dwelling to trustees to hold upon discretionary trusts for a class of beneficiaries that includes **S**. Because **S** does not then have a right to occupy under the trust, an IPDI is not created, and the trustees can grant her a licence to occupy.

Partial or total intestacy

A total intestacy occurs where **T** fails to make an effective disposition of any property. A partial intestacy occurs where **T** makes gifts which fail to dispose of part or of some interest in all or part of the property of which he is competent to dispose by his will. This can occur, for example, where a beneficiary of an absolute gift of the whole or part of **T's** residuary estate dies before the expiry of a survivorship period and the will does not contain a substitutional gift. **T's** estate is then held under a trust for sale by his PR's, who after making the payments prescribed by **s.33 AEA 1925** (as amended by **TLATA 1996**), distribute the net estate in accordance with the intestacy rules.

Phizackerley

In the **Phizackerley** case the Special Commissioner found as a fact that the consideration given for the debt was *'the half-share in the house.'* Whilst appearing to accept that **s.11** applied for the purposes of **s.103 (4) FA 1986**, which switches off the provisions of **s.103(1)**. On the facts of the case he found that the purpose of the gift was not within the relieving section on the pleaded ground of *'maintenance'*. He held that whilst the concept *'is wide enough to cover the transfer of a house or part interest in a house [it does so] only if it relieves the recipient from income expenditure, for example on rent...the only evidence of their purpose [a statement by their daughter who said she believed her parents had severed the joint-tenancy in order to create a tenancy in common to enjoy security of joint-ownership],'* indicated that this was not done for the purpose of maintenance. At paragraph 10, the Special Commissioner stated, *'I do not consider that when a husband puts a house in joint names for himself and his wife during their marriage it is within the ordinary meaning of maintenance.'* The decision is not being appealed. See NRB Discretionary Trusts in **Chapter 3**.

Revocation

A will or codicil is revoked: (i) where **T** marries or forms a civil partnership; (ii) it is destroyed by **T** or by some other person in his presence, and by his direction; and (iii) where **T** executes another valid will or codicil. Note that the execution of a will by **T** in England can inadvertently revoke a foreign will made previously by **T** over assets situated outside the UK. The same applies in reverse if the intention is found to exist, see ***Lamothe v Lamothe*** (2006). To avoid this outcome the draftsman must enquire about the existence of any foreign will(s). The burden of proving revocation falls on the person alleging it.

SDLT trap

There is no general exemption from SDLT for inter-spouse dealing, including the severance of a beneficial joint-tenancy to put the matrimonial home into joint-names as tenants in common in equity. See Nock, paragraphs 10.27 – 10.28.There is a chargeable transaction for SDLT where the property transferred is subject to a mortgage, (which includes contingent debts such as a charge by way of guarantee of the debts of a company of which the transferor may be a director). However these rules do not apply to an appropriation of property by executors in satisfaction of a legacy. **Paragraph 8(1B), Sch 4, FA 2003** provides, that where there is a debt charged on the property and the liability is assumed and either:

1. immediately before the transaction there are two or more persons holding individual shares; or
2. immediately after the transaction there are two or more persons holding an individual share,

the amount of the secured debt brought into charge is the proportion of the debt corresponding to his undivided share of the property at that time. Where the mortgage is less than £250K, a transfer of a half share in the house will be taxable upon one-half i.e. a sum of less than £125K so that the parties can take advantage of the nil rate of SDLT.

Paragraph 8 Sch 4, FA 2003 provides that,

> (1) *Where the chargeable consideration for a land transaction consists in whole or in part of –*
>> *(a) the satisfaction or release of debt due to the purchaser or owed by the vendor, or*
>> *(b) the assumption of existing debt by the purchaser,*
>> *the amount of debt satisfied, released or assumed shall be taken to be the whole or, as the case may be, part of the chargeable consideration for the transaction.*
> (2) *If the effect of sub-paragraph (1) would be that the amount of the chargeable consideration for the transaction exceeded the market value of the subject-matter of the transaction, the amount of the chargeable consideration is treated as limited to that value.*
> (3) *In this paragraph–*
>> *(a) 'debt' means an obligation, whether certain or contingent, to pay a sum of money either immediately or at a future date,*
>> *(b) 'existing debt', in relation to a transaction, means debt created or arising before the effective date of, and otherwise than in connection with, the transaction, and*
>> *(c) references to the amount of a debt are to the principal amount payable or, as the case may be, the total of the principal amounts payable, together with the amount of any interest that has accrued due on or before the effective date of the transaction.'*

Self-dealing rule

If **S** is a NRA trustee then the purchase by her of **T's** share of the equitable interest in the matrimonial home is potentially voidable at the instance of any beneficiary as a self-dealing transaction. Note **Kane v Radley-Kane** (1998). The will may contain provisions authorising such a self-dealing transaction (subject to safe-guards) e.g. through the appointment of an independent trustee to consider whether or not the proposed transaction is contrary to the general interests of the other beneficiaries.

Sham attack

A document or a provision in a document is a sham if it is not intended to be acted on in accordance with its terms, i.e. where a trust is a cloak for something else behind it. For a comprehensive discussion of the practical planning issues surrounding sham trusts see the author's article '*The Concept of Sham In Relation To Offshore Trusts, How Such A Situation Can Arise, And How It Can Best Be Avoided*', published in the Journal of International Trust and Corporate Planning Vol 14, Issue 3, 2007. By definition a trust cannot be created where a sham exists because at the time of creation there was no intention to fulfil the requirements for creation of a valid trust, which requires certainty of intention. If when executing his will **T** genuinely intends the documentation to take effect according to the tenor of its terms and those terms are such as to create a trust, then nothing **T** or the trustees do thereafter can render a valid trust a sham, and the court will not enquire into the motive underlying **T's** intention. The court distinguishes between:

1. a written document deliberately framed with the object of deceiving third parties as to the true nature and effect of the legal relations between the parties – which is a sham ; and
2. situations where '*the [instrument] does precisely reflect the true agreement between the parties, but where the language of the document (and in particular its title or description) superficially indicate that it falls into one legal category, whereas properly analysed in the light of surrounding circumstances it can be seen to fall into another*' – which is not a sham. See *Hadjiloucas v Crean* (1998).

The fact that a deed has been executed with the benefit of legal advice does not affect the status of a transaction as a sham.

A trust instrument will not be a sham simply because:

1. the parties do not know its effects; or
2. it is not commercial, or even artificial - for example a tax-avoidance scheme that relies upon the individual steps making up the scheme to be legal.

If a trust is found to be a sham, then it will be a sham for all purposes. A successful sham attack does not by itself establish the claimant's right to the property held within the trust. Hence a claim for a declaration that a trust is a sham is likely to be accompanied by an alternative recovery claim, the nature of which will depend upon the particular facts of the case and the party bringing the claim.

s.39a trap

A gift of qualifying business or agricultural property should always be made by way of a specific gift to a chargeable beneficiary, because any relief on relevant property not specifically given is apportioned throughout the estate under **s.39A**.

S.199 trap

Under **s.199** PR's have a secondary liability to pay IHT chargeable on lifetime transfers made by **T** before his death (including the amount of any failed PET). Personal liability arises under **s.204 (6) (as amended by Sch 19 para 28 FA 1986)** if the tax remains due 12 months after **T's** death. Therefore careful enquiries need to be made before making any distributions(s) that would not leave the PR's with sufficient funds to pay the IHT. To protect themselves the PR's should consider insurance and the taking of an indemnity or other adequate security. In addition a secondary liability arises under **s.204 (9)** in relation to any unpaid tax chargeable on a gift with reservation under **s.102 FA 1986**.

Unincorporated associations

The validity of the gift depends upon its construction. This is a drafting minefield. Depending upon how the legacy has been drafted, a gift to an unincorporated association may be construed by the court as a gift made to:

- the individual members as beneficial joint-tenants on the date of the gift (or if words of severance are used, as tenants in common). Then every member is entitled to sever his share and claim the value of it (whether or not he continues to be a member);
- all members beneficially, but on the basis that the gift is to be held as an accretion to the funds of the association. The gift is then held by members subject to their contractual rights and liabilities to each other. Contrary to **T's** wishes this may result in a cash distribution to members in the event that the association is wound-up;
- the trustees of the association to be held on trust for the purposes of the association, in which case the gift will fail as an invalid purpose trust; or
- as a gift to the present and future members, then unless the gift is limited in time by reference to the perpetuity period, it will fail.

Valuation reports

On **T's** death it is important that the assets comprising his death estate are valued on a market value basis. HMRC will usually want to see a statement (i.e. a professional valuation report), which confirms that the valuation was prepared on that basis, or a letter instructing the valuer to prepare the valuation on a market value basis. Note that in the case of land HMRC's guidance in relation to the completion of Form IHT 400 states that the valuer should be asked to take any development and hope value into account. It also states that when property is marketed at the valuation price, and offers are made in excess of the valuation, this is indicative that the true value of the land is higher. A valuation report headed *'valuation for probate purposes'* will therefore be viewed with suspicion by HMRC, as not truly reflecting the market value of those assets at the date of **T's** death.

7

Update

- Recent Cases
- UK Budget 2011

Recent cases

The following recent cases have a particular bearing on current legal interpretation. Key passages from the judgments in these cases are set out in Appendix 7:

Pitt v Holt (2011) (Court of Appeal)

The **Hastings-Bass** rule. Note also the article by Andrew Cosedge 'The 'u-turn' in Futter v Futter' in the Trust Quarterly Review (Volume 9, Issue 2, 2011).

RSPCA v Sharp (2011) (Court of Appeal)

Dispute about the construction of a nil rate band gift. At paragraph 18.16, on page 278 of their book Drafting Trusts and Will Trusts (10th edition) James Kessler QC, and Leon Sartin state that in **RSPCA v Sharp** (2010), the Judge at first instance 'misconstrued the NRB gift as a gift of the full statutory NRB... without any allowance for the second gift. That is wrong, because (among other reasons) on that view IHT did 'become payable' - and it did so, in part, 'in respect of' the NRB gift. The correct construction was that the will made a gift of the NRB remaining available after allowing for the second gift...But even if (contrary to our view) the decision were right, the position would be different if the testator had used the form of this book because the maximum amount of cash which could be given without incurring 'any liability to IHT' could only be the net amount.' Please note that the drafting of the Kessler & Sartin 'nil rate formula' is discussed in paragraph 1.16 on page 276 of their book. Note also the article by Amanda Hardy 'A discussion of RSPCA v Sharp' in the Trust Quarterly Review (Volume 9, Issue 1, 2011).

Price v HMRC (2010) (Fist Tier Tribunal Tax Chamber)

The proper construction of the words *'the appropriate portion of the value of the aggregate of that and any related property'* in **s.161(1)** (related property).

Key v Key (2010) (Chancery Division

The Golden Rule.

UK BUDGET 2011

Rates of IHT and CGT

1. IHT

	Cumulative chargeable transfers [gross]		Tax rate on death %	Tax rate in lifetime %
	2010/11 £	2011/12 £		
Nil rate band	325,000	325,000	0	0
Excess	No Limit	No Limit	40	20

Note:
1. Chargeable lifetime transfers only.
2. NRB frozen until 2015. From 2015/16 increases in this figure will be based on CPI.
3. The Coalition Government has announced that a reduced rate of IHT will apply where 10% or more of **T's** net estate (after deducting IHT exemptions, reliefs and the NRB) is left to charity. In those cases the current 40% rate will be reduced to 36%. The new rate will apply to deaths occurring on or after 6 April 2012. A consultation document on the implementation of this measure will be issued in the summer.

2. CGT

2.1 Principal exemptions and reliefs

	2010/11 £	2011/12 £
Annual exemption	10,100	10,600
Principal private residence exemption	No Limit	No Limit
Chattels exemption	6,000	6,000
Entrepreneurs' relief Lifetime limit	All business gain taxed at 10% £5,000,000	All business gain taxed at 10% £10,000,000
Note that £10,600 is the annual exemption for an individual with effect from 6 April 2011. For most trusts the exempt limit in 2011/2012 is £5,300.		

2.2 Tax rates

	2010/11 from 23 June 2010 onwards	2011/12
Individual	Below higher rate band: 18% Within higher or additional rate bands: 28%	Below higher rate band: 18% Within higher or additional rate bands: 28%
Trustees and personal representatives	28%	28%

Appendix 1
Diagrams

DIAGRAM No.1 – TESTAMENTARY PLANNING PROCESS

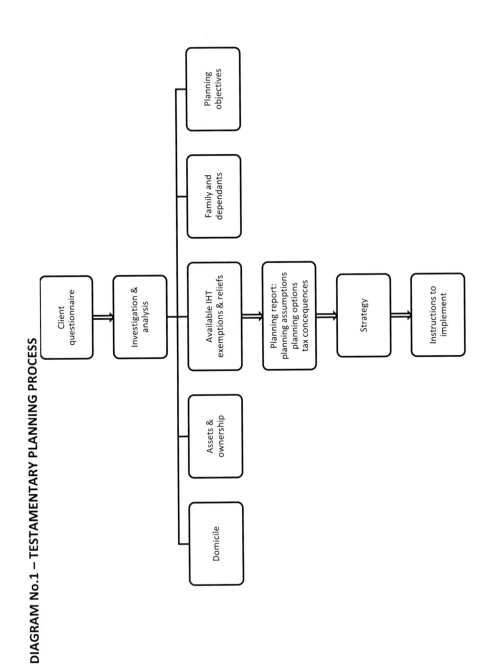

DIAGRAM No.2 – IHT CALCULATIONS

Taxable estate	IHT bill
£325 K	£0
£500 K	£70 K
£750 K	£170 K
£1 M	£270 K
£2 M	£670 K
£4 M	£1,470,000
£10 M	£3,870,000
£20 M	£7,870,000

DIAGRAM NO.3 – WEALTH TRIANGLE

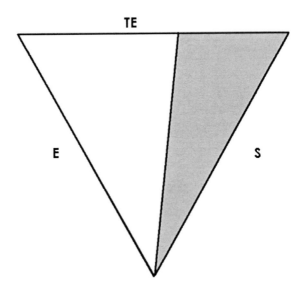

E   = Earn

S   = Spend or give away

TE   = T's taxable estate

       = Reduction of T's taxable estate by IHT

DIAGRAM NO.4 – IHT CATEGORIES OF LIFETIME TRANSFER

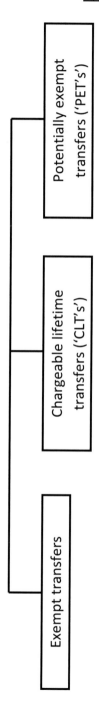

DIAGRAM NO.5 – KEY CATEGORIES OF T'S DEATH ESTATE

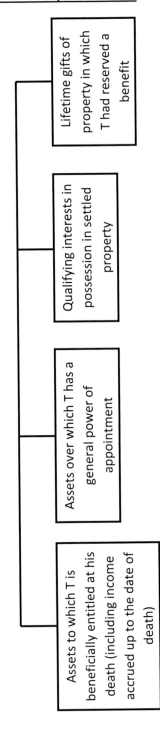

Assets to which T is beneficially entitled at his death (including income accrued up to the date of death)

Assets over which T has a general power of appointment

Qualifying interests in possession in settled property

Lifetime gifts of property in which T had reserved a benefit

DIAGRAM NO.6 – IHT PRIVILEGED WILL/TRUSTS POST 22.03.2006

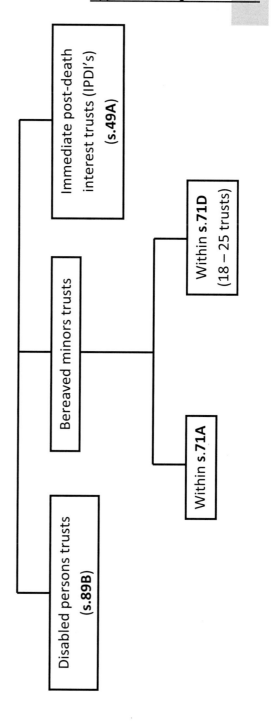

DIAGRAM No.7

WEALTH AND FAMILY TREE

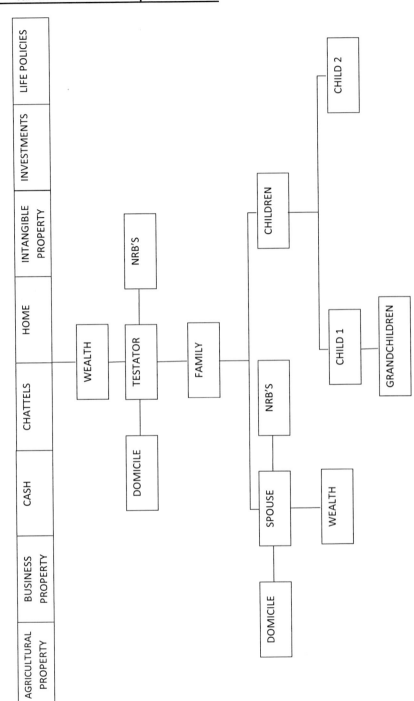

DIAGRAM No.8 – POST-DEATH ALTERATIONS

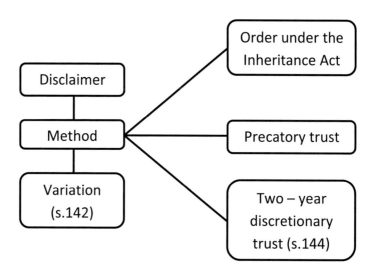

DIAGRAM No.9 - PENALTIES

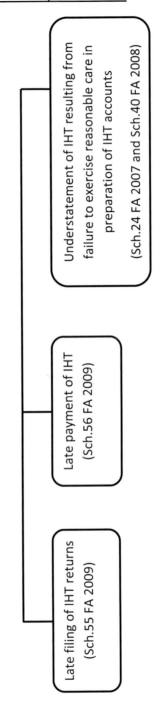

Late filing of IHT returns
(Sch.55 FA 2009)

Late payment of IHT
(Sch.56 FA 2009)

Understatement of IHT resulting from failure to exercise reasonable care in preparation of IHT accounts

(Sch.24 FA 2007 and Sch.40 FA 2008)

DIAGRAM No.10 – INTESTACY RULES (s.46 AEA 1925 as amended by the Family Provision (Intestate Succession) Order 2009 (S/2009/135))

Surviving relative(s)	Person(s) entitled to the estate	Person(s) entitled to grant of letters of administration
1. Spouse only	Surviving spouse absolutely	Surviving spouse
2. Spouse and issue	(a) Surviving spouse takes: (i) personal chattels (ii) £250K (iii) life interest in half residuary estate (b) Issue take residuary estate at age 18 subject to life interest in half of surviving spouse in equal shares *per stirpes*	Surviving spouse and one other person
3. Spouse and parent(s)	(a) Surviving spouse takes: (i) personal chattels (ii) £450K (iii) half residuary estate absolutely (b) Parent(s) take half residuary estate in equal shares	Surviving spouse
4. Spouse and brother(s) and/or sister(s) of the whole blood and/or issue of such who predeceased the intestate	(a) Surviving spouse takes: (i) personal chattels (ii) £450K (iii) half residuary estate absolutely (b) Brother(s) and sister(s) and/or issue takes half residuary estate at age 18 in equal shares *per stirpes*	Surviving spouse (one other person)

DIAGRAM No.11 – FISCAL CONNECTING FACTORS

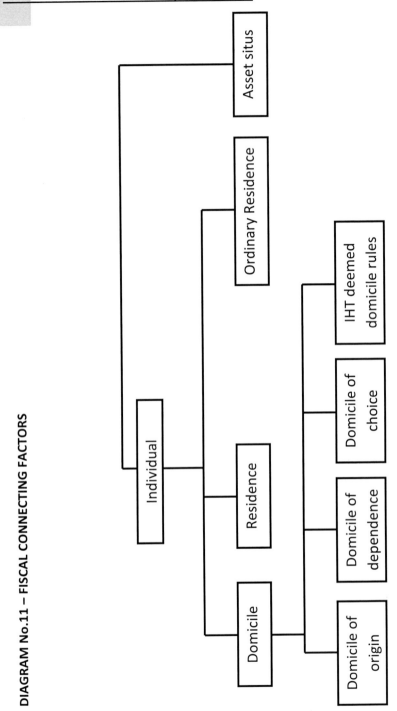

DIAGRAM No. 12 – MASTER PLAN

APPOINTMENT OF PROFESSIONAL ADVISORS

- Capital tax planning (including life-time planning)
- Drafting wills and trusts (including life-time trusts)
- Tax-efficient investments
- Offshore service providers (in relation to planning for non-doms)

INVESTIGATION AND ANALYSIS

WEALTH PLANNING REPORT

DEVELOPMENT OF A HOLISTIC WEALTH PLANNING STRAGETY (including life-time planning)

DRAFTING A TAX-EFFICIENT WILL

- Form of will
- Appointment of executors, trustees, guardians, and a protector (in relation to offshore planning for a non-dom)
- Terms (NB the drafting of additional Trustee's powers)

REVIEW, CONFIRMATION, AND EXECUTION

TWO-YEAR PLANNING REVIEWS AND RECORD | KEEPING

IMPLEMENTATION AFTER DEATH (NB the winding-up of an obsolete NRB discretionary will trust)

POST-DEATH ALTERATIONS

DIAGRAM NO.13 – TRUST FUND

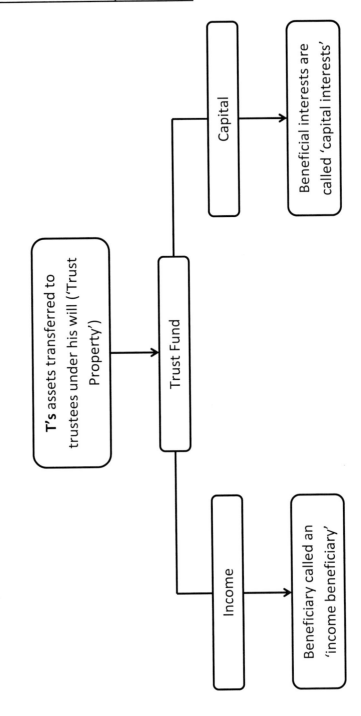

T's assets transferred to trustees under his will ('Trust Property')

Trust Fund

Capital

Income

Beneficial interests are called 'capital interests'

Beneficiary called an 'income beneficiary'

DIAGRAM No.14 – GIFTS OF RESIDUE

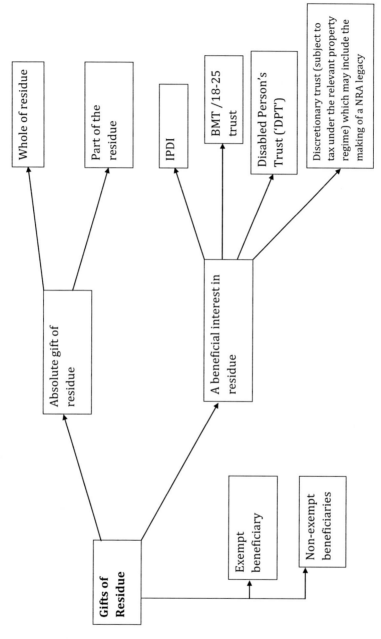

DIAGRAM NO.15 – DISCRETIONARY TRUST STRUCTURE

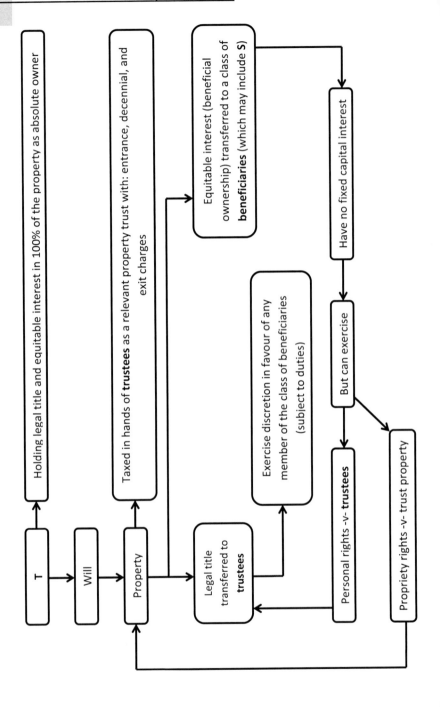

DIAGRAM No.16

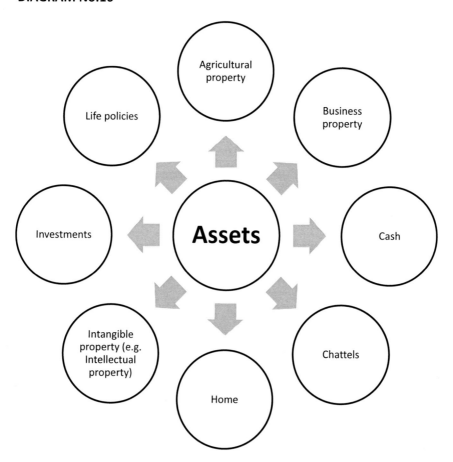

DIAGRAM NO.17 – INTEREST IN POSSESSION TRUSTS

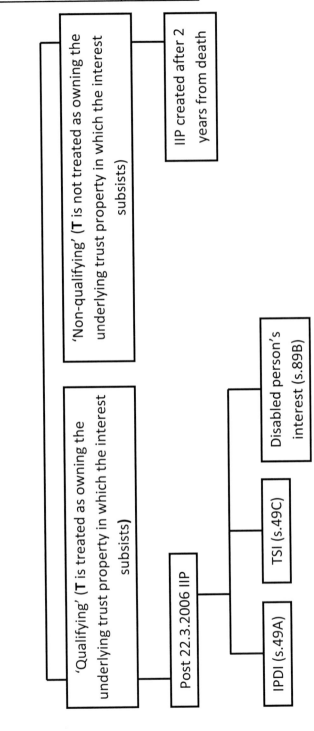

'Qualifying' (**T** is treated as owning the underlying trust property in which the interest subsists)

- Post 22.3.2006 IIP
  - IPDI (s.49A)
  - TSI (s.49C)
  - Disabled person's interest (s.89B)

'Non-qualifying' (**T** is not treated as owning the underlying trust property in which the interest subsists)

- IIP created after 2 years from death

DIAGRAM No.18 – QUALIFYING INTERESTS IN POSSESSION

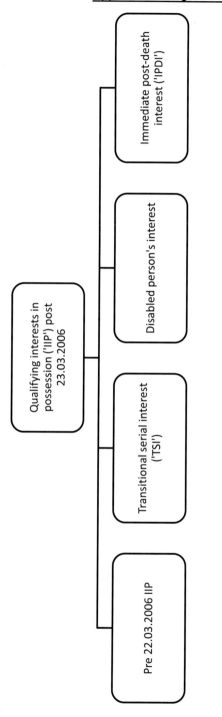

Qualifying interests in possession ('IIP') post 23.03.2006

- Pre 22.03.2006 IIP
- Transitional serial interest ('TSI')
- Disabled person's interest
- Immediate post-death interest ('IPDI')

DIAGRAM No.19 – READING-BACK

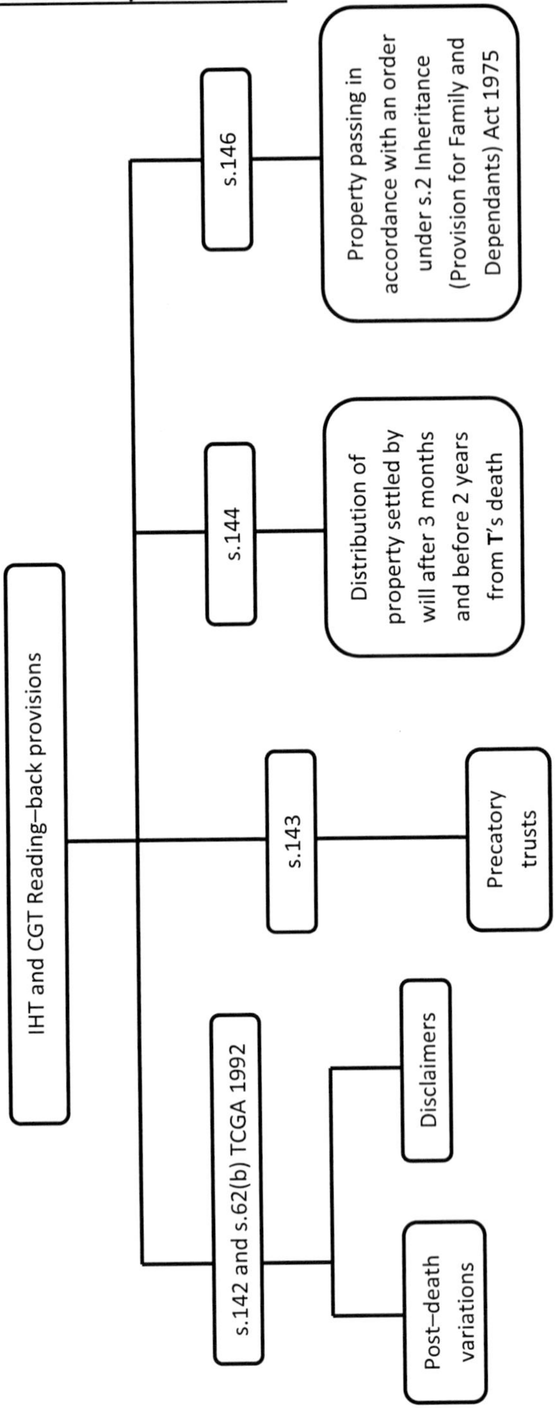

IHT and CGT Reading–back provisions

- s.142 and s.62(b) TCGA 1992
  - Post–death variations
  - Disclaimers
- s.143
  - Precatory trusts
- s.144
  - Distribution of property settled by will after 3 months and before 2 years from T's death
- s.146
  - Property passing in accordance with an order under s.2 Inheritance (Provision for Family and Dependants) Act 1975

DIAGRAM No.20 – TRUSTS FOR CHILDREN AND GRANDCHILDREN

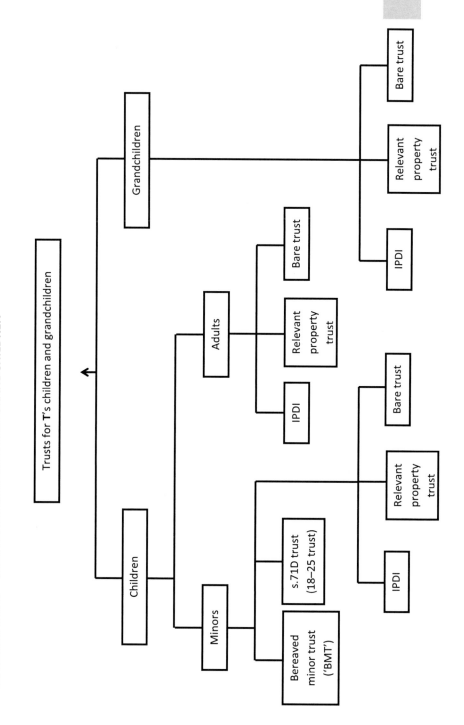

DIAGRAM No.21 – UK SITUS ASSETS DESIGNATED AS EXCLUDED PROPERTY (s.6 and s.157)

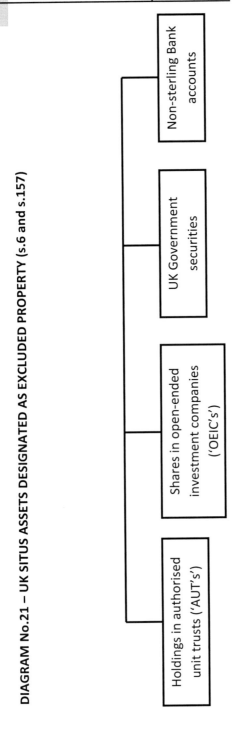

DIAGRAM No.22 – SCHEME OF DISPOSITIONS

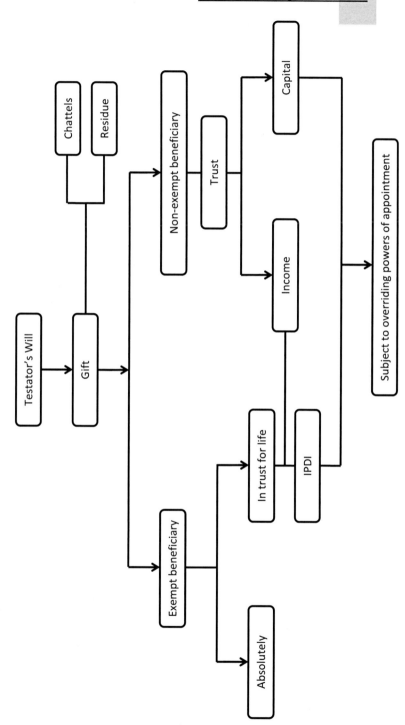

DIAGRAM No.23 – TRUSTEE'S POWERS

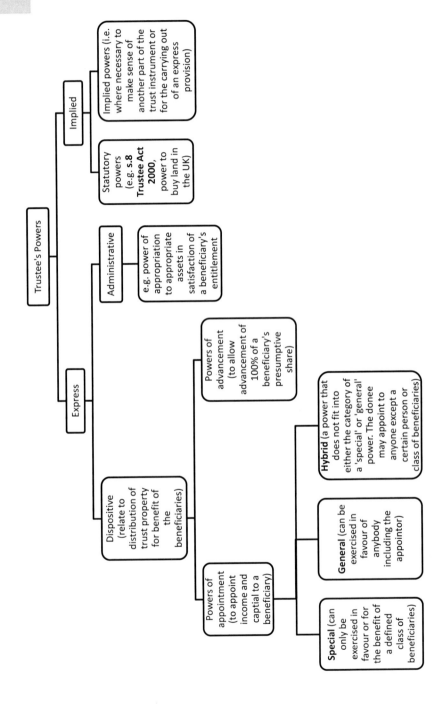

DIAGRAM No.24 – BENEFICIARY'S ENTITLEMENT TO INCOME AND PROFITS GENERATED BY A TRUST ASSET FROM THE DATE OF **T**'s DEATH

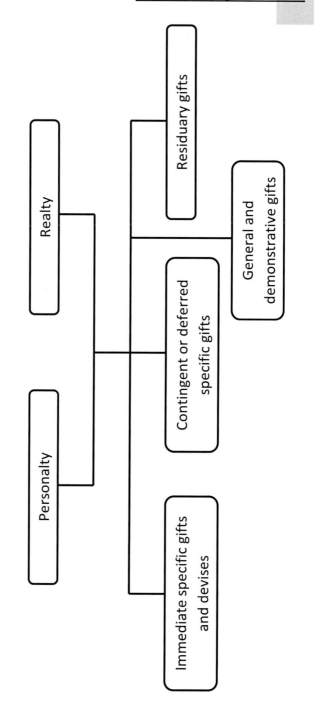

DIAGRAM No. 25 – FAILURE OF LEGACIES

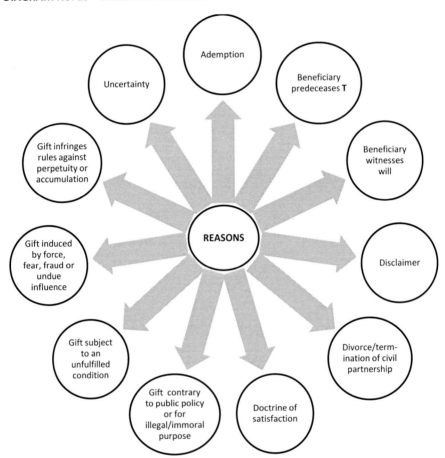

Appendix 2

Note on Trustees' Duties and Powers

- Introduction
- Creation of powers
- Appropriation
- The statutory power of advancement
- General duties
- Exercise
- Vesting and class closure
- Delegation
- Fraud on a power
- Applications to the court
- The *Hastings-Bass* principle

Introduction

The draftsman of a will/trust must ensure that sufficient powers are available to the trustees to enable them to administer the trusts created by the testator's will. For this purpose the draftsman must also consider the modification or exclusion of any relevant statutory powers. Administrative powers are conferred on trustees (which also apply to executors) under: (i) the **Administration of Estates Act 1925** (the '**AEA 1925**'); the **Trustee Act 1925** (the '**TA 1925**'); and (iii) the **TA 2000**. These include the power to:

- acquire land (**s.8 TA 2000**);
- advance capital (**s.32 TA 1925**);
- appropriate any part of **T's** estate in or towards satisfaction of any legacy, interest, or share in **T's** estate, provided any specific bequest or devise is not thereby prejudiced (**s.41 AEA 1925**);
- delegate and appoint agents (**sections 11 – 27 TA 2000**);
- insure (**s.19 TA 1925** (as substituted by **s.34 TA 2000**));
- invest (**Part II TA 2000**, sections 3-7);
- postpone distribution (**s.44 AEA 1925**);
- reimburse: (i) trustees expenses (**s.31 TA 2000**); and (ii) expenses of agents, nominees, and custodians (**s.32 TA 2000**); and
- sell, mortgage, or lease both personal and real property comprised in **T's** estate (see **s.39 AEA 1925** amended by **TLATA 1996**).

Where a power is conferred on a trustee in his *'fiduciary'* capacity fiduciary duties attach to the power and:

1. the trustee owes the following duties:
   (a) to periodically consider the exercise of the power;
   (b) to consider the range of objects;
   (c) to consider whether an individual appointment is appropriate; and
2. there is a corresponding disability from releasing the power (unless authorised by the will).

Creation of powers

A power (i.e. *'the trustee may...'*) confers the capacity to do something, whereas a duty (i.e. *'the trustee must...'*) imposes an obligation to act in a particular way. No technical or express words are necessary in a will to create a power. Any words, however informal, which in their context clearly indicate an intention to give or reserve a power are sufficient for the purpose. Powers may be conferred by reference, for example by incorporating the **Standard Provisions of the Society of Trust and Estate Practitioners**. A power may be held to exist by implication where that is reasonably necessary for making sense of another part of the will, or for the carrying out of some express provision. Rules of equity also confer certain powers, even if the will is silent. For example, a trustee's powers of appropriation derive from rules of equity, where the will makes no express provision.

Appropriation

Following appropriation, an asset is no longer held by executors in their capacity as PR's, and therefore is no longer available to meet the general liabilities and expenses of the estate. If the asset is not immediately transferred to a beneficiary or trustee (in the case of a settled legacy), it is held as trustee for the beneficiary and not for the estate. Under **s. 41 AEA 1942** when making an appropriation an executor must consider the interests of all present and future beneficiaries, and is under a duty to act fairly between all the interests, see **Lloyd's Bank v Duker** (1981). An executor may appropriate assets at any time after the grant of representation has been obtained.

The statutory power of advancement

Under a will the statutory power of advancement under **s.32 TA 1925** may be modified (i) to allow the whole of the share (or presumptive share) to be advanced, and (ii) to allow application for maintenance or education in addition to advancement or benefit. Note that the phrase *'advancement of benefit'* has been given a wide meaning, see **Pilkington v IRC** (1964). This can be coupled with an overriding power of advancement. This is also a power to apply capital for *'benefit'*. The guiding principle is that an application of capital will be for the benefit of the beneficiary concerned if it is used in a way that will improve the material situation of the beneficiary. However, a trustee must not thereby enable a beneficiary to benefit a person who is not a beneficiary (except incidentally). A beneficiary cannot be advanced under the statutory power unless entitled to capital. **Proviso (c) to s.32 (1) TA 1925** also requires the consent of any person with a prior interest in capital, in addition to that of a prior life tenant. Note that a power of advancement in *'pay or apply'* form is sufficiently exercised by a trustee's resolution allocating property to the beneficiary.

General duties

Before accepting his appointment a trustee should check that there is no conflict of interest between himself and the beneficiary or at the very least disclose the existence of any actual or potential conflict. Where a trustee has an absolute discretion and exercises it in good faith (with no improper motive), the court will not interfere even though it might have exercised the discretion differently, **Re Londonderry's Wills** (1965). Subject to any express terms of the will, a trustee must consider the exercise of his discretion on a regular basis, and cannot fetter the future exercise of his discretion by committing in advance to the future exercise of his powers, **Re Gibson's Will Trusts** (1981). In the performance of his duties, a trustee is expected to attain certain standards. There is a general duty imposed on a trustee to ensure fairness between beneficiaries. Failure to manage the trust fund, or to exercise reasonable skill and care, may result in a beneficiary action for breach of trust.

The fiduciary duty of care imposed by equity on a trustee is supplemented in relation to specific duties (including investment) by a new statutory duty of care imposed by **s.1 TA 2000**, which under **Schedule 1** applies to:

1. investment matters;
2. acquisition of land;
3. dealings with agents, nominees and custodians;
4. insuring trust assets; and
5. dealing with reversionary interests, valuation, and audit.

Unless excluded or modified by the will, the duty of care extends to all aspects of the performance of a trustee's duties.

The conduct of a trustee is to be judged in the light of the knowledge possessed by the trustee, and of the standards and practice obtaining at the relevant time. As Mr Justice Hoffman stated in **Nestle v National Westminister Bank** (2000), *'One must be careful not to endow the prudent trustee with prophetic vision or expect him to ignore the received wisdom of his time.'* The fact that a trustee has made an error of judgement is not sufficient to fix him with liability. The usual overriding obligation of a trustee is to preserve and safeguard trust property:

1. first by placing it under his own personal custody and control;
2. then by taking proper care of the property; and
3. by preserving and managing trust property for the benefit of the beneficiaries.

A trustee is under a positive duty to make the trust fund productive for the beneficiaries by investing it. The trustee should consider what investments are open to him. In exercising his powers and duties a trustee has a general duty to exercise care (subject to the terms of the will).

A trustee must adopt a relatively cautious approach to his management of the trust. It is not the case that a trustee can take no risks in his dealings with the trust funds, but he must curb any impulse to risk trust funds in speculative ventures, even where the ventures are of a sort in which a hypothetical prudent businessman may be prepared to risk his own money. However wide the scope of the investment clause, the trustee should not be reckless with trust money, **Re Whitely** (1886). The distinction is between a prudent degree of risk on the one hand and hazard on the other. The level of prudence to be observed depends upon the economic and financial conditions of the time, and not on what judges have held to be the prudent course in the past.

s.1 TA 2000 provides,

'Whenever the duty under this subsection applies to a trustee, he must exercise such care and skill as is reasonable in the circumstances, having regard in particular: –

(i) to any special knowledge or experience that he has or holds himself out as having and

(ii) if he acts as trustee in the course of a business or profession, to any special knowledge or experience that it is reasonable to expect of a person acting in the course of that kind of business or profession.'

A distinction is drawn between (i) a trustee who undertakes trust business in the course of general practice; and (ii) a trustee who specialises or holds himself out as specialising in trust work, or a particular type of trust work.

The former is governed by the general professional standard, while the latter is governed by the higher standard that might be expected of him through the special knowledge or experience that he has or holds himself out as having. A higher standard of care may also be expected of a trustee who is remunerated for his services to the trust, whether or not he holds himself out as a trust professional. The duty of care applies when a trustee:

1. exercises the general power of investment, (conferred by **s.3 TA 2000**);
2. exercises the power under **s.8 TA 2000** to acquire land;

3. enters into arrangements for the appointment of agents, nominees, or custodians, under **sections 11, 16, 17, or 18 TA 2000**;
4. exercises powers of compromise (and other powers conferred by **s.15 TA 1925**);
5. exercises his power under **s.19 TA 1925** to insure property; and
6. exercises the powers conferred by **sections 22(1)**, and **22(3) TA 1925**.

At common law a trustee must exercise the same degree of diligence and care that a man of ordinary prudence would in the management of his own affairs, **Speight v Gaunt** (1883). By **s.1** *'a trustee may make any kind of investment that he could make if he were absolutely entitled to the assets of the trust.'* However, *'investment'* does not include non-income or profit-making assets. A power to invest implies a power to vary investments, including power to resell land held as an investment.

s.5 TA 2000 provides:

'(1) Before exercising any power of investment, whether arising under this Part or otherwise, a trustee must (unless the exception applies) obtain and consider proper advice about the way in which, having regard to the standard investment criteria, the power should be exercised.

(2) When reviewing the investments of the trust, a trustee must (unless the exception applies) obtain and consider proper advice about whether having regard to the standard investment criteria, the investments should be varied.

(3) The exception is that a trustee need not obtain such advice if he reasonably concludes that in all the circumstances it is unnecessary or inappropriate to do so.

(4) Proper advice is the advice of a person who is reasonably believed by the trustee to be qualified to give it by his ability in and practical experience of financial and other matters relating to the proposed investment.'

A trustee should not make an interest-free loan to a beneficiary unless he has an express power to do so. The statutory power does not authorise such loans. The only land that may be acquired under **s.8 (1) TA 2000** is freehold or leasehold land in the United Kingdom. Without express wording expanding the meaning of *'investment'* the purchase of land for an occupational purpose is not authorised by an express investment power. A trustee must account to the beneficiaries for his dealings with the trust assets, and:

1. keep accurate records of all transactions involving trust monies (including receipts);
2. provide information to the beneficiaries on request; and
3. explain, and if necessary justify his dealings with the trust assets.

If a beneficiary requests information, before refusing production, a trustee must consider whether there is a proper reason for refusing the disclosure of each document (or category of documents) requested.

Exercise

In order to consider meaningfully whether or not to exercise a discretion, the trustee must be aware of the extent of the class of beneficiaries. In **Re Hay's Will Trusts** (1981) Megarry VC said, a trustee, *'must make such survey of the range of objects or possible beneficiaries as will enable him to carry out his fiduciary duty. He must find out the permissible area of selection and then consider responsibly, in individual cases, whether, in relation to the possible claimants, a particular grant was appropriate.'*

Duties vary according to the nature of the power. If a power is construed as a trust the trustee is required to exercise it. Administrative powers are generally discretionary. A trustee must from time to time form a judgement in good faith as to whether to exercise his powers. In the case of a trust corporation, it is also necessary to ascertain who can exercise the power on behalf of the company. Ratification is effective to legitimate the actions of a trustee, and for breach of any statutory duty imposed on a director of a trust corporation under the **Companies Act 2006**. Therefore a dog-leap claim brought against a director of a trust corporation will fail.

Where the subsistence of the power or duty depends upon the existence of facts, a trustee must properly consider whether they exist (which in the case of a fiduciary power is inseparable from the duty to consider the exercise of the power from time to time). In considering the facts a trustee must:

1. act honestly and in good faith;
2. ask the correct question – which requires identification of the question **T** has committed to his discretion;
3. make a reasonable decision (a perverse decision is one that no reasonable body of trustees could reach on the information before them); and
4. consider all relevant matters (to the exclusion of irrelevant considerations).

For these purposes the trustee must construe the will correctly (ascribing the sense to it that the court would). Note that honesty and sincerity are not the same as prudence and reasonableness, **Cowan v Scargill** (1985). A trustee acts dishonestly if he pursues a particular course of action, either knowing that it is contrary to the interests of the beneficiaries or being recklessly indifferent as to whether it is contrary to their interests or not, **Armitage v Nurse** (1998). Dishonest conduct is usually advertent. Negligence or carelessness is not dishonesty unless it is so gross as to amount to recklessness. In considering the exercise of a dispositive power a trustee must:

1. act responsibly and in good faith – he must give genuine and responsible consideration to the exercise of his powers, and must not act capriciously;
2. take only relevant matters into account (including directions left by **T** in a letter of wishes);
3. act impartially, balancing the interests of all of the beneficiaries in the estate (except in so far as the will authorises him to discriminate); and
4. not act for an ulterior motive.

Note that the duty to treat all beneficiaries impartially gives rise to the issue of apportionment under the **Apportionment Act 1870**. What are known as the rules in (i) *Howe v. Lord Dartmouth* (1802); (ii) *Allhusen v. Whittell* (1867); and (iii) *Re Earl of Chesterfield's Trusts* (1883) are usually expressly excluded from application by the terms of the will. These principles apply to administrative powers. However, in practice the key power, investment, must be exercised solely for the benefit of the beneficiaries, the trustee owing a duty of care and other duties concerning suitability and diversification.

A trustee must form his own judgement and is not bound by the beneficiaries' wishes. An intention to exercise must be apparent. Reference to property subject to a dispositive power is generally sufficient to indicate the intention to exercise the power. Where a trustee has a discretionary power to distribute income, he must decide about distribution within a reasonable time from receipt. When considering an exercise of his discretion, the trustee should think through the potential consequences of his decision. If he does not do so, then the action he takes may be set aside. A trustee is not obliged to give reasons for the exercise of his discretion. However, these may be discoverable in the course of litigation. Note that in *Re Londonderry's Will* (1965), Lord Justice Harman stated that, '*...if trustees do give reasons, their soundness can be considered by the court.*'

Vesting and class closing

A trustee must ensure that any legacy is paid over:

1. at the right time;
2. in the correct shares; and
3. to the proper person(s).

He is obliged to satisfy himself that:

1. he has correctly identified the beneficiary (or class) who can benefit, and of the nature of each beneficiary's interest in the legacy fund;
2. in the case of a class gift, that the class has closed;
3. the gift has vested because a beneficiary's interest in capital is no

longer dependent upon any uncertainty; and

4.   that any conditions attached to the gift have been fulfilled.

As a general rule a trustee who pays funds to the wrong person is personally liable to make good the loss. Not only must the trustee identify the beneficial class, he must also properly identify the actual individuals to whom funds will be paid over. In a fixed interest trust, the trustee must ensure that every member of the class can be identified by name, and must be able to draw up a list of all members of the class with an interest in capital prior to distribution. If he is in any doubt about the identity of a beneficiary or about their entitlement he should apply to the court for directions. Where the extent of a class is known, but the trustee does not know whether any member of the class is missing he should apply for a Benjamin Order authorising him to distribute to the other beneficiaries on the assumption that the missing beneficiary has died. Note that **s.27 TA** also offers statutory protection, see **Re Aldhous** (1955). To ensure that the correct sum is paid to each beneficiary the trustee must take into account:

1.   *'hotchpot'* (previous advances of capital made to a beneficiary out of his share);
2.   whether it is impossible or inequitable to divide a particular asset into shares; and
3.   retention to pay for future costs and expenses, because a trustee is personally liable for the trust's dealings with third parties.

The date upon which payment must be made (the *'vesting date'*) must also be correctly identified. Early payment may be demanded by a beneficiary under what is known as the rule in **Saunders v Vautier** (1841).

Delegation

If a trustee wrongfully delegates discretion, then: (i) the trustee is liable for all wrongful consequences; and (ii) the exercise of the discretion is void. Under **s.25 TA 1925** (which is the principal source of authority for delegation by an individual), delegation of all or any of the trustee's powers and discretions is permitted. Sub-delegation is not.

Fraud on a power

This occurs where a power is exercised for a purpose or with an intention beyond its scope under the will, or in a manner that is not justified by the will. In **Re Clore's Will Trusts** [1966] it was held, *'it was not open to the trustees to pay away the beneficiary's prospective capital over his head or against his will in discharge of what they consider to be his moral obligations.'* The exercise is void in equity, *Vatcher v Paull* (1915). Three general indicia of fraud on a power can be drawn from *Re Crawshay* (1948):

1. the trustee must have made an appointment intended to benefit someone who is not an object of the power, or for a purpose extraneous to the power;
2. the trustee's motive must exist at the date of the appointment, even if it is later abandoned, or its object can never be carried into effect; and
3. there is no need to establish agreement or even knowledge on the part of the appointee as to the trustee's motive, whatever it might be.

Applications to the Court

When a trustee is '*in genuine doubt about the propriety of any contemplated course of action in the exercise of his fiduciary duties and discretions [he] is always entitled to take proper professional guidance and, if so advised, to protect his position by seeking guidance of the court.*' (per Lord Oliver in *Marley v Mutual Security Merchant Bank* (1991). The orders that the court can make include:

1. giving directions as to whether the power may properly be exercised;
2. if the matter relates to an improper non-exercise of discretion the court may direct the trustee to consider exercising it;
3. if the court believes a past exercise of discretion was tainted, it will declare that the exercise was void from the outset and may then:
   (a) require nothing further of the trustee (where an exercise of discretion has been overturned entirely); or
   (b) require the trustee to consider the discretion anew (or replace the trustee with another who can be relied upon to do so properly);
4. only in rare circumstances will the court exercise the discretion in place of the trustee, such as:
   (a) where the trustee has surrendered his discretion to the court for a proper reason; or
   (b) where the trustee has unreasonably refused to exercise his discretion; and
5. in such cases, the court may (either on the application of a beneficiary, or on its own motion) remove a trustee whom it believes would be unlikely to exercise the discretion honestly and properly in the future.

It is not normally proper for the trustee to propose a variation of trust by applying to the court under the **VOTA 1958**. A trustee should not be an applicant unless satisfied that:

1. the proposals are beneficial to the persons interested;
2. the proposals have a good prospect of being approved by the court;

and
3. that if he (as the trustee) does not make the application, no-one else will, *Re Druce's Will Trusts* (1962).

The Hastings-Bass Principle

The *Hastings-Bass* principle and the equitable jurisdiction in relation to voluntary dispositions made under a mistake was fully examined by the Court of Appeal in the *Pitt* and *Futter* appeals (and note that extracts from the judgment in these appeals appear in **Appendix 7**). The leading speech was given by Lord Justice Lloyd (who had heard *Sieff v Fox* (2005), and elected not to recuse himself from the case). The decision of the court was unanimous. At paragraph 64 the Judge stated the ratio of *Hastings-Bass* in the following terms,

'trustees considering an advancement by way of sub-settlement must apply their minds to the question whether the sub-settlement as a whole will operate for the benefit of the person to be advanced. If one or more aspects of the provisions intended to be created cannot take effect, it does not follow that those which can take effect should not be regarded as having been brought into being by an exercise of the discretion. The fact, and the misapprehension on the part of the trustees as to the effect that it would have, is not by itself fatal to the effectiveness of the advancement…If the provisions that can and would take effect cannot reasonably be regarded as being for the benefit of the person to be advanced, then the exercise fails as not being within the scope of the power of advancement. Otherwise it takes effect to the extent that it can.'

The Judge identified two scenarios in which a purported exercise by trustees of a discretionary power can be set aside applying the *Hastings-Bass* principle. These are where:

1. the purported exercise of a discretionary power on the part of trustees will be void, if what is done is not within the scope of the power; and
2. what is done is within the terms of the power, but the trustees have in some way breached their duties in respect of that exercise, then (unless it is a case of fraud on a power) the trustees' act is not void but it may be voidable at the instance of a beneficiary who is adversely affected.

See paragraphs 102 – 113 for the Judge's comments about the relevant duties of trustees to:

1. exercise such skill and care as is reasonable in the circumstances;
2. weigh benefits and take into account relevant factors when exercising a discretionary power; and
3. consider fiscal consequences.

Appendix 3

1st Edition of the STEP Standard[1] Provisions

Standard Provisions of the Society of Trust and Estate Practitioners

1. INTRODUCTORY

1*(1)*   These Provisions may be called the standard provisions of the Society of Trust and Estate Practitioners (1st Edition).

1*(2)*   These Provisions may be incorporated in a document by the words:-

The standard provisions of the Society of Trust and Estate Practitioners (1st Edition) shall apply

or in any manner indicating an intention to incorporate them.

2. INTERPRETATION

2*(1)*   In these Provisions, unless the context otherwise requires:-
  (a) **Income Beneficiary,** in relation to Trust Property, means a Person to whom income of the Trust Property is payable (as of right or at the discretion of the Trustees).
  (b) **Person** includes a person anywhere in the world and includes a Trustee.
  (c) **The Principal Document** means the document in which these Provisions are incorporated.
  (d) **The Settlement** means any settlement created by the Principal Document and an estate of a deceased Person to which the Principal Document relates.
  (e) **The Trustees** means the personal representatives or trustees of the Settlement for the time being.
  (f) **The Trust Fund** means the property comprised in the Settlement for the time being.
  (g) **Trust Property** means any property comprised in the Trust Fund.

---

[1]   Note that a second edition is expected to be published sometime this year, and that James Kessler QC and STEP have granted the author a licence to include the second edition in a further edition of this book.

(h) **A Professional Trustee** means a Trustee who is or has been carrying on a business which consists of or includes the management of trusts or the administration of estates.

2(2)   These Provisions have effect subject to the provisions of the Principal Document.

3. ADMINISTRATIVE POWERS

The Trustees shall have the following powers:

3(1)   *Investment*
   (a) The Trustees may invest Trust Property in any manner as if they were beneficial owners. In particular the Trustees may invest in unsecured loans.
   (b) The Trustees may decide not to diversify the Trust Fund.

3(2)   *Management*
   The Trustees may effect any transaction relating to the management administration or disposition of Trust Property as if they were beneficial owners. In particular:
   (a) The Trustees may repair and maintain Trust Property.
   (b) The Trustees may develop or improve Trust Property.

3(3)   *Joint property*
   The Trustees may acquire property jointly with any Person.

3(4)   *Income and capital*
   The Trustees may decide not to hold a balance between conflicting interests of Persons interested in Trust Property. In particular:
   (a) The Trustees may acquire
      (i) wasting assets and
      (ii) assets which yield little or no income for investment or any other purpose.
   (b) The Trustees may decide not to procure distributions from a company in which they are interested.
   (c) The Trustees may pay taxes and other expenses out of income although they would otherwise be paid out of capital.

3(5)   *Accumulated income*
   The Trustees may apply accumulated income as if it were income arising in the current year.

3(6)   *Use of trust property*
   The Trustees may permit an Income Beneficiary to occupy or enjoy the use of Trust Property on such terms as they think fit. The Trustees may acquire any property for this purpose.

3(7)   *Application of trust capital*

The Trustees may:

    (a) lend money which is Trust Property to an Income Beneficiary without security, on such terms as they think fit,

    (b) charge Trust Property as security for debts or obligations of an Income Beneficiary, or

    (c) pay money which is Trust Property to an Income Beneficiary as his income, for the purpose of augmenting his income

Provided that:

    (i) the Trustees have power to transfer such Property to that Beneficiary absolutely; or

    (ii) the Trustees have power to do so with the consent of another Person and the Trustees act with the written consent of that Person.

3(8)   *Trade*

The Trustees may carry on a trade, in any part of the world, alone or in partnership.

3(9)   *Borrowing*

The Trustees may borrow money for investment or any other purpose. Money borrowed shall be treated as Trust Property.

3(10)   *Insurance*

The Trustees may insure Trust Property for any amount against any risk.

3(11)   *Delegation*

A Trustee may delegate in writing any of his functions to any Person. A Trustee shall not be responsible for the default of that Person (even if the delegation was not strictly necessary or expedient) provided that he took reasonable care in his selection and supervision.

3(12)   *Deposit of documents*

The Trustees may deposit documents relating to the Settlement (including bearer securities) with any Person.

3(13)   *Nominees*

The Trustees may vest Trust Property in any Person as nominee, and may place Trust Property in the possession or control of any Person.

3(14)   *Offshore administration*

The Trustees may carry on the administration of the trusts of the Settlement outside the United Kingdom.

3(15)   *Payment of tax*

The Trustees may pay tax liabilities of the Settlement (and interest on such tax) even though such liabilities are not enforceable against the Trustees.

3(16) *Indemnities*
The Trustees may indemnify any Person for any liability properly chargeable against Trust Property.

3(17) *Security*
The Trustees may charge Trust Property as security for any liability properly incurred by them as Trustees.

3(18) *Supervision of company*
The Trustees are under no duty to enquire into the conduct of a company in which they are interested, unless they have knowledge of circumstances which call for enquiry.

3(19) *Appropriation*
The Trustees may appropriate Trust Property to any Person or class of Persons in or towards the satisfaction of their interest in the Trust Fund.

3(20) *Receipt by charities*
Where Trust Property is to be paid or transferred to a charity, the receipt of the treasurer or appropriate officer of the charity shall be a complete discharge to the Trustees.

3(21) *Release of powers*
The Trustees may by deed release any of their powers wholly or in part so as to bind future trustees.

3(22) *Ancillary powers*
The Trustees may do anything which is incidental or conducive to the exercise of their functions.

4. POWERS OF MAINTENANCE AND ADVANCEMENT

Sections 31 and 32 Trustee Act 1925 shall apply with the following modifications:
(a) The Proviso to section 31(1) shall be deleted.
(b) The words one-half of in section 32(1)(a) shall be deleted.

5. TRUST FOR SALE

The Trustees shall hold land in England and Wales on trust for sale.

6. MINORS

6(1)   Where the Trustees may apply income for the benefit of a minor, they may do so by paying the income to the minor's parent or guardian on behalf of the minor, or to the minor if he has attained the age of 16. The Trustees are under no duty to enquire into the use of the income unless they have knowledge of circumstances which call for enquiry.

6(2)   Where the Trustees may apply income for the benefit of a minor, they may do so by resolving that they hold that income on trust for the minor absolutely and:
   (a) The Trustees may apply that income for the benefit of the minor during his minority.
   (b) The Trustees shall transfer the residue of that income to the minor on attaining the age of 18.
   (c) For investment and other administrative purposes that income shall be treated as Trust Property.

7. DISCLAIMER

A Person may disclaim his interest under the Settlement wholly or in part.

8. APPORTIONMENT

Income and expenditure shall be treated as arising when payable, and not from day to day, so that no apportionment shall take place.

9. CONFLICTS OF INTEREST

9(1)   In this paragraph:
   (a) **A Fiduciary** means a Person subject to fiduciary duties under the Settlement.
   (b) **An Independent Trustee**, in relation to a Person, means a Trustee who is not:
      (i) a brother, sister, ancestor, descendant or dependant of the Person;
      (ii) a spouse of the Person or of (i) above; or
      (iii) a company controlled by one or more of any of the above.

9(2)   A Fiduciary may:
   (a) enter into a transaction with the Trustees, or
   (b) be interested in an arrangement in which the Trustees are or might have been interested, or
   (c) act (or not act) in any other circumstances

even though his fiduciary duty under the Settlement conflicts with other duties or with his personal interest;

Provided that:—
> (i) The Fiduciary first discloses to the Trustees the nature and extent of any material interest conflicting with his fiduciary duties, and
> (ii) there is an Independent Trustee in respect of whom there is no conflict of interest, and he considers that the transaction arrangement or action is not contrary to the general interest of the Settlement.

9(3)   The powers of the Trustees may be used to benefit a Trustee (to the same extent as if he were not a Trustee) provided that there is an Independent Trustee in respect of whom there is no conflict of interest.

10. POWERS OF TRUSTEES

The powers of the Trustees may be exercised:
> (a) at their absolute discretion; and
> (b) from time to time as occasion requires.

11. TRUSTEE REMUNERATION

11(1)   A Trustee who is a solicitor or an accountant or who is engaged in a business may charge for work done by him or his firm in connection with the Settlement, including work not requiring professional assistance. This has priority to any disposition made in the Principal Document.

11(2)   The Trustees may make arrangements to remunerate themselves for work done for a company connected with the Trust Fund.

12. LIABILITY OF TRUSTEES

12(1)   A Trustee (other than a Professional Trustee) shall not be liable for a loss to the Trust Fund unless that loss was caused by his own fraud or negligence.

12(2)   A Trustee shall not be liable for acting in accordance with the advice of Counsel of at least five years standing, with respect to the Settlement, unless, when he does so:—
> (a) he knows or has reasonable cause to suspect that the advice was given in ignorance of material facts; or
> (b) proceedings are pending to obtain the decision of the court on the matter.

13. APPOINTMENT AND RETIREMENT OF TRUSTEES

13(1)   A Person may be appointed trustee of the Settlement even though he has no connection with the United Kingdom.

13(2)   A Professional Trustee who is an individual who has reached the age of 65 shall retire if:—
   (a) he is requested to do so by his co-trustees, or by a Person interested in Trust Property; and
   (b) he is effectually indemnified against liabilities properly incurred as Trustee.

On that retirement a new Trustee shall be appointed if necessary to ensure that there will be two individuals or a Trust Corporation to act as Trustee.

In this sub-paragraph Trust Corporation has the same meaning as in the Trustee Act 1925.

This sub-paragraph does not apply to a Professional Trustee who is:
   (a) a personal representative
   (b) the settlor of the Settlement or
   (c) a spouse or former spouse of the settlor or testator.

14. PROTECTION FOR LIFE INTEREST AND ACCUMULATION AND MAINTENANCE SETTLEMENTS

These Provisions shall not have effect:
   (a) so as to prevent a Person from being entitled to an interest in possession in Trust Property (within the meaning of the Inheritance Tax Act 1984);
   (b) so as to cause the Settlement to be an accumulation or discretionary settlement (within the meaning of section 5 Taxation of Chargeable Gains Act 1992);
   (c) so as to prevent the conditions of section 71(1) Inheritance Tax Act 1984 from applying to Trust Property.

Appendix 4
Table of Statutes

AEA 1925	Administration of Estates Act 1925
FA	Finance Act
Inheritance Act	Inheritance (Provision for Family and Dependants) Act 1975
ICTA 1988	Income and Corporation Taxes Act 1988
IHTA 1984	Inheritance Tax Act 1984
ITA 2007	Income Tax Act 2007
ITTOIA 2005	Income Tax (Trading and Other Income) Act 2005
LPA 1925	Law of Property Act 1925
LP(MP)A 1989	Law of Property (Miscellaneous Provisions) Act 1989
TA 1925	Trustee Act 1925
TA 2000	Trustee Act 2000
TCGA 1992	Taxation of Chargeable Gains Act 1992
TLATA 1996	Trusts of Land and Appointment of Trustees Act 1996
VOTA 1958	Variation of Trusts Act 1958
WA 1837	Wills Act 1837

Appendix 5

Statutory Extracts

- **FINANCE ACT 1986**
s.102   Gifts with reservation
s.102ZA Gifts with reservation: termination of interests in possession
s.102A Gifts with reservation: interest in land
s.102B Gifts with reservation: share of interest in land
s.102C Sections 102A and 102B: supplemental
s.103   Treatment of certain debts and incumbrances
s.104   Regulations for avoiding double charges etc

- **IHTA 1984**
s.2   Chargeable transfers and exempt transfers
s.3   Transfers of value
s.3A   Potentially exempt transfers
s.4   Transfers on death
s.5   Meaning of estate
s.8A   Transfer of unused nil-rate band between spouses and civil partners
s.8B   Claims under section 8A
s.8C   Section 8A and subsequent charges
s.18   Transfers between spouses [or civil partners]
s.49   Treatment of interests in possession
s.49A Immediate post-death interest
s.51   Disposal of interest in possession
s.52   Charge on termination of interest in possession
s.53   Exceptions from charge under section 52
s.54   Exceptions from charge on death
s.54A Special rate of charge where settled property affected by potentially exempt transfer
s.54B Provisions supplementary to section 54A
s.55   Reversionary interest acquired by beneficiary
s.71A Trusts for bereaved minors
s.71B Charge to tax on property to which Section 71A applies
s.71C Sections 71A and 71B: meaning of 'bereaved minor'
s.71D Age 18-to-25 trusts
s.71E Charge to tax on property to which Section 71D applies
s.71F Calculation of tax charged under Section 71E in certain cases
s.71G Calculation of tax charged under Section 71E in all other cases
s.71H Sections 71A to 71G: meaning of 'parent'

s.92   Survivorship clauses
s.142   Alteration of dispositions taking effect on death
s.143   Compliance with testator's request
s.144   Distribution etc from property settled by will
s.145   Redemption of surviving spouse's [or civil partner's] life interest
s.160   Market value
s.161   Related property
s.162   Liabilities
s.199   Dispositions by transferor
s.200   Transfer on death
s.267   Persons treated as domiciled in United Kingdom
s.268   Associated operations

FINANCE ACT 1986

102. Gifts with reservation

(1) Subject to subsections (5) and (6) below, this section applies where, on or after 18th March 1986, an individual disposes of any property by way of gift and either—

    (a) possession and enjoyment of the property is not bona fide assumed by the donee at or before the beginning of the relevant period; or

    (b) at any time in the relevant period the property is not enjoyed to the entire exclusion, or virtually to the entire exclusion, of the donor and of any benefit to him by contract or otherwise;

and in this section 'the relevant period' means a period ending on the date of the donor's death and beginning seven years before that date or, if it is later, on the date of the gift.

(2) If and so long as—

    (a) possession and enjoyment of any property is not bona fide assumed as mentioned in subsection (1)(a) above, or

    (b) any property is not enjoyed as mentioned in subsection (1)(b) above,

the property is referred to (in relation to the gift and the donor) as property subject to a reservation.

(3) If, immediately before the death of the donor, there is any property which, in relation to him, is property subject to a reservation then, to the extent that the property would not, apart from this section, form part of the donor's estate immediately before his death, that property shall be treated for the purposes of the 1984 Act as property to which he was beneficially entitled immediately before his death.

(4) If, at a time before the end of the relevant period, any property ceases to be property subject to a reservation, the donor shall be treated for the purposes of the 1984 Act as having at that time made a disposition of the property by a disposition which is a potentially exempt transfer.

(5) This section does not apply if or, as the case may be, to the extent that the disposal

of the property by way of gift is an exempt transfer by virtue of any of the following provisions of Part II of the 1984 Act,–

(a) section 18 (transfers between spouses) [or civil partners]) [, except as provided by subsections (5A) and (5B) below];

(b) section 20 (small gifts);

(c) section 22 (gifts in consideration of marriage) [or civil partnership];

(d) section 23 (gifts to charities);

(e) section 24 (gifts to political parties);

[(ee) section 24A (gifts to housing associations);]

(f) section 25 (gifts for national purposes, etc);

(g) [   ];

(h) section 27 (maintenance funds for historic buildings); and

(i) section 28 (employee trusts).

[(5A) Subsection (5)(a) above does not prevent this section from applying if or, as the case may be, to the extent that–

(a) the property becomes settled property by virtue of the gift,

(b) by reason of the donor's spouse [or civil partner] ('the relevant beneficiary') becoming beneficially entitled to an interest in possession in the settled property, the disposal is or, as the case may be, is to any extent an exempt transfer by virtue of section 18 of the 1984 Act in consequence of the operation of section 49 of that Act (treatment of interests in possession),

(c) at some time after the disposal, but before the death of the donor, the relevant beneficiary's interest in possession comes to an end, and

(d) on the occasion on which that interest comes to an end, the relevant beneficiary does not become beneficially entitled to the settled property   or to another interest in possession in the settled property.)

[(5B) If or, as the case may be, to the extent that this section applies by virtue of subsection (5A) above, it has effect as if the disposal by way of gift had been made immediately after the relevant beneficiary's interest in possession came to an end.]

[(5C) For the purposes of subsections (5A) and (5B) above–

(a) section 51(1)(b) of the 1984 Act (disposal of interest in possession treated as coming to end of interest) applies as it applies for the purposes of Chapter 2 of Part 3 of that Act; and

(b) references to any property or to an interest in any property include references to part of any property or interest.]

(6) This section does not apply if the disposal of property by way of gift is made under the terms of a policy issued in respect of an insurance made before 18th March 1986 unless the policy is varied on or after that date so as to increase the benefits secured or to extend the term of the insurance; and, for this purpose, any change in the terms of the policy which is made in pursuance of an option or other power conferred by the policy shall be deemed to be a variation of the policy.

(7) If a policy issued as mentioned in subsection (6) above confers an option or other power under which benefits and premiums may be increased to take account of

increases in the retail price index (as defined in section 8(3) of the 1984 Act) or any similar index specified in the policy, then, to the extent that the right to exercise that option or power would have been lost if it had not been exercised on or before 1st August 1986, the exercise of that option or power before that date shall be disregarded for the purposes of subsection (6) above.

(8) Schedule 20 to this Act has effect for supplementing this section.

[102ZA Gifts with reservation: termination of interests in possession

(1) Subsection (2) below applies where–
   (a) an individual is beneficially entitled to an interest in possession in settled property,
   (b) either–
      (i) the individual became beneficially entitled to the interest in possession before 22nd March 2006, or
      (ii) the individual became beneficially entitled to the interest in p o s s e s s i o n on or after 22nd March 2006 and the interest is an immediate post-death interest, a disabled person's interest or a transitional serial interest,[or falls within section 5(1B) of the 1984 Act], and
   (c) the interest in possession comes to an end during the individual's life.
(2) For the purposes of–
   (a) section 102 above, and
   (b) Schedule 20 to this Act,
   the individual shall be taken (if, or so far as, he would not otherwise be) to dispose, on the coming to an end of the interest in possession, of the no-longer-possessed property by way of gift.
(3) In subsection (2) above 'the no-longer-possessed property' means the property in which the interest in possession subsisted immediately before it came to an end, other than any of it to which the individual becomes absolutely and beneficially entitled in possession on the coming to an end of the interest in possession.]

[102A Gifts with reservation: interest in land

[(1) This section applies where an individual disposes of an interest in land by way of gift on or after 9th March 1999.
(2) At any time in the relevant period when the donor or his spouse [or civil partner] enjoys a significant right or interest, or is party to a significant arrangement, in relation to the land–
   (a) the interest disposed of is referred to (in relation to the gift and the donor) as property subject to a reservation; and
   (b) section 102(3) and (4) above shall apply.
(3) Subject to subsections (4) and (5) below, a right, interest or arrangement in relation to land is significant for the purposes of subsection (2) above if (and only if) it entitles or enables the donor to occupy all or part of the land, or to enjoy some right in relation to all or part of the land, otherwise than for full consideration in money or money's worth.

(4) A right, interest or arrangement is not significant for the purposes of subsection (2) above if–
   (a) it does not and cannot prevent the enjoyment of the land to the entire exclusion, or virtually to the entire exclusion, of the donor; or
   (b) it does not entitle or enable the donor to occupy all or part of the land immediately after the disposal, but would do so were it not for the interest disposed of.
(5) A right or interest is not significant for the purposes of subsection (2) above if it was granted or acquired before the period of seven years ending with the date of the gift.
(6) Where an individual disposes of more than one interest in land by way of gift, whether or not at the same time or to the same donee, this section shall apply separately in relation to each interest.]

[102B Gifts with reservation: share of interest in land
[(1) This section applies where an individual disposes, by way of gift on or after 9th March 1999, of an undivided share of an interest in land.
(2) At any time in the relevant period, except when subsection (3) or (4) below applies–
   (a) the share disposed of is referred to (in relation to the gift and the donor) as property subject to a reservation; and
   (b) section 102(3) and (4) above shall apply.
(3) This subsection applies when the donor–
   (a) does not occupy the land; or
   (b) occupies the land to the exclusion of the donee for full consideration in money or money's worth.
(4) This subsection applies when–
   (a) the donor and the donee occupy the land; and
   (b) the donor does not receive any benefit, other than a negligible one, which is provided by or at the expense of the donee for some reason connected with the gift.]

102C Sections 102A and 102B: supplemental
[(1) In sections 102A and 102B above 'the relevant period' has the same meaning as in section 102 above.
(2) An interest or share disposed of is not property subject to a reservation under section 102A(2) or 102B(2) above if or, as the case may be, to the extent that the disposal is an exempt transfer by virtue of any of the provisions listed in section 102(5) above.
(3) In applying sections 102A and 102B above no account shall be taken of–
   (a) occupation of land by a donor, or
   (b) an arrangement which enables land to be occupied by a donor,
   in circumstances where the occupation, or occupation pursuant to the arrangement, would be disregarded in accordance with paragraph 6(1)(b) of Schedule 20 to this Act.
(4) The provisions of Schedule 20 to this Act, apart from paragraph 6, shall have effect for the purposes of sections 102A and 102B above as they have effect for the

purposes of section 102 above; and any question which falls to be answered under section 102A or 102B above in relation to an interest in land shall be determined by reference to the interest which is at that time treated as property comprised in the gift.

(5) …

(6) …

(7) Section 102A above shall not apply to a case to which section 102 above applies.]

103. Treatment of certain debts and incumbrances

(1) Subject to subsection (2) below, if, in determining the value of a person's estate immediately before his death, account would be taken, apart from this subsection, of a liability consisting of a debt incurred by him or an incumbrance created by a disposition made by him, that liability shall be subject to abatement to an extent proportionate to the value of any of the consideration given for the debt or incumbrance which consisted of–

   (a) property derived from the deceased; or

   (b) consideration (not being property derived from the deceased) given by any person who was at the time entitled to, or amongst whose resources there was at any time included, any property derived from the deceased.

(2) If, in the case where the whole or part of the consideration given for a debt or incumbrance consisted of such consideration as is mentioned in subsection (1)(b) above, it is shown that the value of the consideration given, or of that part thereof, as the case may be, exceeded that which could have been rendered available by application of all the property derived from the deceased, other than such (if any) of that property–

   (a) as is included in the consideration given, or

   (b) as to which it is shown that the disposition of which it, or the property which it represented, was the subject matter was not made with   reference to, or with a view to enabling or facilitating, the giving of the consideration or the recoupment in any manner of the cost thereof,

   no abatement shall be made under subsection (1) above in respect of the excess.

(3) In subsections (1) and (2) above 'property derived from the deceased' means, subject to subsection (4) below, any property which was the subject matter of a disposition made by the deceased, either by himself alone or in concert or by arrangement with any other person or which represented any of the subject matter of such a disposition, whether directly or indirectly, and whether by virtue of one or more intermediate dispositions.

(4) If the disposition first-mentioned in subsection (3) above was not a transfer of value and it is shown that the disposition was not part of associated operations which included–

   (a) a disposition by the deceased, either alone or in concert or by arrangement with any other person, otherwise than for full consideration in money or money's worth paid to the deceased for his own use or benefit; or

   (b) a disposition by any other person operating to reduce the value of the property of the deceased,

that first-mentioned disposition shall be left out of account for the purposes of subsections (1) to (3) above.

(5) If, before a person's death but on or after 18th March 1986, money or money's worth is paid or applied by him—

(a) in or towards the satisfaction or discharge of a debt or incumbrance in the case of which subsection (1) above would have effect on his death if the debt or incumbrance had not been satisfied or discharged, or

(b) in reduction of debt or incumbrance in the case of which that subsection has effect on his death,

the 1984 Act shall have effect as if, at the time of the payment or application, the person concerned had made a transfer of value equal to the money or money's worth and that transfer were a potentially exempt transfer.

(6) Any reference in this section to a debt incurred is a reference to a debt incurred on or after 18th March 1986 and any reference to an incumbrance created by a disposition is a reference to an incumbrance created by an disposition made on or after that date; and in this section 'subject matter' includes, in relation to any disposition, any annual or periodical payment made or payable under or by virtue of the disposition.

(7) In determining the value of a person's estate immediately before his death, no account shall be taken (by virtue of section 5 of the 1984 Act) of any liability arising under or in connection with a policy of life insurance issued in respect of an insurance made on or after 1st July 1986 unless the whole of the sums assured under that policy form part of that person's estate immediately before his death.

104. Regulations for avoiding double charges etc

(1) For the purposes of the 1984 Act the Board may by regulations make such provision as is mentioned in subsection (2) below with respect to transfers of value made, and other events occurring, on or after 18th March 1986 where—

(a) a potentially exempt transfer proves to be a chargeable transfer and, immediately before the death of the transferor, his estate includes property acquired by him from the transferee otherwise than for full consideration in money or money's worth;

(b) an individual disposes of property by a transfer of value which is or proves to be a chargeable transfer and the circumstances are such that subsection (3) or subsection (4) of section 102 above applies to the property as being or having been property subject to a reservation;

(c) in determining the value of a person's estate immediately before his death, a liability of his to any person is abated as mentioned in section 103 above and, before his death, the deceased made a transfer of value by virtue of which the estate of that other person was increased or by virtue of which property becomes comprised in a settlement of which that other person is a trustee; or

(d) the circumstances are such as may be specified in the regulations for the purposes of this subsection, being circumstances appearing to the Board to be similar to those referred to in paragraphs (a) to (c) above.

(2) The provision which may be made by regulations under this section is provision for either or both of the following,–

(a) treating the value transferred by a transfer of value as reduced by reference to the value transferred by another transfer of value ; and

(b) treating the whole or any part of the tax paid or payable on the value transferred by a transfer of value as a credit against the tax payable on the value transferred by another transfer of value.

(3) The power to make regulations under this section shall be exercisable by statutory instrument subject to annulment in pursuance of a resolution of the Commons House of Parliament.

IHTA 1984

2.   Chargeable transfers and exempt transfers

(1) A chargeable transfer is a transfer of value which is made by an individual but is not (by virtue of Part II of this Act or any other enactment) an exempt transfer.

(2) A transfer of value made by an individual and exempt only to a limited extent–

(a) is, if all the value transferred by it is within the limit, an exempt transfer, and

(b) is, if that value is partly within and partly outside the limit, a chargeable transfer of so much of that value as is outside the limit as well as an exempt transfer of so much of that value as is within the limit.

(3) Except where the context otherwise requires, references in this Act to chargeable transfers, to their making or to the values transferred by them shall be construed as including references to occasions on which tax is chargeable under Chapter III of Part III of this Act (apart from section 79), to their occurrence or to the amounts on which tax is then chargeable.

3.   Transfers of value

(1) Subject to the following provisions of this Part of this Act, a transfer of value is a disposition made by a person (the transferor) as a result of which the value of his estate immediately after the disposition is less than it would be but for the disposition; and the amount by which it is less is the value transferred by the transfer.

(2) For the purposes of subsection (1) above no account shall be taken of the value of excluded property which ceases to form part of a person's estate as a result of a disposition.

(3) [Where the value of a person's estate is diminished, and the value–

(a) of another person's estate, or

(b) of any settled property, other than settled property treated by section 49(1) below as property to which a person is beneficially entitled,

is increased] by the first-mentioned person's omission to exercise a right, he shall be treated for the purposes of this section as having made a disposition at the time (or latest time) when he could have exercised the right, unless it is shown that the omission was not deliberate.

(4) Except as otherwise provided, references in this Act to a transfer of value made, or made by any person, include references to events on the happening of which tax is chargeable as if a transfer of value had been made, or, as the case may be, had been made by that person; and 'transferor' shall be construed accordingly.

[3A.   Potentially exempt transfers

(1) Any reference in this Act to a potentially exempt transfer is a reference to a transfer of value–
  (a) which is made by an individual on or after 18th March 1986 [but before 22nd March 2006]; and
  (b) which, apart from this section, would be a chargeable transfer (or to the extent to which, apart from this section, it would be such a transfer); and
  (c) to the extent that it constitutes either a gift to another individual or a gift into an accumulation and maintenance trust or a disabled trust; . . .

[(1A) Any reference in this Act to a potentially exempt transfer is also a reference to a transfer of value–
  (a) which is made by an individual on or after 22nd March 2006,
  (b) which, apart from this section, would be a chargeable transfer (or to the extent to which, apart from this section, it would be such a transfer), and
  (c) to the extent that it constitutes–
    (i) a gift to another individual,
    (ii) a gift into a disabled trust, or
    (iii) a gift into a bereaved minor's trust on the coming to an end of an immediate post-death interest.]

[(1B) Subsections (1) and (1A) above have effect subject to any provision of this Act which provides that a disposition (or transfer of value) of a particular description is not a potentially exempt transfer.]

(2) Subject to subsection (6) below, a transfer of value falls within subsection (1)(c)[or (1A)(c)(i)] above, as a gift to another individual,–
  (a) to the extent that the value transferred is attributable to property which, by virtue of the transfer, becomes comprised in the estate of that other individual, . . . or
  (b) so far as that value is not attributable to property which becomes comprised in the estate of another person, to the extent that, by virtue of the transfer, the estate of that other individual is increased, . . .

(3) Subject to subsection (6) below, a transfer of value falls within subsection (1)(c) above, as a gift into an accumulation and maintenance trust or a disabled trust, to the extent that the value transferred is attributable to property which, by virtue of the transfer, becomes settled property to which section 71 or 89 of this Act applies.

[(3A) Subject to subsection (6) below, a transfer of value falls within subsection (1A)(c) (ii) above to the extent that the value transferred is attributable to property which, by virtue of the transfer, becomes settled property to which section 89 below applies.]

[(3B) A transfer of value falls within subsection (1A)(c)(iii) above to the extent that the value transferred is attributable to settled property (whenever settled) that becomes property to which section 71A below applies in the following circumstances–

(a) under the settlement, a person ('L') is beneficially entitled to an interest in possession in the settled property,

(b) the interest in possession is an immediate post-death interest,

(c) on or after 22nd March 2006, but during L's life, the interest in possession comes to an end,

(d) L is beneficially entitled to the interest in possession immediately before it comes to an end, and

(e) on the interest in possession coming to an end, the property–

    (i) continues to be held on the trusts of the settlement, and

    (ii) becomes property to which section 71A below applies.]

(4) A potentially exempt transfer which is made seven years or more before the death of the transferor is an exempt transfer and any other potentially exempt transfer is a chargeable transfer.

(5) During the period beginning on the date of a potentially exempt transfer and ending immediately before–

(a) the seventh anniversary of that date, or

(b) if it is earlier, the death of the transferor,

it shall be assumed for the purposes of this Act that the transfer will prove to be an exempt transfer.

(6) Where, under any provision of this Act [other than section 52] tax is in any circumstances to be charged as if a transfer of value had been made, that transfer shall be taken to be a transfer which is not a potentially exempt transfer.]

[(6A) The reference in subsection (6) above to any provision of this Act does not include section 52 below except where the transfer of value treated as made by that section is one treated as made on the coming to an end of an interest which falls within section 5(1B) below.]

[(7) In the application of this section to an event on the happening of which tax is chargeable under section 52 below, the reference in subsection (1)(a) [or (1A)(a)] above to the individual by whom the transfer of value is made is a reference to the person who, by virtue of section 3(4) above, is treated as the transferor.]

4.   Transfers on death

(1) On the death of any person tax shall be charged as if, immediately before his death, he had made a transfer of value and the value transferred by it had been equal to the value of his estate immediately before his death.

(2) For the purposes of this section, where it cannot be known which of two or more persons who have died survived the other or others they shall be assumed to have died at the same instant.

5.   Meaning of estate

(1) For the purposes of this Act a person's estate is the aggregate of all the property to which he is beneficially entitled, [except that–

(a) the estate of a person–

(i) does not include an interest in possession in settled property to which section 71A or 71D below applies, and

(ii) does not include an interest in possession that falls within subsection (1A) below [unless it falls within subsection (1B) below], and

(b) the estate of a person immediately before his death does not include excluded property [or a foreign-owned work of art which is situated in the United Kingdom for one or more of the purposes of public display,cleaning and restoration (and for no other purpose)]...

[(1A) An interest in possession falls within this subsection if–

(a) it is an interest in possession in settled property,

(b) the settled property is not property to which section 71A or 71D below applies,

(c)the person is beneficially entitled to the interest in possession,

(d) the person became beneficially entitled to the interest in possession on or after 22nd March 2006, and

(e) the interest in possession is–

(i) not an immediate post-death interest,

(ii) not a disabled person's interest, and

(iii) not a transitional serial interest.]

[(1B) An interest in possession falls within this subsection if the person –

(a) was domiciled in the United Kingdom on becoming beneficially entitled to it, and

(b) became beneficially entitled to it by virtue of a disposition which was prevented from being a transfer of value by section 10 below.]

(2) A person who has a general power which enables him, or would if he were sui juris enable him, to dispose of any property other than settled property, or to charge money on any property other than settled property, shall be treated as beneficially entitled to the property or money; and for this purpose 'general power' means a power or authority enabling the person by whom it is exercisable to appoint or dispose of property as he thinks fit.

(3) In determining the value of a person's estate at any time his liabilities at that time shall be taken into account, except as otherwise provided by this Act.

(4) The liabilities to be taken into account in determining the value of a transferor's estate immediately after a transfer of value include his liability for capital transfer tax on the value transferred but not his liability (if any) for any other tax or duty resulting from the transfer.

(5) Except in the case of a liability imposed by law, a liability incurred by a transferor shall be taken into account only to the extent that it was incurred for a consideration in money or money's worth.

[8A Transfer of unused nil-rate band between spouses and civil partners

(1) This section applies where–

(a) immediately before the death of a person (a 'deceased person'),the deceased person had a spouse or civil partner ('the survivor'), and

(b) the deceased person had unused nil-rate band on death.

(2) A person has unused nil-rate band on death if–

$$M > VT$$

where–

M is the maximum amount that could be transferred by a chargeable transfer made (under section 4 above) on the person's death if it were to be wholly chargeable to tax at the rate of nil per cent (assuming, if necessary, that the value of the person's estate were sufficient but otherwise having regard to the circumstances of the person); and

VT is the value actually transferred by the chargeable transfer so made (or nil if no chargeable transfer is so made).

(3) Where a claim is made under this section, the nil-rate band maximum at the time of the survivor's death is to be treated for the purposes of the charge to tax on the death of the survivor as increased by the percentage specified in subsection (4) below (but subject to subsection (5) and section 8C below).

(4) That percentage is–

$$\frac{E}{NRBMD} \times 100$$

where–

E is the amount by which M is greater than VT in the case of the deceased person; and NRBMD is the nil-rate band maximum at the time of the deceased person's death.

(5) If (apart from this subsection) the amount of the increase in the nil-rate band maximum at the time of the survivor's death effected by this section would exceed the amount of that nil-rate band maximum, the amount of the increase is limited to the amount of that nil-rate band maximum.

(6) Subsection (5) above may apply either–

    (a) because the percentage mentioned in subsection (4) above as reduced under section 8C below where that section applies) is more than 100 because of the amount by which M is greater than VT in the case of one deceased person, or

    (b) because this section applies in relation to the survivor by reference to the death of more than one person who had unused nil-rate band on death.

(7) In this Act 'nil-rate band maximum' means the amount shown in the second column in the first row of the Table in Schedule 1 to this Act (upper limit of portion of value charged at rate of nil per cent) and in the first column in the second row of that Table (lower limit of portion charged at next rate).]

[8B Claims under section 8A

(1) A claim under section 8A above may be made–

    (a) by the personal representatives of the survivor within the permitted period, or

    (b) (if no claim is so made) by any other person liable to the tax chargeable on the survivor's death within such later period as an officer of Revenue and Customs may in the particular case allow.

(2) If no claim under section 8A above has been made in relation to a person (P) by reference to whose death that section applies in relation to the survivor, the claim under that section in relation to the survivor may include a claim under that section in relation to P if that does not affect the tax chargeable on the value transferred by the chargeable transfer of value made on P's death.

(3) In subsection (1) (a) above 'the permitted period' means–

   (a) the period of two years from the end of the month in which the survivor dies or (if it ends later) the period of three months beginning with the date on which the personal representatives first act as such, or

   (b) such longer period as an officer of Revenue and Customs may in the particular case allow.

(4) A claim made within either of the periods mentioned in subsection (3)(a) above may be withdrawn no later than one month after the end of the period concerned.]

[8C Section 8A and subsequent charges

(1) This section applies where–

   (a) the conditions in subsection (I) (a) and (b) of section 8A above are met, and

   (b) after the death of the deceased person, tax is charged on an amount under any of sections 32, 32A and 126 below by reference to the rate or rates that would have been applicable to the amount if it were included in the value transferred by the chargeable transfer made (under section 4 above) on the deceased person's death.

(2) If the tax is charged before the death of the survivor, the percentage referred to in subsection (3) of section 8A above is (instead of that specified in subsection (4) of that section) –

$$\left(\frac{E}{NRBMD} - \frac{TA}{NRBME} \right) \times 100$$

where –

E and NRBMD have the same meaning as in subsection (4) of that section; TA is the amount on which tax is charged; and

NRBME is the nil-rate band maximum at the time of the event occasioning the charge.

(3) If this section has applied by reason of a previous event or events, the reference in subsection (2) to the fraction

$$\frac{TA}{NRBME}$$

is to the aggregate of that fraction in respect of the current event and the previous event (or each of the previous events).

(4) If the tax is charged after the death of the survivor, it is charged as if the personal nil-rate band maximum of the deceased person were appropriately reduced.

(5) In subsection (4) above–

'the personal nil-rate band maximum of the deceased person' is the nil rate band maximum which is treated by Schedule 2 to this Act as applying in relation to the deceased person's death, increased in accordance with section 8A above where that section effected an increase in that nil-rate band maximum in the case of the deceased person (as survivor of another deceased person), and

'appropriately reduced' means reduced by the amount (if any) by which the amount on which tax was charged at the rate of nil per cent on the death of the survivor was increased by reason of the operation of section 8A above by virtue of the position of the deceased person.]

18.   Transfers between spouses [or civil partners]

(1) A transfer of value is an exempt transfer to the extent that the value transferred is attributable to property which becomes comprised in the estate of the transferor's spouse [or civil partner] or, so far as the value transferred is not so attributable, to the extent that that estate is increased.

(2) If, immediately before the transfer, the transferor but not the transferor's spouse [or civil partner] is domiciled in the United Kingdom the value in respect of which the transfer is exempt (calculated as a value on which no tax is chargeable) shall not exceed £55,000 less any amount previously taken into account for the purposes of the exemption conferred by this section.

(3) Subsection (1) above shall not apply in relation to property if the testamentary or other disposition by which it is given–

   (a) takes effect on the termination after the transfer of value of any interest or period, or

   (b) depends on a condition which is not satisfied within twelve months after the transfer;

   but paragraph (a) above shall not have effect by reason only that the property is given to a spouse [or civil partner] only if he survives the other spouse [or civil partner] for a specified period.

(4) For the purposes of this section, property is given to a person if it becomes his property or is held on trust for him.

49.   Treatment of interests in possession

(1) A person beneficially entitled to an interest in possession in settled property shall be treated for the purposes of this Act as beneficially entitled to the property in which the interest subsists.

[(1A) Where the interest in possession mentioned in subsection (1) above is one to which the person becomes beneficially entitled on or after 22nd March 2006, subsection (1) above applies in relation to that interest only if, and for so long as, it is–

   (a) an immediate post-death interest,

   (b) a disabled person's interest, or

   (c) a transitional serial interest.]

   [or falls within section 5(1B) above].

[(1B) Where the interest in possession mentioned in subsection (1) above is one to which the person became beneficially entitled before 22nd March, subsection (1) above does not apply in relation to that interest at any time when section 71A below applies to the property in which the interest subsists.]

(2) Where a person becomes entitled to an interest in possession in settled property as a result of a disposition for a consideration in money or money's worth, any question whether and to what extent the giving of the consideration is a transfer of value or chargeable transfer shall be determined without regard to subsection (1) above.

[49A. Immediate post-death interest

(1) Where a person ('L') is beneficially entitled to an interest in possession in settled property, for the purposes of this Chapter that interest is an 'immediate post-death interest' only if the following conditions are satisfied.

(2) Condition 1 is that the settlement was effected by will or under the law relating to intestacy.

(3) Condition 2 is that L became beneficially entitled to the interest in possession on the death of the testator or intestate.

(4) Condition 3 is that–

    (a) section 71A below does not apply to the property in which the interest subsists, and

    (b) the interest is not a disabled person's interest.

(5) Condition 4 is that Condition 3 has been satisfied at all times since L became beneficially entitled to the interest in possession.]

51.   Disposal of interest in possession

(1) Where a person beneficially entitled to an interest in possession in settled property disposes of his interest the disposal–

    (a) is not a transfer of value, but

    (b) shall be treated for the purposes of this Chapter as the coming to an end of his interest;

and tax shall be charged accordingly under section 52 below.

[(1A) Where the interest disposed of is one to which the person became beneficially entitled on or after 22nd March 2006, subsection (1) above applies in relation to the disposal only if the interest is–

    (a) an immediate post-death interest,

    (b) a disabled person's interest within section 89B(1)(c) or (d) below, or

    (c) a transitional serial interest]

    [or falls within section 5(1B) above].

(1B) Where the interest disposed of is one to which the person became beneficially entitled before 22nd March 2006, subsection (1) above does not apply in relation to the disposal if, immediately before the disposal, section 71A or 71D below applies to the property in which the interest subsists.]

(2) Where a disposition satisfying the conditions of section 11 above is a disposal of an interest in possession in settled property, the interest shall not by virtue of subsection (1) above be treated as coming to an end.

(3) References in this section to any property or to an interest in any property include references to part of any property or interest.

52.   Charge on termination of interest in possession

(1) Where at any time during the life of a person beneficially entitled to an interest in possession in settled property his interest comes to an end, tax shall be charged, subject to section 53 below, as if at that time he had made a transfer of value and the value transferred had been equal to the value of the property in which his interest subsisted.

(2) If the interest comes to an end by being disposed of by the person beneficially entitled to it and the disposal is for a consideration in money or money's worth, tax shall be chargeable under this section as if the value of the property in which the interest subsisted were reduced by the amount of the consideration; but in determining that amount the value of a reversionary interest in the property or of any interest in other property comprised in the same settlement shall be left out of account.

[(2A) Where the interest mentioned in subsection (1) or (2) above is one to which the person became beneficially entitled on or after 22nd March 2006, that subsection applies in relation to the coming to an end of the interest only if the interest is–

(a) an immediate post-death interest,

(b) a disabled person's interest, or

(c)a transitional serial interest]

[or falls within section 5(1B) above].

(3) Where a transaction is made between the trustees of the settlement and a person who is, or is connected with,–

(a) the person beneficially entitled to an interest in the property, or

(b) a person beneficially entitled to any other interest in that property or to any interest in any other property comprised in the settlement, or

(c)a person for whose benefit any of the settled property may be applied,

and, as a result of the transaction, the value of the first-mentioned property is less than it would be but for the transaction, a corresponding part of the interest shall be deemed for the purposes of this section to come to an end, unless the transaction is such that, were the trustees beneficially entitled to the settled property, it would not be a transfer of value.

[(3A) Where the interest mentioned in paragraph (a) of subsection (3) above is one to which the person mentioned in that paragraph became beneficially entitled on or after 22nd March 2006, that subsection applies in relation to the transaction only if the interest is–

(a) an immediate post-death interest,

(b) a disabled person's interest, or

(c)a transitional serial interest.]

[or falls within section 5(1B) above].

(4) References in this section or section 53 below to any property or to an interest in any property include references to part of any property or interest; and–

(a) the tax chargeable under this section on the coming to an end of part of an interest shall be charged as if the value of the property (or part) in which the interest subsisted were a corresponding part of the whole; and

(b) if the value of the property (or part) to which or to an interest in which a person becomes entitled as mentioned in subsection (2) of section 53 below is less than the value on which tax would be chargeable apart from that subsection, tax shall be chargeable on a value equal to the difference.

53.   Exceptions from charge under section 52

(1) Tax shall not be chargeable under section 52 above if the settled property is excluded property.

[(1A)Tax shall not be chargeable under section 52 above if–

(a) the person whose interest comes to an end became beneficially entitled to the interest before 22nd March 2006,

(b) the interest comes to an end on or after that day, and

(c)immediately before the interest comes to an end, section 71A or 71D below applies to the property in which the interest subsists.]

(2) Tax shall not be chargeable under section 52 above (except in the case mentioned in subsection (4)(b) of that section) if the person whose interest in the property comes to an end becomes on the same occasion beneficially entitled to the property or to another interest in possession in the property.

[(2A) Subsection (2) above applies by virtue of the person becoming beneficially entitled on or after 12th March 2008 to another interest in possession in the property only if that other interest is–

(a) a disabled person's interest, or

(b) a transitional serial interest;

and that is the case irrespective of whether the person's beneficial entitlement to the interest in possession in the property which comes to an end is one which began before, or on or after, 22nd March 2006.],

(3) Tax shall not be chargeable under section 52 above if the interest comes to an end during the settlor's life and on the same occasion the property in which the interest subsisted reverts to the settlor.

(4) Tax shall not be chargeable under section 52 above if on the occasion when the interest comes to an end–

(a) the settlor's spouse [or civil partner], or

(b) where the settlor has died less than two years earlier, the settlor's widow or widower [or surviving civil partner],

becomes beneficially entitled to the settled property and is domiciled in the United Kingdom.

(5) Subsections (3) and (4) above shall not apply in any case where–

(a) the settlor or the spouse [or civil partner] (or in a case within subsection (4)(b), the widow or widower [or surviving civil partner]) of the settlor had acquired a reversionary interest in the property for a consideration in money or money's worth, or

(b) their application depends upon a reversionary interest having been transferred into a settlement on or after 10th March 1981.

(6) For the purposes of subsection (5) above a person shall be treated as acquiring an interest for a consideration in money or money's worth if he becomes entitled to it as a result of transactions which include a disposition for such consideration (whether to him or another) of that interest or of other property.

(7) Where the acquisition of the interest was before 12th April 1978, subsection (5) (a) above shall have effect, so far as it relates to subsection (3) above, with the omission of the reference to the spouse [or civil partner] of the settlor.

(8) Subsection (6) above shall not apply where the person concerned became entitled to the interest before 12th April 1978.

54.   Exceptions from charge on death

(1) Where a person is entitled to an interest in possession in settled property which on his death, but during the settlor's life, reverts to the settlor, the value of the settled property shall be left out of account in determining for the purposes of this Act the value of the deceased's estate immediately before his death.

(2) Where on the death of a person entitled to an interest in possession in settled property–
(a) the settlor's spouse [or civil partner], or
(b) if the settlor has died less than two years earlier, the settlor's widow or widower [or surviving civil partner],

becomes beneficially entitled to the settled property and is domiciled in the United Kingdom, the value of the settled property shall be left out of account in determining for the purposes of this Act the value of the deceased's estate immediately before his death.

[(2A) Where a person becomes beneficially entitled on or after 22nd March 2006 to an interest in possession in settled property, subsections (1) and (2) above apply in relation to the interest only if it is–
(a) a disabled person's interest, or
(b) a transitional serial interest.]

[(2B) Where–
(a) a person ('B') becomes beneficially entitled on or after 22nd March 2006 to an interest in possession in settled property,
(b) B dies,
(c) the interest in possession, throughout the period beginning with when B becomes beneficially entitled to it and ending with B's death, is an immediate post-death interest,
(d) the settlor died before B's death but less than two years earlier, and
(e) on B's death, the settlor's widow or widower, or surviving civil partner, becomes beneficially entitled to the settled property and is domiciled in the United Kingdom,

the value of the settled property shall be left out of account in determining for the purposes of this Act the value of B's estate immediately before his death.]

(3) Subsections (5) and (6) of section 53 above shall apply in relation to subsections [(1), (2) and (2B)] above as they apply in relation to section 53(3) and (4) [, but as if the reference in section 53(5)(a) above to section 53(4)(b) above were to subsection (2)(b) or (2B) above.] .

(4) For the purposes of this section, where it cannot be known which of two or more persons who have died survived the other or others they shall be assumed to have died at the same instant.

[**54A. Special rate of charge where settled property affected by potentially e x - empt transfer**

(1) If the circumstances fall within subsection (2) below, this section applies to any chargeable transfer made–

   (a) under section 52 above, on the coming to an end of an interest in possession in settled property during the life of the person beneficially entitled to it, or

   (b) on the death of a person beneficially entitled to an interest in possession in settled property;

   and in the following provisions of this section the interest in possession mentioned in paragraph (a) or paragraph (b) above is referred to as 'the relevant interest'.

[(1A) Where a person becomes beneficially entitled on or after 22nd March 2006 to an interest in possession in settled property, subsection (1)(b) above applies in relation to the person's death only if the interest is–

   (a) a disabled person's interest, or

   (b) a transitional serial interest.]

(2) The circumstances referred to in subsection (1) above are–

   (a) that the whole or part of the value transferred by the transfer is attributable to property in which the relevant interest subsisted and which became settled property in which there subsisted an interest in possession whether the relevant interest or any previous interest) on the making by the settlor of a potentially exempt transfer at any time on or after 17th March 1987 and within the period of seven years ending with the date of the chargeable transfer; and

   (b) that the settlor is alive at the time when the relevant interest comes to an end; and

   (c)that, on the coming to an end of the   relevant interest, any of the property in which that interest subsisted becomes settled property in which no qualifying interest in possession (as defined in section 59 below) subsists ... ; and

   (d) that, within six months of the coming to an end of the relevant interest, any of the property in which that interest subsisted has neither–

      (i) become settled property in which a qualifying interest in possession subsists ... , nor

      (ii) become property to which an individual is beneficially entitled.

(3) In the following provisions of this section 'the special rate property', in relation to a chargeable transfer to which this section applies, means the property in which the relevant interest subsisted or, in a case where–

   (a) any part of that property does not fall within subsection (2)(a) above, or

(b) any part of that property does not become settled property of the kind mentioned in subsection (2)(c) above,

so much of that property as appears to the Board or, on appeal, to the [tribunal] to be just and reasonable.

(4) Where this section applies to a chargeable transfer (in this section referred to as 'the relevant transfer'), the tax chargeable on the value transferred by the transfer shall be whichever is the greater of the tax that would have been chargeable apart from this section and the tax determined in accordance with subsection (5) below.

(5) The tax determined in accordance with this subsection is the aggregate of–

(a) the tax that would be chargeable on a chargeable transfer of the description specified in subsection (6) below, and

(b) so much (if any) of the tax that would, apart from this section, have been chargeable on the value transferred by the relevant transfer as is attributable to the value of property other than the special rate property.

(6) The chargeable transfer postulated in subsection (5)(a) above is one–

(a) the value transferred by which is equal to the value transferred by the relevant transfer or, where only part of that value is attributable to the special rate property, that part of that value;

(b) which is made at the time of the relevant transfer by a transferor who has in the preceding seven years made chargeable transfers having an aggregate value equal to the aggregate of the values transferred by any chargeable transfers made by the settlor in the period of seven years ending with the date of the potentially exempt transfer; and

(c) for which the applicable rate or rates are one-half of the rate or rates referred to in section 7(1) above.

(7) This section has effect subject to section 54B below.]

[54B. Provisions supplementary to section 54A

(1) The death of the settlor, at any time after a chargeable transfer to which section 54A above applies, shall not increase the tax chargeable on the value transferred by the transfer unless, at the time of the transfer, the tax determined in accordance with subsection (5) of that section is greater than the tax that would be chargeable apart from that section.

(2) The death of the person who was beneficially entitled to the relevant interest, at any time after a chargeable transfer to which section 54A above applies, shall not increase the tax chargeable on the value transferred by the transfer unless, at the time of the transfer, the tax that would be chargeable apart from that section is greater than the tax determined in accordance with subsection (5) of that section.

(3) Where the tax chargeable on the value transferred by a chargeable transfer to which section 54A above applies falls to be determined in accordance with subsection (5) of that section, the amount referred to in paragraph (a) of that subsection shall be treated for the purposes of this Act as tax attributable to the value of the property in which the relevant interest subsisted.

(4) Subsection (5) below shall apply if–

(a) during the period of seven years preceding the date on which a chargeable transfer to which section 54A above applies ('the current transfer') is made, there has been another chargeable transfer to which that section applied, and

(b) the person who is for the purposes of the current transfer the settlor mentioned in subsection (2)(a) of that section is the settlor for the purposes of the other transfer (whether or not the settlements are the same);

and in subsections (5) and (6) below the other transfer is referred to as the 'previous transfer'.

(5) Where this subsection applies, the appropriate amount in relation to the previous transfer (or, if there has been more than one previous transfer, the aggregate of the appropriate amounts in relation to each) shall, for the purposes of calculating the tax chargeable on the current transfer, be taken to be the value transferred by a chargeable transfer made by the settlor immediately before the potentially exempt transfer was made.

(6) In subsection (5) above 'the appropriate amount', in relation to a previous transfer, means so much of the value transferred by the previous transfer as was attributable to the value of property which was the special rate property in relation to that transfer.

(7) In this section–

'the relevant interest' has the meaning given by subsection (1) of section 54A above; and

'the special rate property' has the meaning given by subsection (3) of that section.]

55. Reversionary interest acquired by beneficiary

(1) Notwithstanding section 5(1) above, where a person entitled to an interest (whether in possession or not) in any settled property acquires a reversionary interest expectant (whether immediately or not) on that interest, the reversionary interest is not part of his estate for the purposes of this Act.

(2) Section 10(1) above shall not apply to a disposition by which a reversionary interest is acquired in the circumstances mentioned in subsection (1) above.

[71A. Trusts for bereaved minors

(1) This section applies to settled property (including property settled before 22nd March 2006) if–

(a) it is held on statutory trusts for the benefit of a bereaved minor under sections 46 and 47(1) of the Administration of Estates Act 1925 (succession on intestacy and statutory trusts in favour of issue of intestate), or

(b) it is held on trusts for the benefit of a bereaved minor and subsection (2) below applies to the trusts,

but this section does not apply to property in which a disabled person's interest subsists.

(2) This subsection applies to trusts–

(a) established under the will of a deceased parent of the bereaved minor, or

(b) established under the Criminal Injuries Compensation Scheme, [or (c)established under the Victims of Overseas Terrorism Compensation Scheme,] which secure that the conditions in subsection (3) below are met.

(3) Those conditions are—

    (a) that the bereaved minor, if he has not done so before attaining the age of 18, will on attaining that age become absolutely entitled to—

        (i) the settled property,

        (ii) any income arising from it, and

        (iii) any income that has arisen from the property held on the trusts for his benefit and been accumulated before that time,

    (b) that, for so long as the bereaved minor is living and under the age of 18, if any of the settled property is applied for the benefit of a beneficiary, it is applied for the benefit of the bereaved minor, and

    (c) that, for so long as the bereaved minor is living and under the age of 18, either—

        (i) the bereaved minor is entitled to all of the income (if there is any) arising from any of the settled property, or

        (ii) no such income may be applied for the benefit of any other person.

(4) Trusts such as are mentioned in paragraph (a) [,(b) or (c)] of subsection (2) above are not to be treated as failing to secure that the conditions in subsection (3) above are met by reason only of—

    (a) the trustees' having the powers conferred by section 32 of the Trustee Act 1925 (powers of advancement),

    (b) the trustees' having those powers but free from, or subject to a less restrictive limitation than, the limitation imposed by proviso (a) of subsection (1) of that section,

    (c) the trustees' having the powers conferred by section 33 of the Trustee Act (Northern Ireland) 1958 (corresponding provision for Northern Ireland),

    (d) the trustees' having those powers but free from, or subject to a less restrictive limitation than, the limitation imposed by subsection (1)(a) of that section, or

    (e) the trustees' having powers to the like effect as the powers mentioned in any of paragraphs (a) to (d) above.

(5) In this section 'the Criminal Injuries Compensation Scheme' means—

    (a) the schemes established by arrangements made under the Criminal Injuries Compensation Act 1995,

    (b) arrangements made by the Secretary of State for compensation for criminal injuries in operation before the commencement of those schemes, and

    (c) the scheme established under the Criminal Injuries Compensation (Northern Ireland) Order 2002.

[71B. Charge to tax on property to which section 71A applies

(1) Subject to subsections (2) and (3) below, there shall be a charge to tax under this section—

    (a) where settled property ceases to be property to which section 71A above applies, and

(b) in a case where paragraph (a) above does not apply, where the trustees make a disposition as a result of which the value of settled property to which section 71A above applies is less than it would be but for the disposition.

(2) Tax is not charged under this section where settled property ceases to be property to which section 71A applies as a result of–
  (a) the bereaved minor attaining the age of 18 or becoming, under that age, absolutely entitled as mentioned in section 71A(3)(a) above, or
  (b) the death under that age of the bereaved minor, or
  (c) being paid or applied for the advancement or benefit of the bereaved minor.

(3) Subsections (3) to (8) and (10) of section 70 above apply for the purposes of this section as they apply for the purposes of that section, but–
  (a) with the substitution of a reference to subsection (1)(b) above for the reference in subsection (4) of section 70 above to subsection (2)(b) of that section,
  (b) with the substitution of a reference to property to which section 71A above applies for each of the references in subsections (3), (5) and (8) of section 70 above to proper to which that section applies,
  (c) as if, for the purposes of section 70(8) above as applied by this subsection, property–
    (i) which is property to which section 71A above applies,
    (ii) which, immediately before it became property to which section 71A above applies, was property to which section 71 above applied, and
    (iii) which, by the operation of section 71(1B) above, ceased on that occasion to be property to which section 71 above applied,
    had become property to which section 71A above applies not on that occasion but on the occasion (or last occasion) before then when it became property to which section 71 above applied, and
  (d) as if, for the purposes of section 70(8) above as applied by this subsection, property–
    (i) which is property to which section 71A above applies,
    (ii) which, immediately before it became property to which section 71A above applies, was property to which section 71D below applied, and
    (iii) which, by the operation of section 71D(5)(a) below, ceased on that occasion ('the 71D-to-71A occasion') to be property to which section 71D below applied,
    had become property to which section 71A above applies not on the 71D-to-71A occasion but on the relevant earlier occasion.

(4) In subsection (3)(d) above–
  (a) 'the relevant earlier occasion' means the occasion (or last occasion) before the 71D-to-71A occasion when the property became property to which section 71D below applied, but
  (b) if the property, when it became property to which section 71D below applied, ceased at the same time to be property to which section 71 above applied without ceasing to be settled property, 'the relevant   earlier   occasion' means

the occasion (or last occasion) when the property became property to which section 71 above applied.]

[71C. Sections 71A and 71B: meaning of 'bereaved minor'

In sections 71A and 71B above 'bereaved minor' means a person–

    (a) who has not yet attained the age of 18, and

    (b) at least one of whose parents has died.]

[71D. Age 18-to-25 trusts

(1) This section applies to settled property (including property settled before 22nd March 2006), but subject to subsection (5) below, if–

    (a) the property is held on trusts for the benefit of a person who has not yet attained the age of 25,

    (b) at least one of the person's parents has died, and

    (c) subsection (2) below applies to the trusts.

(2) This subsection applies to trusts–

    (a) established under the will of a deceased parent of the person mentioned in subsection (1)(a) above, or

    (b) established under the Criminal Injuries Compensation Scheme, [or

    (c) established under the Victims of Overseas Terrorism Compensation Scheme,]

which secure that the conditions in subsection (6) below are met.

(3) Subsection (4) has effect where–

    (a) at any time on or after 22nd March 2006 but before 6th April 2008, or on the coming into force of paragraph 3(1) of Schedule 20 to the Finance Act 2006, any property ceases to be property to which section 71 above applies without ceasing to be settled property, and

    (b) immediately after the property ceases to be property to which section 71 above applies–

        (i) it is held on trusts for the benefit of a person who has not yet attained the age of 25, and

        (ii) the trusts secure that the conditions in subsection (6) below are met.

(4) From the time when the property ceases to be property to which section 71 above applies, but subject to subsection (5) below, this section applies to the property (if it would not apply to the property by virtue of subsection (1) above) for so long as–

    (a) the property continues to be settled property held on trusts such as are mentioned in subsection (3)(b)(i) above, and

    (b) the trusts continue to secure that the conditions in subsection (6) below are met.

(5) This section does not apply–

    (a) to property to which section 71A above applies,

    (b) to property to which section 71 above, or section 89 below, applies, or

    (c) to settled property if a person is beneficially entitled to an interest in possession in the settled property and–

        (i) the person became beneficially entitled to the interest in possession before 22nd March 2006, or

    (ii) the interest in possession is an immediate post-death interest, or a transitional serial interest, and the person became beneficially entitled to it on or after 22nd March 2006.

(6) Those conditions are–

  (a) that the person mentioned in subsection (1)(a) or (3)(b)(i) above ('B'), if he has not done so before attaining the age of 25, will on attaining that age become absolutely entitled to–

    (i) the settled property,

    (ii) any income arising from it, and

    (iii) any income that has arisen from the property held on the trusts for his benefit and been accumulated before that time,

  (b) that, for so long as B is living and under the age of 25, if any of the settled property is applied for the benefit of a beneficiary, it is applied for the benefit of B, and

  (c) that, for so long as B is living and under the age of 25, either–

    (i) B is entitled to all of the income (if there is any) arising from any of the settled property, or

    (ii) no such income may be applied for the benefit of any other person.

(7) For the purposes of this section, trusts are not to be treated as failing to secure that the conditions in subsection (6) above are met by reason only of–

  (a) the trustees' having the powers conferred by section 32 of the Trustee Act 1925 (powers of advancement),

  (b) the trustees' having those powers but free from, or subject to a less restrictive limitation than, the limitation imposed by proviso (a) of subsection (1) of that section,

  (c) the trustees' having the powers conferred by section 33 of the Trustee Act (Northern Ireland) 1958 (corresponding provision for Northern Ireland),

  (d) the trustees' having those powers but free from, or subject to a less restrictive limitation than, the limitation imposed by subsection (1)(a) of that section, or

  (e) the trustees' having powers to the like effect as the powers mentioned in any of paragraphs (a) to (d) above.

(8) In this section 'the Criminal Injuries Compensation Scheme' means–

  (a) the schemes established by arrangements made under the Criminal Injuries Compensation Act 1995,

  (b) arrangements made by the Secretary of State for compensation for criminal injuries in operation before the commencement of those schemes, and

  (c) the scheme established under the Criminal Injuries Compensation (Northern Ireland) Order 2002.

[71E. Charge to tax on property to which section 71D applies

(1) Subject to subsections (2) to (4) below, there shall be a charge to tax under this section–

  (a) where settled property ceases to be property to which section 71D above applies, or

    (b) in a case where paragraph (a) above does not apply, where the trustees make a disposition as a result of which the value

of the settled property to which section 71D above applies is less than it would be but for the disposition.

(2) Tax is not charged under this section where settled property ceases to be property to which section 71D above applies as a result of–

    (a) B becoming, at or under the age of 18, absolutely entitled as mentioned in section 71D(6)(a) above,

    (b) the death, under the age of 18, of B,

    (c) becoming, at a time when B is living and under the age of 18, property to which section 71A above applies, or

    (d) being paid or applied for the advancement or benefit of B–

        (i) at a time when B is living and under the age of 18, or

        (ii) on B's attaining the age of 18.

(3) Tax is not charged under this section in respect of–

    (a) a payment of costs or expenses (so far as they are fairly attributable to property to which section 71D above applies), or

    (b) a payment which is (or will be) income of any person for any of the purposes of income tax or would for any of those purposes be income of a person not resident in the United Kingdom if he were so resident,

or in respect of a liability to make such a payment.

(4) Tax is not charged under this section by virtue of subsection (1)(b) above if the disposition is such that, were the trustees beneficially entitled to the settled property, section 10 or section 16 above would prevent the disposition from being a transfer of value.

(5) For the purposes of this section the trustees shall be treated as making a disposition if they omit to exercise a right (unless it is shown that the omission was not deliberate) and the disposition shall be treated as made at the time or latest time when they could have exercised the right.]

[71F. Calculation of tax charged under section 71E in certain cases

(1) Where–

    (a) tax is charged under section 71E above by reason of the happening of an event within subsection (2) below, and

    (b) that event happens after B has attained the age of 18,

the tax is calculated in accordance with this section.

(2) Those events are–

    (a) B becoming absolutely entitled as mentioned in section 71D(6)(a) above,

    (b) the death of B, and

    (c) property being paid or applied for the advancement or benefit of B.

(3) The amount of the tax is given by–

Chargeable amount x Relevant fraction x Settlement rate

(4) For the purposes of subsection (3) above, the 'Chargeable amount' is–

    (a) the amount by which the value of property which is comprised in the settlement and to which section 71D above applies is less immediately after the event giving rise to the charge than it would be but for the event, or

    (b) where the tax is payable out of settled property to which section 71D above applies immediately after the event, the amount which, after deducting the tax, is equal to the amount on which tax would be charged by virtue of paragraph (a) above.

(5) For the purposes of subsection (3) above, the 'Relevant fraction' is three tenths multiplied by so many fortieths as there are complete successive quarters in the period–

    (a) beginning with the day on which B attained the age of 18 or, if later, the day on which the property became property to which section 71D above applies, and

    (b) ending with the day before the occasion of the charge.

(6) Where the whole or part of the Chargeable amount is attributable to property that was excluded property at any time during the period mentioned in subsection (5) above then, in determining the 'Relevant fraction' in relation to that amount or part, no quarter throughout which that property was excluded property shall be counted.

(7) For the purposes of subsection (3) above, the 'Settlement rate' is the effective rate (that is to say, the rate found by expressing the tax chargeable as a percentage of the amount on which it is charged) at which tax would be charged on the value transferred by a chargeable transfer of the description specified in subsection (8) below.

(8) The chargeable transfer postulated in subsection (7) above is one–

    (a) the value transferred by which is equal to an amount determined in accordance with subsection (9) below,

    (b) which is made at the time of the charge to tax under section 71E above by a transferor who has in the period of seven years ending with the day of the occasion of the charge made chargeable transfers having an aggregate value equal to that of any chargeable transfers made by the settlor in the period of seven years ending with the day on which the settlement commenced, disregarding transfers made on that day, and

    (c) on which tax is charged in accordance with section 7(2) above.

(9) The amount referred to in subsection (8)(a) above is equal to the aggregate of–

    (a) the value, immediately after the settlement commenced, of the property then comprised in it,

    (b) the value, immediately after a related settlement commenced, of the property then comprised in it, and

    (c) the value, immediately after it became comprised in the settlement, of any property which became so comprised after the settlement commenced and before the occasion of the charge under section 71E above (whether or not it has remained so comprised).]

[71G. Calculation of tax charged under section 71E in all other cases

(1) Where–

    (a) tax is charged under section 71E above, and

    (b) the tax does not fall to be calculated in accordance with section 71F above,

the tax is calculated in accordance with this section.

(2) The amount on which the tax is charged is–

    (a) the amount by which the value of property which is comprised in the settlement and to which section 71D above applies is less immediately after the event giving rise to the charge than it would be but for the event, or

    (b) where the tax is payable out of settled property to which section 71D above applies immediately after the event, the amount which, after deducting the tax, is equal to the amount on which tax would be charged by virtue of paragraph (a) above.

(3) The rate at which the tax is charged is the rate that would be given by subsections (6) to (8) of section 70 above–

    (a) if the reference to section 70 above in subsection (8)(a) of that section were a reference to section 71D above,

    (b) if the other references in those subsections to section 70 above were references to section 71E above, and

    (c) if, for the purposes of section 70(8) above, property–

        (i) which is property to which section 71D above applies,

        (ii) which, immediately before it became property to which section 71D above applies, was property to which section 71 applied, and

        (iii) which ceased on that occasion to be property to which section 71 above applied without ceasing to be settled property,

had become property to which section 71D above applies not on that occasion but on the occasion (or last occasion) before then when it became property to which section 71 above applied.]

[71H. Sections 71A to 71G: meaning of 'parent'

(1) In sections 71A to 71G above 'parent' includes step-parent.

(2) For the purposes of sections 71A to 71G above, a deceased individual ('D') shall be taken to have been a parent of another individual ('Y') if, immediately before D died, D had–

    (a) parental responsibility for Y under the law of England and Wales,

    (b) parental responsibilities in relation to Y under the law of Scotland, or

    (c) parental responsibility for Y under the law of Northern Ireland.

(3) In subsection (2)(a) above 'parental responsibility' has the same meaning as in the Children Act 1989.

(4) In subsection (2)(b) above 'parental responsibilities' has the meaning given by section 1(3) of the Children (Scotland) Act 1995.

(5) In subsection (2)(c) above 'parental responsibility' has the same meaning as in the Children (Northern Ireland) Order 1995.]

92.   Survivorship clauses

(1) Where under the terms of a will or otherwise property is held for any person on condition that he survives another for a specified period of not more than six months, this Act shall apply as if the dispositions taking effect at the end of the period or, if he does not survive until then, on his death (including any such disposition which has effect by operation of law or is a separate disposition of the income from the property) had had effect from the beginning of the period.

(2) Subsection (1) above does not affect the application of this Act in relation to any distribution or application of property occurring before the dispositions there mentioned take effect.

142.   Alteration of dispositions taking effect on death

(1) Where within the period of two years after a person's death–

    (a) any of the dispositions (whether effected by will, under the law relating to intestacy or otherwise) of the property comprised in his estate immediately before his death are varied, or

    (b) the benefit conferred by any of those dispositions is disclaimed,

by an instrument in writing made by the persons or any of the persons who benefit or would benefit under the dispositions, this Act shall apply as if the variation had been effected by the deceased or, as the case may be, the disclaimed benefit had never been conferred.

[(2) Subsection (1) above shall not apply to a variation unless the instrument contains a statement, made by all the relevant persons, to the effect that they intend the subsection to apply to the variation.]

[(2A) For the purposes of subsection (2) above the relevant persons are–

    (a) the person or persons making the instrument, and

    (b) where the variation results in additional tax being payable, the personal representatives.

Personal representatives may decline to make a statement under subsection (2) above only if no, or no sufficient, assets are held by them in that capacity for discharging the additional tax.]

(3) Subsection (1) above shall not apply to a variation or disclaimer made for any consideration in money or money's worth other than consideration consisting of the making, in respect of another of the dispositions, of a variation or disclaimer to which that subsection applies.

(4) Where a variation to which subsection (1) above applies results in property being held in trust for a person for a period which ends not more than two years after the death, this Act shall apply as if the disposition of the property that takes effect at the end of the period had had effect from the beginning of the period; but this subsection shall not affect the application of this Act in relation to any distribution or application of property occurring before that disposition takes effect.

(5) For the purposes of subsection (1) above the property comprised in a person's estate includes any excluded property but not any property to which he is treated as entitled by virtue of section 49(1) above [or section 102 of the Finance Act 1986].

(6) Subsection (1) above applies whether or not the administration of the estate is complete or the property concerned has been distributed in accordance with the original dispositions.

143. Compliance with testator's request

Where a testator expresses a wish that property bequeathed by his will should be transferred by the legatee to other persons, and the legatee transfers any of the property in accordance with that wish within the period of two years after the death of the testator, this Act shall have effect as if the property transferred had been bequeathed by the will to the transferee.

144. Distribution etc from property settled by will

(1) [Subsection (2) below applies] where property comprised in a person's estate immediately before his death is settled by his will and, within the period of two years after his death and before any interest in possession has subsisted in the property, there occurs–

    (a) an event on which tax would [(apart from subsection (2) below)] be chargeable under any provision, other than section 64 or 79, of Chapter III of Part III of this Act, or

    (b) an event on which tax would be so chargeable but for section 75 or 76 above or paragraph 16(1) of Schedule 4 to this Act.

[(1A) Where the testator dies on or after 22nd March 2006, subsection (1) above shall have effect as if the reference to any interest in possession were a reference to any interest in possession that is–

    (a) an immediate post-death interest, or

    (b) a disabled person's interest.]

(2) Where [this subsection] applies by virtue of an event within paragraph (a) of subsection (1) above, tax shall not be charged under the provision in question on that event; and in every case in which [this subsection] applies in relation to an event, this Act shall have effect as if the will had provided that on the testator's death the property should be held as it is held after the event.

[(3) Subsection (4) below applies where–

    (a) a person dies on or after 22nd March 2006,

    (b) property comprised in the person's estate immediately before his death is settled by his will, and

    (c)within the period of two years after his death, but before an immediate post-death interest or a disabled person's interest has subsisted in the property, there occurs an event that involves causing the property to be held on trusts that would, if they had in fact been established by the testator's will, have resulted in–

        (i) an immediate post-death interest subsisting in the property, or

        (ii) section 71A or 71D above applying to the property.]

[(4) Where this subsection applies by virtue of an event–

    (a) this Act shall have effect as if the will had provided that on the testator's death the property should be held as it is held after the event, but

(b) tax shall not be charged on that event under any provision of Chapter 3 of Part 3 of this Act.]

[(5) Subsection (4) above also applies where–

(a) a person dies before 22nd March 2006,

(b) property comprised in the person's estate immediately before his death is settled by his will,

(c) an event occurs–

(i) on or after 22nd March 2006, and

(ii) within the period of two years after the testator's death,

that involves causing the property to be held on trusts within subsection (6) below,

(d) no immediate post-death interest, and no disabled person's interest, subsisted in the property at any time in the period beginning with the testator's death and ending immediately before the event, and

(e) no other interest in possession subsisted in the property at any time in the period beginning with the testator's death and ending immediately before 22nd March 2006.]

[(6) Trusts are within this subsection if they would, had they in fact been established by the testator's will and had the testator died at the time of the event mentioned in subsection (5)(c) above, have resulted in–

(a) an immediate post-death interest subsisting in the property, or

(b) section 71A or 71D above applying to the property.]

145. Redemption of surviving spouse's [or civil partner's] life interest

Where an election is made by a surviving spouse [or civil partner] under section 47A of the Administration of Estates Act 1925, this Act shall have effect as if the surviving spouse [or civil partner] , instead of being entitled to the life interest, had been entitled to a sum equal to the capital value mentioned in that section.

160. Market value

Except as otherwise provided by this Act, the value at any time of any property shall for the purposes of this Act be the price which the property might reasonably be expected to fetch if sold in the open market at that time; but that price shall not be assumed to be reduced on the ground that the whole property is to be placed on the market at one and the same time.

161. Related property

(1) Where the value of any property comprised in a person's estate would be less than the appropriate portion of the value of the aggregate of that and any related property, it shall be the appropriate portion of the value of that aggregate.

(2) For the purposes of this section, property is related to the property comprised in a person's estate if–

(a) it is comprised in the estate of his spouse [or civil partner] ; or

(b) it is or has within the preceding five years been–

    (i) the property of a charity, or held on trust for charitable purposes only, or

    (ii) the property of a body mentioned in section 24, [24A,] [or 25] above,

and became so on a transfer of value which was made by him or his spouse [o r civil partner] after 15th April 1976 and was exempt to the extent that the value transferred was attributable to the property.

(3) The appropriate portion of the value of the aggregate mentioned in subsection (1) above is such portion thereof as would be attributable to the value of the first-mentioned property if the value of that aggregate were equal to the sums of the values of that and any related property, the value of each property being determined as if it did not form part of that aggregate.

(4) For the purposes of subsection (3) above the proportion which the value of a smaller number of shares of any class bears to the value of a greater number shall be taken to be that which the smaller number bears to the greater; and similarly with stock, debentures and units of any other description of property.

(5) Shares shall not be treated for the purposes of subsection (4) above as being of the same class unless they are so treated by the practice of a recognised stock exchange or would be so treated if dealt with on such a stock exchange.

162. Liabilities

(1) A liability in respect of which there is a right to reimbursement shall be taken into account only to the extent (if any) that reimbursement cannot reasonably be expected to be obtained.

(2) Subject to subsection (3) below, where a liability falls to be discharged after the time at which it is to be taken into account it shall be valued as at the time at which it is to be taken into account.

(3) In determining the value of a transferor's estate immediately after a transfer of value, his liability for capital transfer tax shall be computed–

    (a) without making any allowance for the fact that the tax will not be due immediately, and

    (b) as if any tax recovered otherwise than from the transferor (or a person liable for it under section 203(1) below) were paid in discharge of a liability in respect of which the transferor had a right to reimbursement.

(4) A liability which is an incumbrance on any property shall, so far as possible, be taken to reduce the value of that property.

(5) Where a liability taken into account is a liability to a person resident outside the United Kingdom which neither–

    (a) falls to be discharged in the United Kingdom, nor

    (b) is an incumbrance on property in the United Kingdom,

it shall, so far as possible, be taken to reduce the value of property outside the United Kingdom.

199. Dispositions by transferor

(1) The persons liable for the tax on the value transferred by a chargeable transfer

made by a disposition (including any omission treated as a disposition under section 3(3) above) of the transferor are–

(a) the transferor;

(b) any person the value of whose estate is increased by the transfer;

(c) so far as the tax is attributable to the value of any property, any person in whom the property is vested (whether beneficially or otherwise) at any time after the transfer, or who at any such time is beneficially entitled to an interest in possession in the property;

(d) where by the chargeable transfer any property becomes comprised in a settlement, any person for whose benefit any of the property or income from it is applied.

[(2) Subsection (1)(a) above shall apply in relation to–

(a) the tax on the value transferred by a potentially exempt transfer; and

(b) so much of the tax on the value transferred by any other chargeable transfer made within seven years of the transferor's death as exceeds what it would have been had the transferor died more than seven years after the transfer,

with the substitution for the reference to the transferor of a reference to his personal representatives.]

(3) A purchaser of property, and a person deriving title from or under such a purchaser, shall not by virtue of subsection (1)(c) above be liable for tax attributable to the value of the property unless the property is subject to an Inland Revenue charge.

(4) For the purposes of this section–

(a) any person who takes possession of or intermeddles with, or otherwise acts in relation to, property so as to become liable as executor or trustee (or, in Scotland, any person who intromits with property or has become liable as a vitious intromitter), and

(b) any person to whom the management of property is entrusted on behalf of a person not of full legal capacity,

shall be treated as a person in whom the property is vested.

(5) References in this section to any property include references to any property directly or indirectly representing it.

200. Transfer on death

(1) The persons liable for the tax on the value transferred by a chargeable transfer made (under section 4 above) on the death of any person are [(subject to subsection (1A) below)]–

(a) so far as the tax is attributable to the value of property which either–

(i) was not immediately before the death comprised in a settlement, or

(ii) was so comprised and consists of land in the United Kingdom which devolves upon or vests in the deceased's personal representatives,

the deceased's personal representatives;

(b) so far as the tax is attributable to the value of property which, immediately before the death, was comprised in a settlement, the trustees of the settlement;

(c) so far as the tax is attributable to the value of any property, any person in whom the property is vested (whether beneficially or otherwise) at any time after the death, or who at any such time is beneficially entitled to an interest in possession in the property;

(d) so far as the tax is attributable to the value of any property which, immediately before the death, was comprised in a settlement, any person for whose benefit any of the property or income from it is applied after the death.

[(1A) The person liable for tax chargeable by virtue of section 151A or 151C above in relation to any registered pension scheme is the scheme administrator of the pension scheme.]

(2) A purchaser of property, and a person deriving title from or under such a purchaser, shall not by virtue of subsection (1)(c) above be liable for tax attributable to the value of the property unless the property is subject to an Inland Revenue charge.

(3) For the purposes of subsection (1) above a person entitled to part only of the income of any property shall, notwithstanding anything in section 50 above, be deemed to be entitled to an interest in the whole of the property.

(4) Subsections (4) and (5) of section 199 above shall have effect for the purposes of this section as they have effect for the purposes of that section.

267. Persons treated as domiciled in United Kingdom

(1) A person not domiciled in the United Kingdom at any time (in this section referred to as 'the relevant time') shall be treated for the purposes of this Act as domiciled in the United Kingdom (and not elsewhere) at the relevant time if—

(a) he was domiciled in the United Kingdom within the three years immediately preceding the relevant time, or

(b) he was resident in the United Kingdom in not less than seventeen of the twenty years of assessment ending with the year of assessment in which the relevant time falls.

(2) Subsection (1) above shall not apply for the purposes of section 6(2) or (3) or 48(4) above and shall not affect the interpretation of any such provision as is mentioned in section 158(6) above.

(3) Paragraph (a) of subsection (1) above shall not apply in relation to a person who (apart from this section) has not been domiciled in the United Kingdom at any time since 9th December 1974, and paragraph (b) of that subsection shall not apply in relation to a person who has not been resident there at any time since that date; and that subsection shall be disregarded—

(a) in determining whether settled property which became comprised in the settlement on or before that date is excluded property,

(b) in determining the settlor's domicile for the purposes of section 65(8) above in relation to settled property which became comprised in the settlement on or before that date, and

(c) in determining for the purposes of section 65(8) above whether the condition in section 82(3) above is satisfied in relation to such settled property.

(4) For the purposes of this section the question whether a person was resident in the United Kingdom in any year of assessment shall be determined as for the purposes of income tax, ...

268.   Associated operations

(1) In this Act 'associated operations' means, subject to subsection (2) below, any two or more operations of any kind, being–

   (a) operations which affect the same property, or one of which affects some property and the other or others of which affect property which represents, whether directly or indirectly, that property, or income arising from that property, or any property representing accumulations of any such income, or

   (b) any two operations of which one is effected with reference to the other, or with a view to enabling the other to be effected or facilitating its being effected, and any further operation having a like relation to any of those two, and so on,

   whether those operations are effected by the same person or different persons, and whether or not they are simultaneous; and 'operation' includes an omission.

(2) The granting of a lease for full consideration in money or money's worth shall not be taken to be associated with any operation effected more than three years after the grant, and no operation effected on or after 27th March 1974 shall be taken to be associated with an operation effected before that date.

(3) Where a transfer of value is made by associated operations carried out at different times it shall be treated as made at the time of the last of them; but where any one or more of the earlier operations also constitute a transfer of value made by the same transferor, the value transferred by the earlier operations shall be treated as reducing the value transferred by all the operations taken together, except to the extent that the transfer constituted by the earlier operations but not that made by all the operations taken together is exempt under section 18 above.

Appendix 6
Table of Cases

Aldhous, Re (1955)2 All ER 80
Allhusen v Whittell (1867) LR 4 Eq 295
Anderson (Anderson's Executor) v CIR (1998) STC (SCD 43)
Andrews v Partington (1791) 29 ER 610
Armitage v Nurse (1998) Ch 241; [1997] 3 WLR 1046
Arnander and others (executors of McKenna, deceased) v Revenue and Customs Commissioners (2007) RVR 208; (2006) STC (SCD) 800 Sp Comm
Arkwright (Williams Personal Representatives) v IRC (2004) STC 1323 (2004) EWHC 1720 (Ch)
Ashcroft v Barnsdale (2010) EWHC 1948 (CH)
Atkinson v HMRC (2010) UKFTT 108 (TC); (2010) WTLR 745

Bacon v Howard Kennedy (2000) WTLR 169 Ch D
Banks v Goodfellow (1869-70) LR5 QB 549
Barclays Bank Trust Co Ltd v Inland Revenue Commissioners (1998) STC (SCD) 125
Barry v Butlin 12 ER 1089 (1838)
Bartlett v Barclays Bank Trust Co Ltd (No2) (1980) Ch 515
Bell v Kennedy (1866 - 69) LR 1 Sc 307 HL
Bennett v IRC (1995) STC 54
Boughton v Knight (1872-75) LR 3 P&D Ct of Probate
Breakspear v Ackland (2009) Ch 32
Burden & Burden v United Kingdom (13378/05) (2008) STC 1305
Buttle v Saunders (1950) 2 All ER 193

Cancer Research Campaign v Ernest Brown & Co (1997) STC 1425
Carr-Glynn v Frearsons (1999) Ch 326
Carradine Properties Ltd v DJ Freeman & Co (1999) Lloyd's Rep PN 483
Casdagli v Casdagli (1919) AC 145 HL
Chicester Diocesan Fund and Board of Finance Inc v Simpson (1944) AC 341
CIR v Lloyd's Private Banking Limited (1998) Ch D STC 559
Clore's Settlement Trusts, Re (1966) 2 All ER 272
Cowan v Scargill (1985) 2 All ER 750
Crawshay, Re (1948) Ch 123

Dobson v North Tyneside Health Authority (1997) 1 WLR 596

Druce's Settlement Trusts (1962) 1 All ER 563

Earl of Chesterfield's Trusts, Re (1883) 24 Ch D 643
Esterhuizen v Allied Dunbar (1998) 2 FLR 668
Estill v Cowling Swift and Kitchen (2000) WTLR 417 Ch D

Forbes v Forbes (1854) Kay 341
Frankland v IRC (1996) STC 735
Freeston's Charity, Re (1978) 1 WLR 741

Gestetner Settlement, Re (1953) Ch 672
Gibson's Setlement Trusts, Re (1981) Ch 179
Grimwood-Taylor and Mallender v CIR (2000) SSCD 39 (Sp C 233)
Gulbenkian's Settlement (No 1), Re (1970) AC 508

Hadjiloucas v Crean (1998) 1 WLR 1006
Hastings-Bass, Re (1975) Ch 25
Hay's Settlement Trusts, Re (1981) 3 All ER 786
H v Mitson (2009) EWHC 3114 (Fam)
Holder v Holder (1968) Ch 353
Holland v IRC (2003) STC (SCD) 43
Howe v Lord Dartmouth (1802) 7 Ves 137
Hurlingham Estates Ltd v Wilde & Partners (1997) 1 Lloyd's Rep 525

Ingram v IRC (2000) 1 AC 293
IRC v Eversden (2003) EWCA Civ 668

Jiggens v Low (2010) EWHC 1566 (Ch)
Judge (Walden's Personal Representative) v HRMC (2005) STC (SCD) 863

Kane v Radley-Kane (1999) Ch 274
Key & Anor v Key & Ors (2010) EWHC 408 (Ch)

Lamothe v Lamothe (2006) EWHC 1387
Lloyd's Bank v Duker (1987) 3 All ER 193
Lloyds TSB Bank Plc (Personal Representative of Antrobus) v IRC (2002) *(Antrobus No.1)* STC (SCD) 486
Londonderry's Settlement, Re (1965) Ch 918

MacNiven v Westmoreland Investments Ltd (2001) UKHL 6
Marley v Mutual Security Merchant Bank (2001) WTLR 483 PC (Jam)
McPhail v Doulton (1970) 2 WLR 1110

Midland Bank v Hett, Stubs, and Kemp (1979) Ch 384

Nathan v Leonard (2002) EWHC 1701
Nestle v Westminister Bank (2000) WTLR 795

Pearson v Inland Revenue Commissioners (1981) AC 753
Phizackerley v HMRC (2007) STC (SCD) 328
Pilkington v IRC (1964) AC 612
Pitt & Anor v Holt & Anor (2011) EWCA Civ 197
Plummer v CIR (1988) 1 WLR 292
Price v Revenue and Customs Commissioners (2010) UKFTT 474 (TC)
  WTLR161 (an application for leave to appeal has been made)

R v. Allen (1999) STC 846
Revenue and Customs Comrs v Brander (2009) UKFTT 101
*Revenue and Customs Comrs v Trustees of the Nelson Dance Family
  Settlement* (2009) EWHC 71 (CH)
RSPCA v Sharp (2010) EWCA Civ 1474
Ruddock, Re (1910) 102 LT 89
Russell v IRC (1998) 2 All ER 405
Rysaffe Trustee Co (CI) Ltd v Inland Revenue Commissioners (2003)
  EWCA Civ 356

Saunders v Vautier (1841) Cr & Ph.240
Schmidt v Rosewood (2003) 2 WLR 1442
Sieff v Fox (2005) WTLR 891
Speight v Gaunt (1883) 9 App Cas 1
Stevenson v Wishhart (1987) 1 WLR 1204
Stoneham's Settlement Trusts, Re (1953) Ch 59

Thompson's Settlement, Re (1986) Ch 99
Tito v Waddell (No.2) (1977) Ch 106
Vatcher v Paull (1915) AC 372
Whicker v Hume (1858) 7 HLC 124
Williams v Williams (1881)17 Ch D 437
Willoughby v IRC (1997) STC 995
Wingham, Re (1949) LJR 695, and 2 All ER 908
Winnans v A.G. (1904) AC 287 HL
Wright v Morgan (1926) AC 788 PC (NZ)
WT Ramsay Ltd v IRC (1982) AC 300

X v Woolcombe Yonge (2001) WTLR 301

Appendix 7
Recent Cases

PITT v HOLT (2011) (COURT OF APPEAL)

Selected extracts from the Judgment

Lord Justice Lloyd

[1]   Two questions arise in these appeals. The first can be stated, broadly, in this way. Trustees of a settlement exercise a discretionary power intending to change the beneficial ownership of trust property, but the effect of what they do turns out to be different from that which they intended. Can their act be set aside by the court? If so, what is the correct legal test to determine in what circumstances and on what basis the court can intervene? The second question concerns the correct legal test to be applied if a donor seeks to have a voluntary disposition set aside as having been made under a mistake.

The appeals

[23]   In each case HMRC appeal, contending that, on a correct view, the *Hastings-Bass* rule does not justify a conclusion that the relevant disposition was void or even voidable. It is not suggested that either Judge was wrong, at first instance, being bound, in effect, to follow the line of decisions that has developed since *Mettoy*. However, it is contended that, looking at the matter in terms of (a) the ratio of *Re Hastings-Bass* itself and (b) relevant principles of trust law, it is wrong to treat the acts of either Mrs *Pitt* or the trustees of the *Futter* settlements as vitiated by the fact that the fiscal consequences of what was done were different from what was expected. The argument on this point requires the court to go back both to **Re Hastings-Bass** itself and to first principles.

[127]   The cases which I am now considering concern acts which are within the powers of the trustees but are said to be vitiated by the failure of the trustees to take into account a relevant factor to which they should have regard - usually tax consequences – or by taking into account some irrelevant matter. It seems to me that the principled and correct approach to these cases is, first, that the trustees' act is not void, but that it may be voidable. It will be voidable if, and only if,

it can be shown to have been done in breach of fiduciary duty on the part of the trustees. If it is voidable, then it may be capable of being set aside at the suit of a beneficiary, but this would be subject to equitable defences and to the court's discretion. The trustees' duty to take relevant matters into account is a fiduciary duty, so an act done as a result of a breach of that duty is voidable. Fiscal considerations will often be among the relevant matters which ought to be taken into account. However, if the trustees seek advice (in general or in specific terms) from apparently competent advisors as to the implications of the course they are considering taking, and follow the advice so obtained, then, in the absence of any other basis for challenge, I would hold that the trustees are not in breach of their fiduciary duty for failure to have regard to relevant matters if the failure occurs because it turns out that the advice given to them was materially wrong. Accordingly, in such a case I would not regard the trustees' act, done in reliance on that advice, as being vitiated by the error and therefore voidable.

[210] I hold that, for the equitable jurisdiction to set aside a voluntary disposition for mistake to be invoked, there must be a mistake on the part of the donor either as to the legal effect of the disposition or as to an existing fact which is basic to the transaction. .... Moreover, the mistake must be of sufficient gravity as to satisfy the *Ogilvie v Littleboy* test, which provides protection to the recipient against too ready an ability of the donor to seek to recall his gift. The fact that the transaction gives rise to unforeseen fiscal liabilities is a consequence, not an effect, for this purpose, and is not sufficient to bring the jurisdiction into play.

[222] The *Hastings-Bass Rule*. The principle promulgated first by Warner J, in *Mettoy*, developed thereafter, and set out by myself in paragraph 119(i) of my judgment in *Sieff v Fox* is not correct. Two kinds of case need to be distinguished.

    (i)   On the one hand there may be a case in which, for example because of an inadvertent misunderstanding of the position, an act done by trustees in the exercise of a dispositive discretion is not within the scope of the relevant power. If so it is void. That was the case in Re Abrahams' Will Trusts, as it was interpreted in *Re Hastings-Bass*. It would have been the case in *Re Hastings-Bass* but for the Court of Appeal having allowed the appeal by the trustees.

    (ii)   On the other hand, the case may be one in which the trustees' act in exercise of their discretion is within the terms of their power, but is said to have been vitiated by their failure to take into account a relevant matter, or their taking something irrelevant into account, when deciding to exercise, and exercising, the discretion. The correct approach to such cases is dealt with at paragraph [127] above. The trustees' act is not void; it may be voidable. To be voidable it must be shown to have been done in breach of a fiduciary duty of the trustees. The duty to take relevant, and no irrelevant, matters into account is a fiduciary duty. Relevant matters may include fiscal consequences of the act in question. However, if the trustees fulfil their duty of skill and care by seeking professional advice (whether in general or specific terms) from a proper source, and act on the advice so obtained, then (in the absence of any other basis for a challenge) they do not commit a breach of trust even if, because of inadequacies of the advice given, they act under a mistake as to a relevant matter, such as tax consequences. In the absence of a breach of trust, the trustees' act is not voidable. Even if it is voidable, it cannot be avoided unless a beneficiary seeks to have it avoided, and a claim to that effect will be subject to the discretion of the court and to the usual range of equitable defences.

   (iii)   The same principles may apply to acts on the part of other persons in a fiduciary position, of whom a receiver appointed under the **Mental Health Act 1983** is an example.

[223]   Mistake. The correct test is set out at paragraph [210] above. If the only ground for invoking equity's jurisdiction is a mistake on the part of the donor, it must be shown that the donor was under a mistake at the time of the disposition, which is either a mistake as to the legal effect of the transaction, or as to an existing fact which is basic to the transaction, and the mistake must be of sufficient gravity to satisfy the *Ogilvie v Littleboy* test, set out in the quotation from Lindley LJ's judgment at paragraph [167] above.

[225]   *Futter v Futter*. The trustees' acts of enlargement and advancement were within their powers under the respective settlements, and cannot be held to be void. The trustees took advice from appropriate solicitors as to the tax consequences of what they were thinking of doing, and acted in accordance with that advice. Therefore they did not act in breach of trust in making the enlargement and the advancements even though, because the advice was wrong, they were mistaken as to the tax consequences. The enlargement and the advancements are therefore not voidable.

[226]   For those reasons, I would allow the appeals by HMRC in *Pitt v Holt* and in *Futter v Futter*, and set aside the order made below in each case.

RSPCA V SHARP (2011) (COURT OF APPEAL)

Lord Justice Patten:

[15]   The difference between the parties really turns on whether the Testator intended to make a tax-efficient disposition of his estate; ie one which avoided IHT entirely by limiting the totality in value of the gifts under clauses 3 and 4 to the nil rate band and leaving the entire residue to charity.

[19]   One thing on which the parties were in agreement was the approach of the court to the construction of a will. As mentioned above, it was common ground before the judge that no extrinsic evidence was admissible. He had therefore to follow the guidance of Lord Simon L.C. in **Perrin v Morgan** [1943] A.C.399 at 406 and to construe the language of the will so as to find:

'... the meaning which, having regard to the terms of the will, the testator intended. The question is not, of course, what the testator meant to do when he made his will, but what the written words he uses mean in the particular case – what are the 'expressed intentions' of the testator.'

[20]   We have therefore to examine the language of the will in its context taking into account the will as a whole; any relevant background circumstances which inform the meaning of the words used; and giving to those words their ordinary meaning unless they are obviously used in some special or technical sense.

[21]   The divide in this case centres on whether the Testator intended to make a will which excluded IHT unless the property exceeded the nil rate band in value. In this event the pecuniary legacies under clause 3 would also be eliminated. The judge largely rejected this construction of the will because he considered it incredible (as he put it) to assume that the Testator would have intended to reduce or eliminate the gifts of money to his brother and to the Sharps in the event that the combined value of the non-exempt transfers should exceed the amount of the nil rate band. But, in the absence of any extrinsic evidence about the Testator or his wishes, this is largely speculation. We know nothing about his brother's financial circumstances; the Testator's degree of commitment to the RSPCA; or the strength of his desire to avoid any charge to IHT on his assets. It is perfectly possible that the second and third of these elements outweighed any perceived risk that the clause 3 legacies would be reduced to nil.

[22]   For these reasons it is dangerous to approach the assessment of the

Testator's intentions other than through the language of his will. The first relevant consideration in my view is that the will was professionally drafted by a solicitor who has to be assumed to be competent. Although solicitors do obviously make mistakes, there needs to be something in the language of the document or its admissible background to justify that inference. More importantly, those factors must be such as to permit the Court to give the words actually used a meaning which is not strictly in accordance with the usual rules of grammar or vocabulary: see *Investors Compensation Scheme Ltd v West Bromwich Building Society* [1998] 1 WLR 896.

[24]   It is true that a gift equal to the nil rate band of IHT cannot be isolated from the application of the charge to tax. But that is not what the draftsman is saying. The words 'in respect of this gift' far from being inconsistent with an understanding of IHT, shows that the draftsman appreciated that the gift of the Property and the legacies under clause 3 would be aggregated in order to calculate what was left of the nil rate band. Clause 3 is therefore limited to what is left of the band before tax would otherwise become payable as a result of this gift. The phrase 'in respect of' is far too general to negative the effect of the words which precede it.

[25]   The language of clause 3 does not therefore disclose a misunderstanding of IHT nor does it permit the clause to be construed as Mr Gordon contends. His construction (which the judge adopted) would involve, in my view, a complete re-drafting of clause 3. Instead of a gift equal to the amount of the nil rate band determined by reference to the other provisions of the will ('which I can give them by this my Will') one has on this argument to read clause 3 simply as a gift of a sum equal to the nil rate band from time to time. There is nothing in clause 3 which indicates that this is what the draftsman and, through him, the Testator intended.

[27]   For those reasons, I consider that the construction adopted by the judge was wrong and that the appeal against his judgment on that issue should be allowed. In these circumstances, it is unnecessary for me to deal with the appeal against his order that the RPSCA should pay the costs of the action on an indemnity basis. The order for costs must be set aside if the appeal on construction is allowed. I would only say that an order for indemnity costs remains an exceptional order and that I do not believe that it was justified in this case.

Lord Justice Black:

[31]   As Patten LJ impliedly acknowledges by his reference to *Investors*

Compensation Scheme Limited v West Bromwich Building Society [1998] 1 WLR 896, the court's approach to the interpretation of wills is, in practice, very similar to its approach to the interpretation of contracts. Of course, in the case of a contract, there are at least two parties involved in negotiating its terms, whereas a will is a unilateral document. However, it is clear from a number of cases that the approach to interpretation of unilateral documents, such as a notice or a patent, is effectively the same, as matter of principle, as the court's approach to the interpretation of a bilateral or multilateral document such as a contract: see *Mannai Investments Ltd v Eagle Star Insurance Co plc* [1997] AC 749 and *Kirin-Amgen Inc v Hoechst Marion Roussel Ltd* [2005] RPC 9.

[37]   Quite apart from this, there is a well established body of authority which establishes that 'prima face, all bequests stand on an equal footing, and it lies upon those who assert the contrary, to prove it. It is not sufficient that the words of the Will should leave the question in doubt. They must positively and clearly establish, that it was the intention of the testator that the bequests should not stand upon an equal footing' – see per Knight Bruce V-C in *Thwaites v Foreman* (1884) 1 Coll. 409, 414, cited by Warrington J in *In re Harris, Harris, v Harris* [1912] 2 Ch.241. See also Blower v Morret (1752) 2 Ves. Sen 420 and In re: *Schweder's Estate; Oppenheim v Schweder* [1891] 3 Ch.44. In those cases (none of which was cited below, it is only fair to say), the court was concerned with a different question from that which arises in this case, namely what to do when an estate is too small to satisfy all the bequests in the Will. However, it seems to me that they underline the general point that a will is to be construed as a whole, and clear words are required before one construes one clause as being subject or subordinate to another, simply because it is later in the Will than the other clause.

[38]   That is to say that the fact that one bequest comes before another in a will must always be wholly disregarded when one has to decide how they interrelate, but, as a free-standing point, the mere fact that one clause precedes another seems to me to be of minor potential relevance on the issue of how they interrelate with each other.

PRICE V HMRC (2010) (FIRST TIER TRIBUNAL TAX CHAMBER)

Extracts from the decision

[54]   Turning to the substantive dispute, the central issue is whether the

Appellant is right in his submission that the expression '*the value of the aggregate of [any property comprised in a person's estate] and any related property [ie, property comprised in the estate of his spouse]*', where it appears in **section 161 (1)**, connotes a valuation of the total of the two properties each taken separately as a unit, or whether the valuation should be of a different item of property formed by the aggregation of the two properties mentioned, and involving their '*notional conversation*' or '*transformation*'.

[55] The Appellant's argument is based on the meaning of '*aggregate*' which is simply the '*bringing together*' or '*total*' as, he says, the word is used in **section 5(1)**. He also refers in support of his argument to the terms of **section 161(4)**, which, he says, provides for the method of valuation for which HMRC argue, but only in the case of the valuation of shares, stock, debentures and units of any other description of property, which language does not include interests in land such as those in the present case. He further supports his argument by reference to the statutory words '*appropriate portion of*' introducing the crucial phrase in **section 161(1)**, asking rhetorically, how, if the valuation is of a species of property which does not in fact exist in the circumstances and **section 161(4)** does not apply, any portion of the resultant value can be determined to be '*appropriate*'.

[56] HMRC's argument in reply was that the words in **section 161(1)** naturally bear the meaning that the value which is required is the value of both properties taken together either forming a new property for valuation purposes or not, as the circumstances indicate. This approach was supported by the Special Commissioner's comment at [46] of her decision in ***Arkwright*** (which recapitulated what she had said in [38].

[57] The Appellant is correct in observing that in ***Arkwright*** the parties agreed that this was the effect of **section 161(1)** – see [39] of the Special Commissioner's Decision.

[58] We do not rely on the Special Commissioner's analysis in ***Arkwright***, but examine further the context of **section 161(1)** in the scheme of IHTA. The related property provisions in **section 161** are supplementary to **section 160**, which is the provision establishing that the open market value of property is the norm for valuation for inheritance tax purposes.

[59] **Section 161** is effectively a special case exception to the norm established by **section 160**, but in the light of **section 160**, **section 161** must be construed by reference to the concept of '*the price which the property might reasonably be expected to fetch if sold in the open market*' (**section 160**).

[60]   There is, therefore, a notional sale implicit in the hypothesis established by the related property provisions.

[61]   *IRC v Gray* was not concerned with the related property provisions, but with how the valuation exercise predicated by **section 38 Finance Act 1975 (now section 160 IHTA)** was to be applied when the deceased herself held two assets (a freehold of an estate subject to a farming partnership, and her 92.5% interest in the partnership which held the tenancy).

[62]   It thus approached essentially the same problem which the Appellant's submissions address. Where there are two properties to be valued at the same time, are they to be taken together, or as amalgamated for the purposes of valuation (if amalgamation would produce a different value)?

[63]   Hoffmann LJ (as he then was) said:-

> '**Section 38** [now **section 160 IHTA**] requires one to consider what a particular item of property would have fetched if sold on the open market. The **Buccleuch** principle may require one to suppose that it was sold alone, split into parts or together with something else. But [Counsel for the executor] says the process must be one of valuation, not the attribution of part of the value of something else. In this case he says that the notice of determination did not value any actual item of property. It proceeded by a 'notional lotting' of the freehold interest with an item of property which had never had a separate existence, namely Lady Fox's interest in the partnership's tenancy to the exclusion of her interest in the other partnership assets, and then attributed part of the value of this imaginary asset to the freehold. [Counsel for the executor] says that this exercise is far removed from the practical and common sense conduct of the hypothetical seller postulated by Lord Wilberfoce in **Buccleuch**. The tribunal agreed. It said that 'if it was permissible to lot the freehold interest and the share in the partnership together as being a single unit of property, then **s.38 [s.160]** requires that that single unit be valued as a single unit and that apportionment is neither permissible not appropriate.
>
> I do not think this fairly reflects what the notice of determination was doing. The only assumption it makes about how the hypothetical sale would have been conducted is that the freehold and Lady Fox's entire interest in the partnership would have been sold together. I shall return in due course to whether such an assumption could be justified under the **Buccleuch** principle [he held that it could be], but there is no doubt that it involves the aggregation of two assets which each had a real existence at the relevant date. Since the two assets

are supposed to have been sold together because this would realise a greater price than selling them separately, the value of each asset must necessarily be an apportioned part of the price which would have been realised for both...

*In my judgment, therefore, the exercise performed by the notice was in accordance with **s.38 [s.160]**.'*

[64] The Court of Appeal thus decided (Waite and Neill LJJ agreed with Hoffman LJ) that it was right to value two assets held in the same estate on the basis that they would achieve a greater price if offered together for sale in the open market than if they were offered separately, even though that would, of necessity, require an apportionment of the price fetched by the aggregate of the assets in ascertaining the price paid for each.

[65] We consider that this reasoning applies equally to the question of what is the valuation called for by the related property provisions in **section 161**.

[66] Where **section 161** applies, the two items of property which are to be valued (on the facts of this case comprised in the estate of Mrs Price and the estate of the Appellant respectively) are to be valued on the basis that they are offered for sale together and at the same time. If a greater price would be achieved *'in real life'* on such a sale, as compared to the price which would be achieved if the items had been offered for sale individually, and such a sale would not have require undue effort or expense (which was not suggested by the Appellant), then that greater price must be attributed to the two items by application of the formula contained in **section 161(3)** (compare *IRC v Gray* at p.378f/g).

[69] We hold that the valuation required ought not to make any allowance for the notional costs and expenses of selling in the hypothetical sale. The statutory language 'the price which the property might reasonably be expected to fetch' does not permit such notional costs or expenses to be taken into account. Nor do we discern any purpose pursuant to which they might be taken into account. The legislature seems, unsurprisingly to us, not have thought it appropriate to reduce the tax base for expenses which have not in fact been incurred.

[70] Likewise, we hold that the valuation required (in terms of the price notionally fetched) ought not to make any allowance for debts or other liabilities charged on the property being valued. There is nothing which suggests to us that in the statutory hypothetical sale of property which is so charged, the notional purchaser is expected himself to

discharge the debts or other liabilities. On the contrary, we consider that the natural assumption would be that the vendor would discharge such debts or other liabilities out of the price fetched in the sale.

[71] Debts and other liabilities are relieved for inheritance tax purposes by separate provision, namely **section 5**, and in the case of liabilities which are an incumbrance on any property, they are, so far as possible to taken to reduce the value of the property pursuant to **section 162(4)**.

The author understands that an application for leave to appeal has been made but not heard at the time of writing.

KEY V KEY (2010) (CHANCERY DIVISION)

Extract from the Judgment of Mr Justice Briggs:

The Golden Rule

[7] The substance of the Golden Rule is that when a solicitor is instructed to prepare a will for an aged testator, or for one who has been seriously ill, he should arrange for a medical practitioner first to satisfy himself as to the capacity and understanding of the testator, and to make a contemporaneous record of his examination and findings: see *Kenward v Adams* (1975) Times 29th November 1975; *Re Simpson* (1977) 121 SJ 224, in both cases per Templeman J, and subsequently approved in *Buckenhan v Dickinson* [2000] WTLR 1083, *Hoff v Atherton* [2005] WTLR 99, *Cattermole v Prisk* [2006] 1 FLR 697, and in *Scammell v Farmer* [2008] EWHC 1100 (Ch), at paragraphs 117 to 123.

[8] Compliance with the Golden Rule does not, of course, operate as a touchstone of the validity of a will, nor does non-compliance demonstrate its invalidity. Its purpose, as has repeatedly been emphasised, is to assist in the avoidance of disputes, or at least in the minimisation of their scope. As the expert evidence in the present case confirms, persons with failing or impaired mental faculties may, for perfectly understandable reasons, seek to conceal what they regard as their embarrassing shortcomings from persons with whom they deal, so that a friend or professional person such as a solicitor may fail to detect defects in mental capacity which would be or become apparent to a trained and experienced medical examiner, to whom a proper description of the legal test for testamentary capacity had first been provided.

Appendix 8
Abbreviations

AOR	Associated operations rules
APR	Agricultural property relief
BMT	Bereaved Minor's Trust
BPR	Business property relief
CGT	Capital Gains Tax
DPT	Disabled person's trust
DT	Discretionary trust
GWR	The IHT gifts with reservation of benefit rules
HMRC	Her Majesty's Revenue and Customs
IHT	Inheritance Tax
IHTM	HMRC's IHT Manual (available to view on www.hmrc.gov.uk/manual/ihtmanual)
IP	An interest in possession (referred to in this book as a life interest)
IPDI	Immediate post death interest trust
NON-DOM	Non-domiciliary
NRA	Nil Rate Amount
NRB	Nil Rate Band
NRBDT	Nil Rate Band Discretionary Trust
PET	Potentially exempt transfer
POAT	Pre-owned assets tax
PR's	Personal representatives
RPR	Relevant Property Regime
SDLT	Stamp duty land tax
SDLTM	HMRC's SDLT Manual
Special Trusts	DPT's; BMT's (including 18-25 trusts); and IPDI's
Spouse	The author uses this term interchangeably to mean both a spouse and a civil partner, where the civil partnership has been registered as such
SVM	HMRC's Shares and Assets Valuation Manual
TSEM	HMRC's Trusts Settlements and Estates Manual
TSI	Transitional serial interest

Bibliography

A Modern Approach to Wills, Administration and Estate Planning (with Precedents), by Christopher Whitehouse and Professor Lesley King (Jordans) (*'Whitehouse & King'*);

A Practitioner's Guide to Beneficiary Actions, by Arabella Saker (with a contribution by Richard Wilson) (Tottel Publishing) (*'Saker'*);

A Practitioner's Guide to Wills (3rd edition), by Lesley King, keith Biggs, and Peter Gausden (Wildy, Simmonds & Hill Publishing) (*'King, Biggs & Gausden'*);

A Practitioner's Guide to Legacies, by Martyn Frost, Paul Saunders, Arabella Saker, Geoffrey Shindler, Tim Stone, and Richard Wilson (Lexis Nexis Tolley) (*'Legacies'*);

A Practitioner's Guide to Powers and Duties of Trustees, by Stephen Bleasdale and Marie-Claire Lloyd (Tottel Publishing) (*'Bleasdale & Lloyd'*);

BDO's Yellow Tax Guide 2010-11, edited by Nigel Eastaway and Jacqueline Kimber (Lexis Nexis) (*'BDO Tax Guide'*);

Capital Gains Tax 2009/2010, by Rebecca Cave, and Iris Wunschmann-Lyall (Bloomsbury Professional) (*'CGT 2010'*);

Drafting Trusts and Will Trusts A Modern Approach (10th edition), by James Kessler QC and Leon Sartin (Sweet & Maxwell) (*'Kessler & Sartin'*);

FL Memo Company Law 2010 ('FL Memo');

Foster's Inheritance Tax, by Richard Wallington (Lexis Nexis Butterworths) (*'Foster'*);

Hutton on Estate Planning, by Matthew Hutton (Hutton Publishing) (*'Hutton'*);

Inheritance Claims and Challenges, by Nazreen Pearce (Callow Publishing) (*'Pearce'*);

Inheritance Tax 2009/2010, by Mark McLaughlin, Toby Harris, and Iris Wunschmann-Lyall (Bloomsbury Professional) (*'IHT 2010'*);

Jackson & Powell on Professional Liability, John Powell and Roger Stewart (general editors) (Thomson Sweet & Maxwell) (*'Jackson'*);

Lewin on Trusts, edited by John Mowbray, Lynton Tucker, Nicholas Le Poidevin, Edwin Simpson, and James Brightwell (Thomson Sweet & Maxwell) (*'Lewin'*);

McCutcheon on Inheritance Tax, by Withers LLP, Aparna Nathan, and, Marika Lemos (Sweet & Maxwell) *('McCutcheon')*;

Parker's Modern Will Precedents, by Michael Waterworth (Tottel Publishing) *('Waterworth')*;

Personal Chattels: Law, Practice and Tax with Precedents, by Ann Stanyer (Sweet & Maxwell) *('Stanyer')*;

Personal Tax Planning: Principles and Practice, by Malcolm Finney (Bloomsbury Professional) *('Finney')*;

Practical Will Precedents, by Murray Hallam, Keith Bruce-Smith, Robin Paul, Paul Clark, and Richard Underwood (Thomson Sweet & Maxwell) *('Practical Will Precedents')*;

Pre-Owned Assets and Estate Planning, by Emma Chamberlain and Chris Whitehouse (Sweet & Maxwell) *('POAT')*;

Ray & McLaughlin's Practical Inheritance Act Planning, by Toby Harris, Mark McLaughlin, and Ralph Ray (Tottel Publishing) *('Harris, McLaughlin,& Ray')*;

Revenue Law – Principles and Practice (28th edition), Natalie Lee (editor) (Tottel Publishing) *('Lee')*;

Risk And Negligence In Wills, Estates, And Trusts, by Martyn Frost, Penelope Reed, and Mark Baxter (Oxford University Press) *('Frost, Reed, & Baxter')*;

Stamp Duty Land Tax, by Reg Nock (Jordans) *('Nock')*;

Tax-Efficient Will Drafting, by Stephen Arthur, Chris Jarman, and John Thurston (Lexis Nexis Tolley) *('Arthur, Jarman, & Thurston')*;

Taxation of Foreign Domiciliaries 2010-2011, by James Kessler QC (Key Haven Publications PLC) *('Taxation of Foreign Domiciliaries 2010-2011')*;

Tax Planning 2010/2011, Mark McLaughlin (general editor) (Bloomsbury Professional) *('Tax Planning 2010/2011')*;

The Solicitor's Handbook 2011, by Andrew Hopper QC and Gregory Treverton-Jones QC (The Law Society) *('Solicitor's Handbook')*;

The Law of Trusts, by Geraint Thomas and Alastair Hudson (Oxford University Press) *('Thomas & Hudson')*;

Theobald on Wills (17th edition), by John G. Ross Martyn, Charlotte Ford, Alexander Learmonth, and Mika Oldham (Sweet & Maxwell) *('Theobald')*;

Thomas on Powers, by Geraint Thomas (Sweet & Maxwell) *('Thomas')*;

Tolley's Estate Planning 2010-2011, by Sharon McKie, and Simon McKie (Lexis Nexis) *('McKie')*;

Tolley's Inheritance Tax 2010-2011, by Jon Golding (Lexis Nexis) *('Golding')*;

Tolley's Inheritance Tax Planning 2009-2010, by Michael Waterworth, Richard Dew, and Ten Old Square (Lexis Nexis) *('Waterworth & Dew')*;

Tolley's Tax Cases 2010, by Alan Dolton and Kevin Walton (Lexis Nexis) *('Dalton & Walton')*;

Tolley's Yellow Tax Handbook 2010 – 2011, Anne Redston (consultant editor) (Tolley Lexis Nexis) *('Yellow Book')*;

Trusts and Estates Law Handbook, by Penelope Reed (Tottel Publishing) *('Reed')*;

Trust Taxation, by Emma Chamberlain and Chris Whitehouse (Thomson Sweet & Maxwell) *('Chamberlain & Whitehouse')*;

Trusts & Trustees Cases & Materials, by Edward Burn, and Graham Virgo (Oxford University Press) *('Burn & Virgo')*;

Wills, Administration and Taxation Law and Practice, by John Barlow, Lesley King, and Anthony King (Sweet & Maxwell) *('Barlow, King, & King')*;

Will Draftsman's Handbook , by Robin Riddett (The Law Society) *('Riddett')*; and

Williams on Wills, by Francis Barlow, Christopher Sherrin, Richard Wallington, Susannah Meadway, and Michael Waterworth (Lexis Nexis Butterworths) *('Williams')*.

Index